The Campus History Series

WESTMINSTER COLLEGE

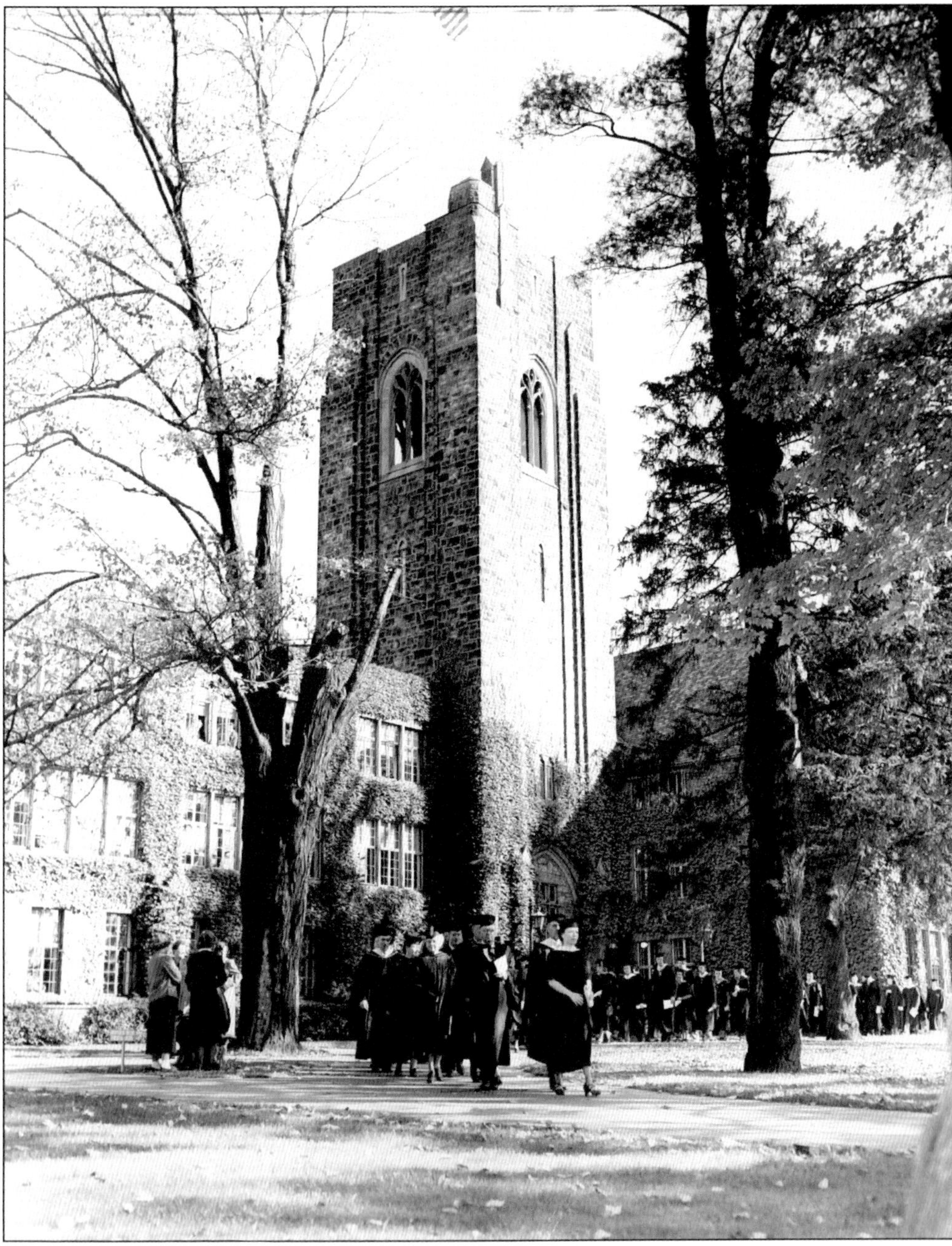

Erected during 1928 in the Collegiate Gothic style, Old Main Memorial stands proudly as a symbol of scholarship and tradition. To this day, it serves as the center for administrative activities and contains classrooms, Wallace Memorial Chapel, and the bell tower, which continually tolls the iconic Westminster chimes on quarter-hour intervals. In 1949, it was the backdrop for the inauguration of Pres. Will W. Orr (above).

On the cover: Eager students streamed into graduation ceremonies in the chapel of newly constructed Old Main Memorial on a rainy spring day around 1928. (Courtesy of the Westminster College archives.)

The Campus History Series

WESTMINSTER COLLEGE

BARBARA BRADEN GUFFEY AND DEBORA SWATSWORTH FOSTER

ARCADIA
PUBLISHING

ISBN 978-0-7385-5477-8

Published by Arcadia Publishing
Charleston SC, Chicago IL, Portsmouth NH, San Francisco CA

Printed in the United States of America

Library of Congress Catalog Card Number: 2007925817

For all general information contact Arcadia Publishing at:
Telephone 843-853-2070
Fax 843-853-0044
E-mail sales@arcadiapublishing.com
For customer service and orders:
Toll-Free 1-888-313-2665

Visit us on the Internet at www.arcadiapublishing.com

To Westminster College students and alums, past and present, who have continued to cherish the gifts provided by our founding fathers, an enlightened administration as well as a learned and caring faculty.

CONTENTS

Acknowledgments 6

Foreword 7

1. In the Beginning 9

2. Traditions and Celebrations 21

3. When Titans Truly Were 47

4. The Arts and the Sciences 55

5. Special Places, Special Memories 83

6. On the Field and on the Court 105

ACKNOWLEDGMENTS

This book became a reality thanks to the dedication and assistance of many people, principle among them Dr. H. Dewey DeWitt, professor emeritus and Westminster College archivist. He led the dig through mountains of documents and photographs, a treasure hunt that resulted in the images included here. Thanks also go to Molly Spinney, librarian, who supported our work and continues to cherish the college's records, photographs, and ephemera. We also are indebted to college historian Paul W. Gamble, whose earlier histories informed our research and contributed valued perspective.

Importantly, we are grateful to Tom Williamson, Westminster's 13th president and a man of great character with a great love for the college. His foreword provides insight into our college's past and its future.

Dorothy Pollock, Darwin Huey, Gloria Cagigas, Sue Rudloff, Mark Meighan, Sandra Chandler, Justin Zackel, Keith McCauley, Bill Foster, Jim Giel, and many others offered advice and guidance. What's more, they opened their files and shared countless stories and photographs.

It is impossible, in 128 pages, to capture the breadth of Westminster's history. We hope that we have included photographs that represent shared memories, favorite events, and significant places.

Works cited in the book include: *The History of New Wilmington, Pennsylvania 1797–2003: The Story of a Small Town*, edited by H. Dewey DeWitt, Paul W. Gamble, Delber L. McKee, Eugene G. Sharkey, and Alan G. Sternbergh in 2004; *The Westminster Story, 1852–2002, Glorious, Grand and True*, by Paul W. Gamble and Richard H. Gamble in 2002; *History of Westminster College, 1852–1992*, by Paul W. Gamble in 1992; and *When Titans Truly Were: Westminster College and the Second World War*, by Eugene G. Sharkey.

All royalties from this book benefit McGill Memorial Library.

FOREWORD

There is a line from an old Beatles song that goes, "There are places I remember, all my life." Westminster has many such places. It is, after all, that sense of place that beckons us to keep coming back to this beautiful campus again and again to experience a certain tranquility that we cannot quite describe.

Fortunately, a picture *is* worth a thousand words, and here are lots of them—carefully selected to freshen our memories, tickle our emotions, and create a record so that all who read this photographic history will have a better understanding of Westminster and its heritage. It is the beauty of this place that has drawn remarkable people to teach and learn here. Many have gone forth to serve and to accomplish great things.

I would like to thank trustee Barbara Braden Guffey, class of 1970, and chair of the board Debora Swatsworth Foster, class of 1974, for this wonderful addition to Westminster's historical record. Through the lens of pictorial history we can better appreciate the 155-year building process that has created the Westminster of today. The current strength of the college is based on the efforts of each generation, each faculty member, staff member, student—each alumna and alumnus, and each trustee. Together they have helped to create a "big picture" for Westminster that none could have envisioned or accomplished alone. The big picture for the college is as bright as can be. A mural, if you will, unfinished, yet well-proportioned and designed with care so that those who will add to the picture will find inspiration and opportunities to make a difference, just as those who preceded us have done.

As you enjoy the pages that follow, I urge you to think about your role in making Westminster ever-better in keeping with its special mission: "To help men and women develop competencies, commitments and characteristics that have distinguished human beings at their best." It is that mission that distinguishes Westminster and sustains it so that it will remain (in the words of our alma mater) "glorious, grand, and true."

R. Thomas Williamson
President of Westminster College

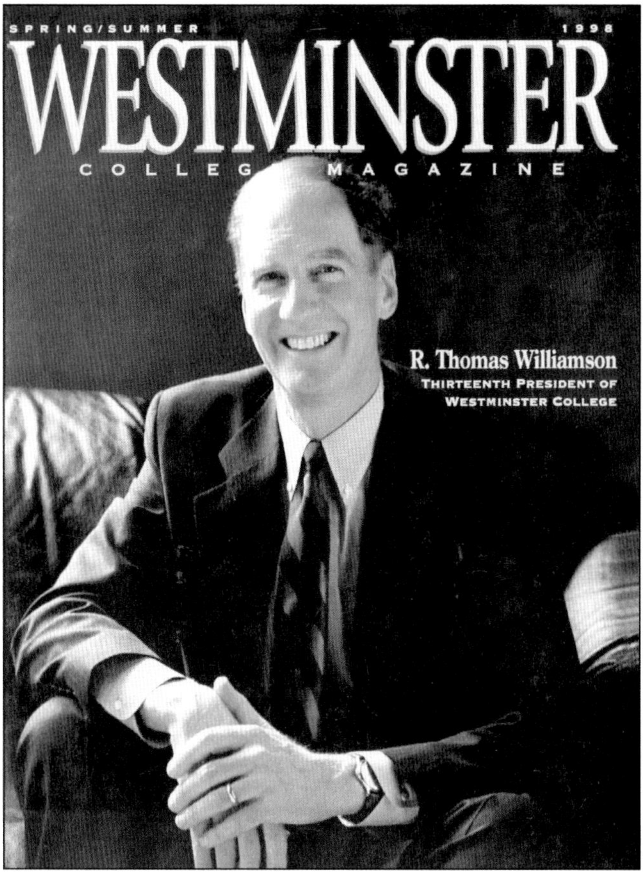
SPRING/SUMMER 1998
WESTMINSTER
COLLEGE MAGAZINE
R. Thomas Williamson
THIRTEENTH PRESIDENT OF WESTMINSTER COLLEGE

R. Thomas Williamson is the 13th president of Westminster College. His acumen for strategic planning and his talents in leadership propelled Westminster into the 21st century.

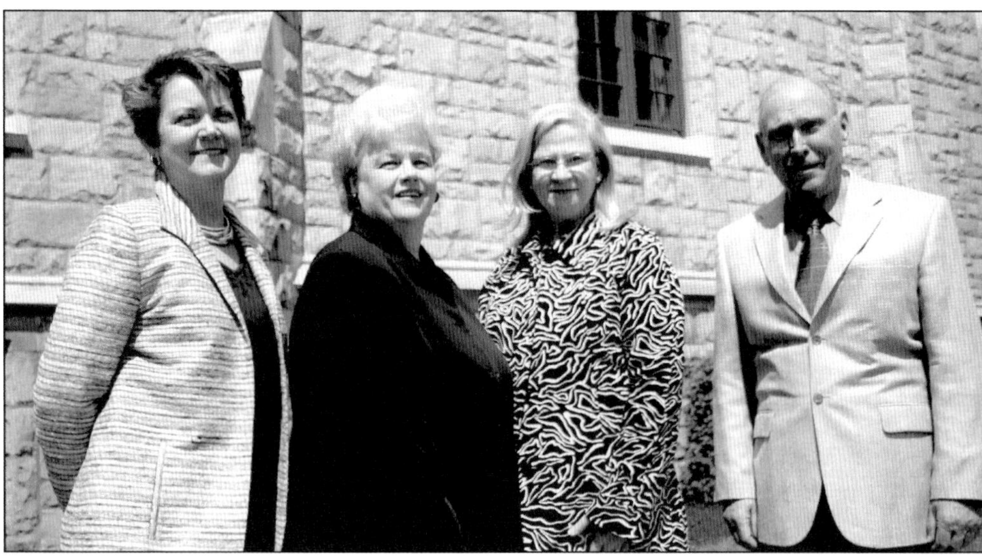

Seen here, from left to right, authors Debora Swatsworth Foster '74, and Barbara Braden Guffey '70, worked with librarian Molley Spinney '72, and archivist Dr. H. Dewey DeWitt, professor emeritus, in selecting photographs and illustrations. Together they share more than 155 years in association with Westminster College.

One

IN THE BEGINNING

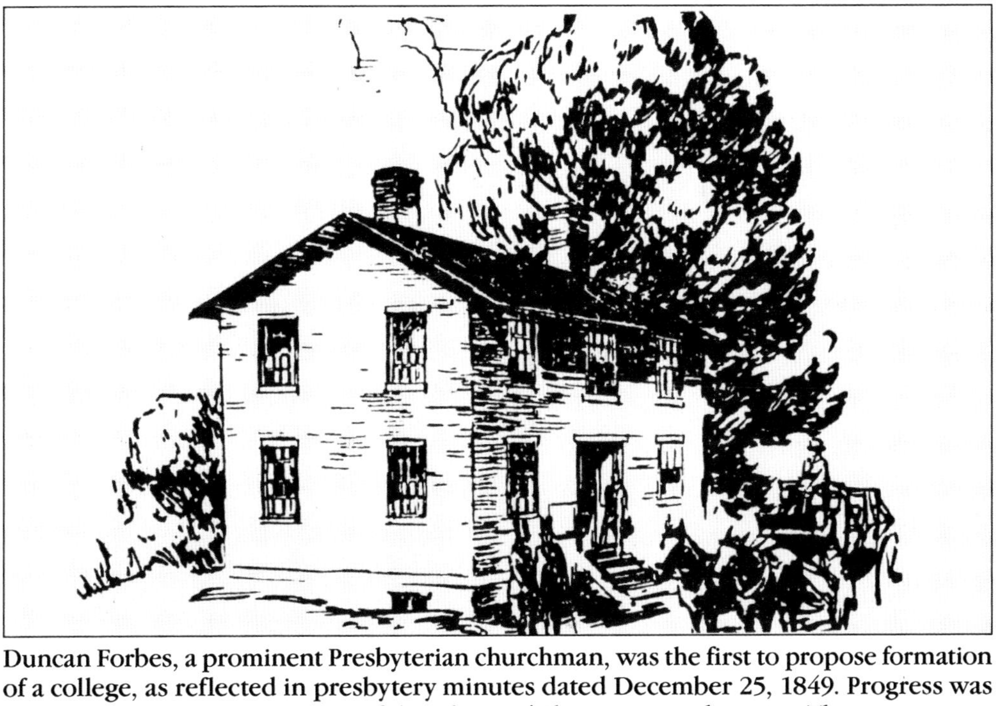

Duncan Forbes, a prominent Presbyterian churchman, was the first to propose formation of a college, as reflected in presbytery minutes dated December 25, 1849. Progress was made at a January 1852 meeting of the Ohio and Shenango presbyteries. The precepts put forth then were revolutionary; the future college would be established for "the mental and moral training of youth of *both* sexes." The name Westminster Collegiate Institute was chosen out of respect for the Westminster Confession of Faith. The founders picked New Wilmington, Pennsylvania, as the site because the town's 200 citizens pledged $10,000. Westminster's first building (above) was erected in 1853. An early proposal called for separate classrooms for men and women. The trustees voted down the idea.

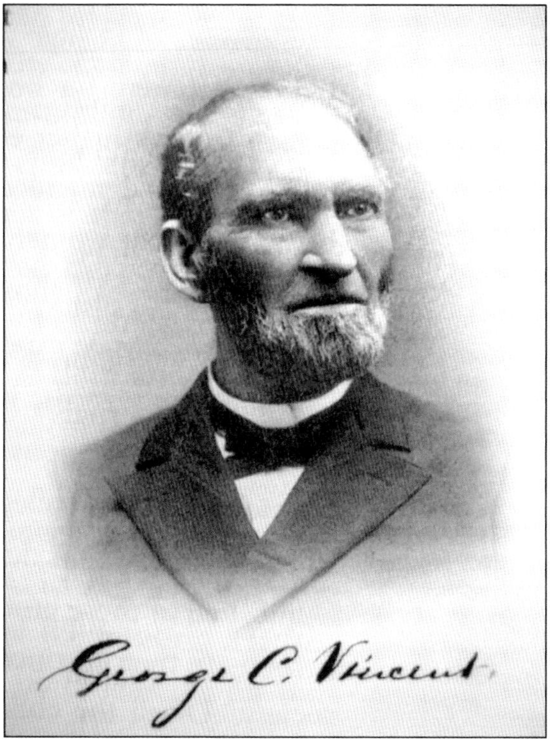

The Rev. George C. Vincent was named the first "principal" of the college by his fellow founders. Two of the primary purposes of the new institute were to educate men for the Presbyterian ministry, and to help expand public schools, which were demanding more teachers. Historian Paul Gamble noted that, at the time, there was growing recognition that women could teach as well as men and at one-quarter to one-half the salaries demanded by male counterparts.

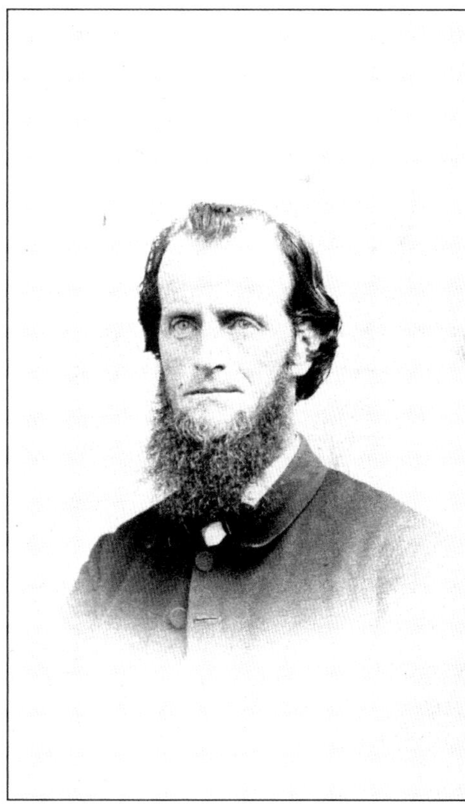

The first graduate of Westminster Collegiate Institute was William P. Shaw, who received a bachelor of arts degree and went on to become a minister. In July 1857, ten young women were among the 21 graduates. Sarah McMichael received a degree for completing the regular Classical Course studied by the men. This was a rare accomplishment, as most educational authorities believed that coeducational learning would not work because women "lacked the mental stamina." Westminster's women were pioneers indeed. In addition, McMichael may have been the very first woman in America to receive such a degree. As Paul Gamble has stated, at Westminster and elsewhere "coeducation prevailed not only because women were given a chance, but because they capitalized on it."

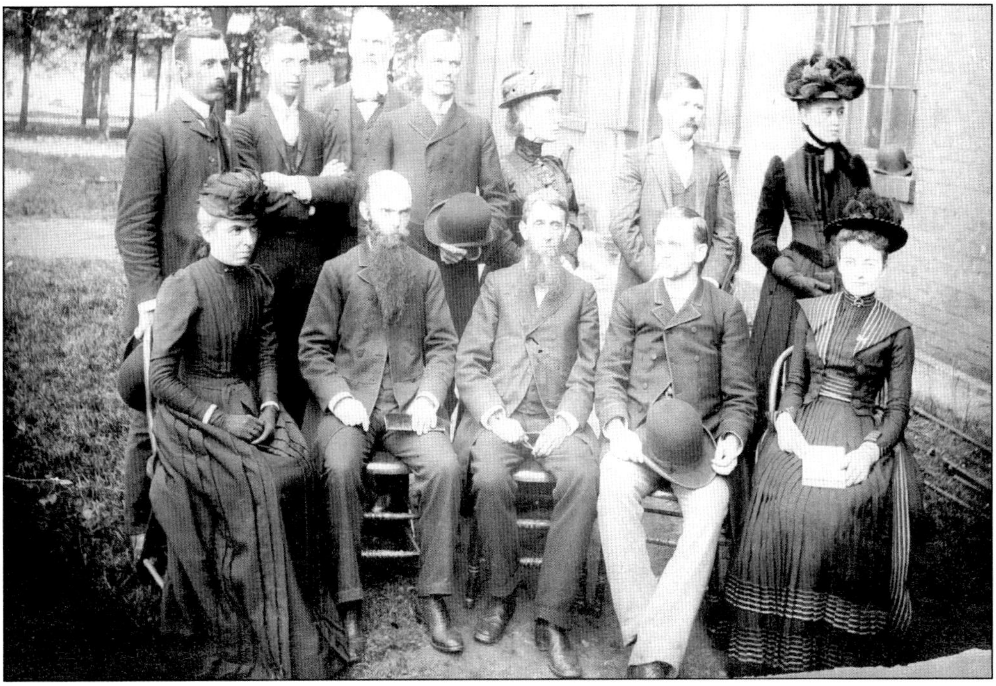

Early faculty members pose in the late 1800s for one of the college's first staff photographs. Rev. Dr. Robert Gracey Ferguson (first row, third from left) served then as Westminster's third president. He was at the helm for 22 years, from 1884 to 1906, longer than any other Westminster president.

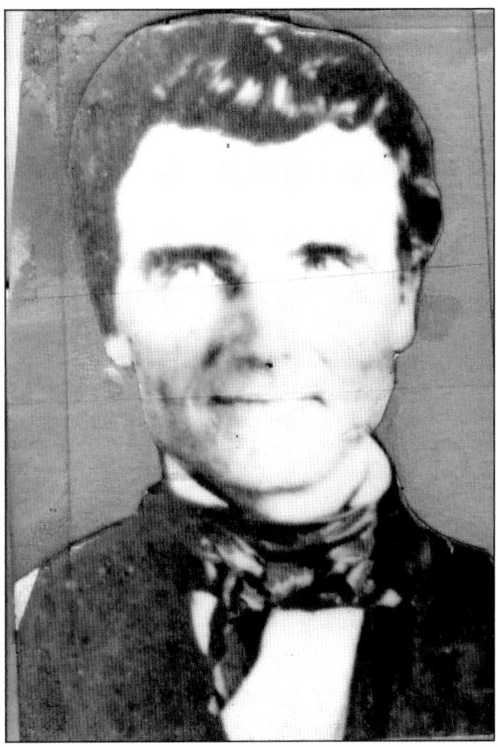

As a founder and early financial agent, William Dickey rode on horseback (one observer called him "weather beaten") throughout western Pennsylvania to solicit funds and to sell "scholarships." At the time, families could purchase perpetual scholarships ranging from $100 to $500 for future generations of students. While the scheme was enticing to parents, it was disastrous for Westminster. An ensuing financial crisis forced the board to rescind the plan.

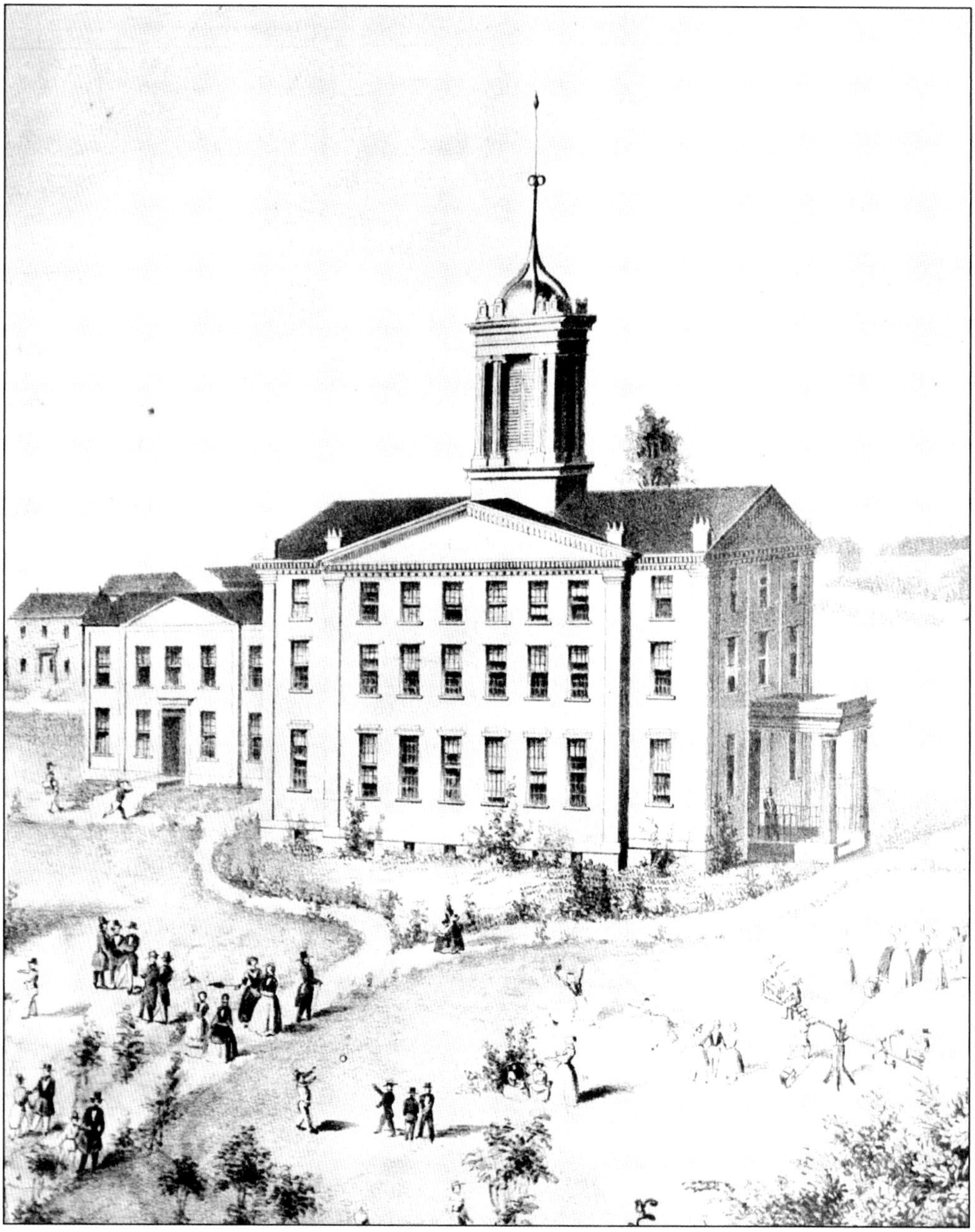

Westminster Collegiate Institute's main building was constructed in 1855, just three years after the college's founding. A relatively small (58 feet by 90 feet), three-story structure, it incorporated a chapel and numerous rooms for literary societies and classes. When it opened, tuition stood at $8.33 per term and room and board fees averaged $1.50 weekly. The student body numbered 100 men and 65 women. The facility lasted for six years until ravaged by fire in 1861. The citizenry of New Wilmington raised $8,000 for rebuilding on the identical site, thus assuring the college's home there.

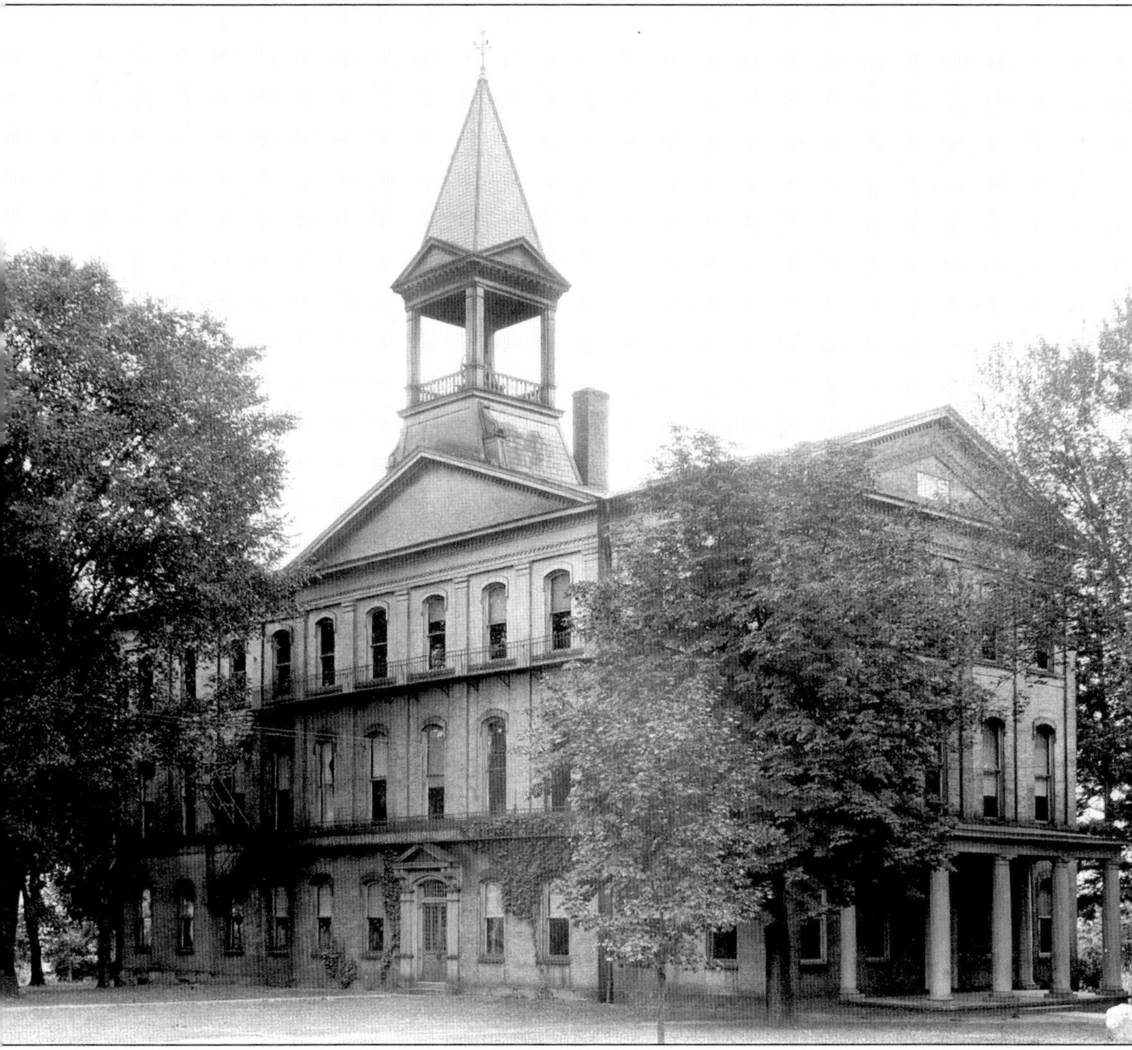

The second administrative building, dubbed Old Main, welcomed scholars starting in the fall of 1862. For decades, its large belfry symbolized Westminster College, as the institution became officially known in 1897.

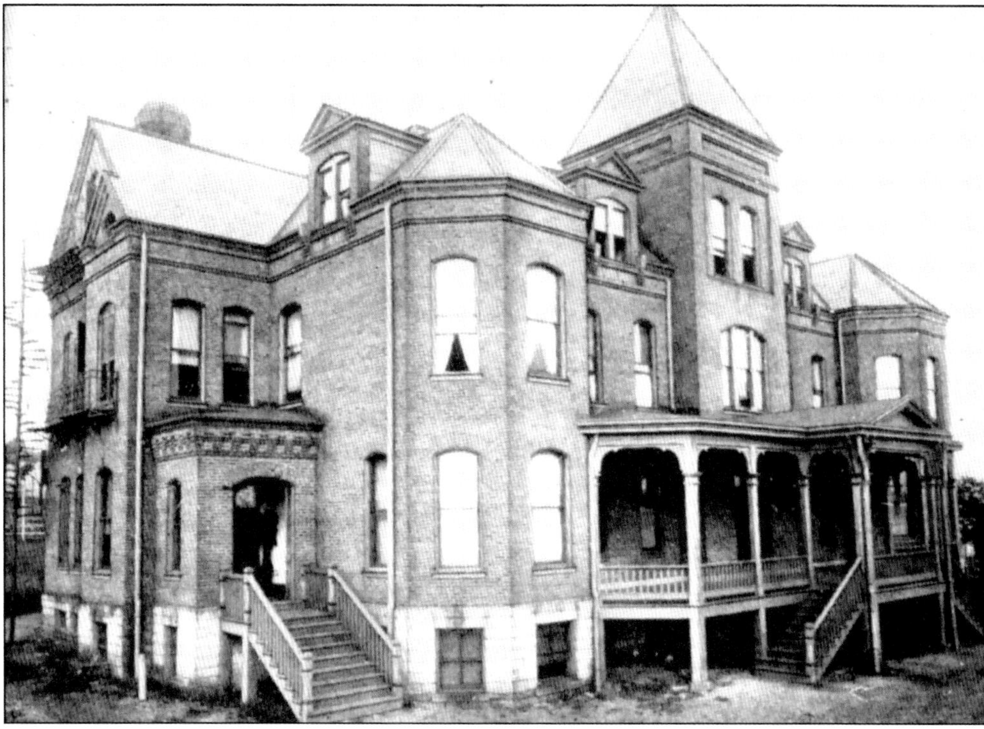

The Conservatory of Music and Ladies Hall went up in January 1885 at a cost of $25,000. It became known affectionately as the "Hillside." Construction of this first conservatory allowed the college to offer a five-year music course. Hillside remains the oldest major building on campus and today serves as a women's dormitory.

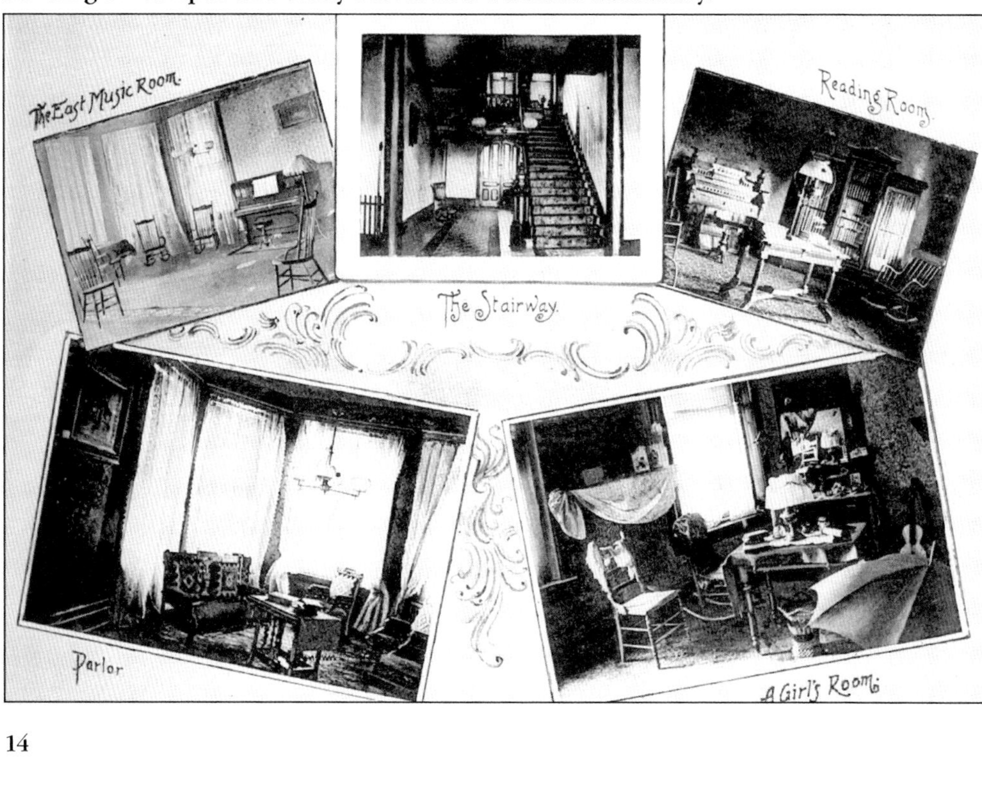

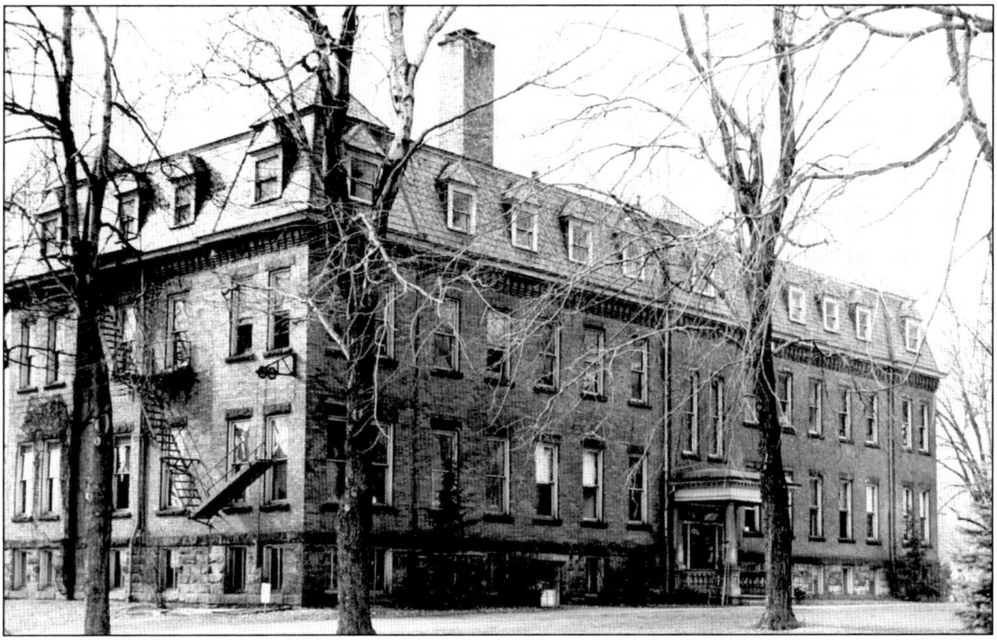

Westminster's 1889–1890 catalogue announced, for the first time, a four-year scientific course. Behind this dramatic move was Prof. S. R. Thompson, an 1863 graduate and beloved faculty member, who was a proponent of the natural sciences and, importantly, laboratory experimentation. Prior to that time, scientific learning was based almost solely upon textbook studies. Thompson was so dedicated to the efficacy of laboratory work that, in 1893, he and his wife offered the college their personal savings of $20,000 to erect a hall for the study of physics and botany. The structure was dedicated in 1894 as Mary Thompson Science Hall in memory of their daughter who had died eight years earlier while a Westminster coed. Gen. W. A. Clark of New Wilmington later funded a chemistry wing; the subsequent addition of laboratories and lecture halls honored chemistry professor Charles C. Freeman. Thompson Clark Hall received an award-winning restoration in 1999 and remains in continuous use.

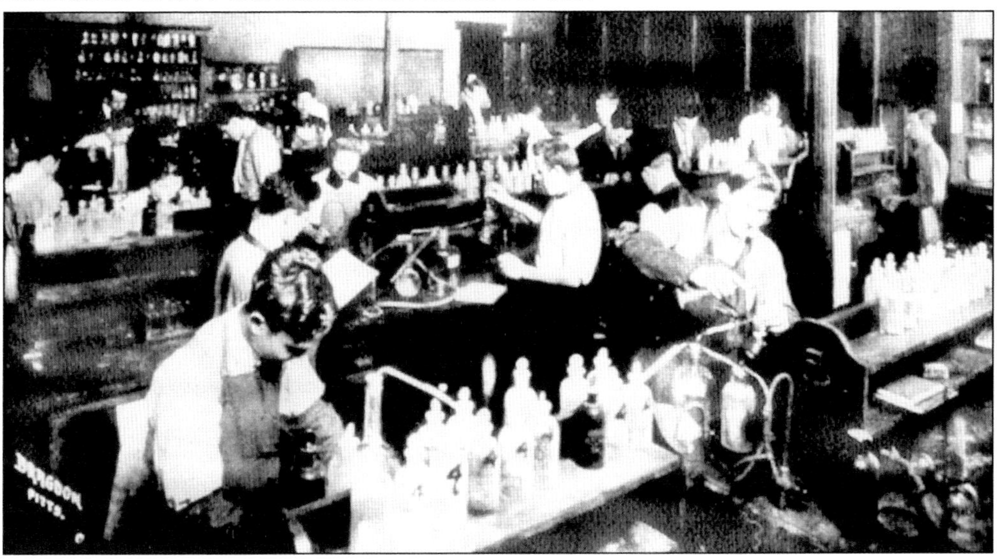

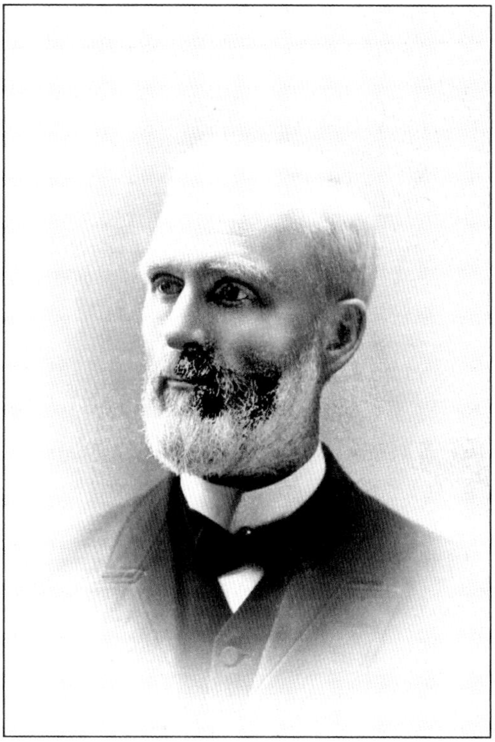

Thompson House, the first area home to boast of electricity and indoor plumbing, has long been a New Wilmington treasure. Listed on the National Register of Historic Places, the Queen Anne dwelling was built in 1884 as a family home by Prof. S. R. Thompson (left). Following Thompson's death, his wife Lucy operated it as a boardinghouse. Subsequently, the landmark served as a dormitory, sorority house, and administrative office. Thompson House was restored to its original splendor in 2006 and now offers coveted dormitory space.

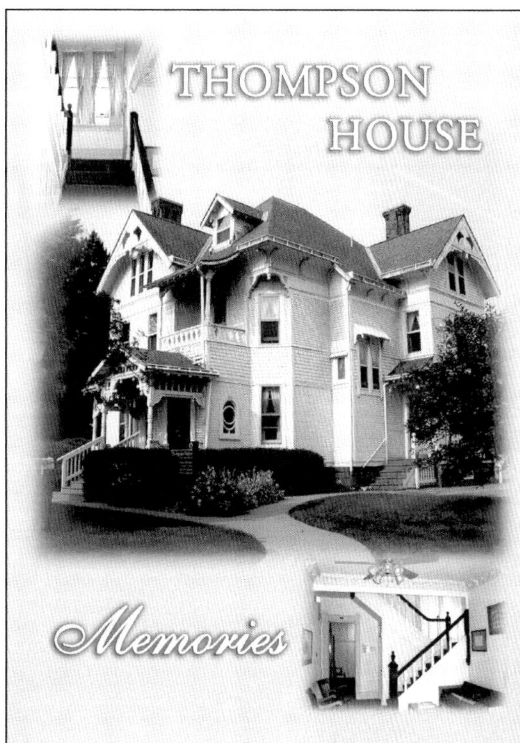

Former trustee Dorothy Pollock '46 edited a booklet of collected stories from men and women who lived or worked in this treasured home.

Like so many of their post–Civil War contemporaries, Westminster coeds were smitten with the new media of photography. College archives contain a wealth of scrapbooks and photograph collections assembled during the late 1870s and beyond. Ermine McElwee, later Mrs. H. D. Gordon, and others in the class of 1886 were the subjects of elaborately posed portraits. During this era, students signed the bylaws of the college, which ruled that they could not "frequent taverns, groceries and places of amusement and vice" and were not permitted out of their rooms after 9:00 p.m.

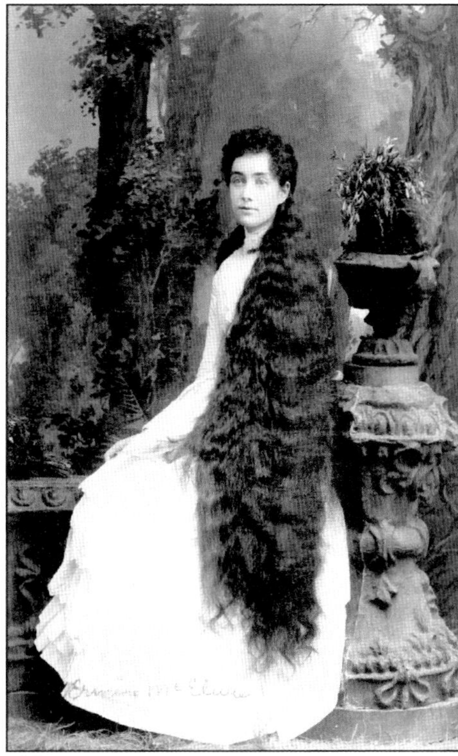

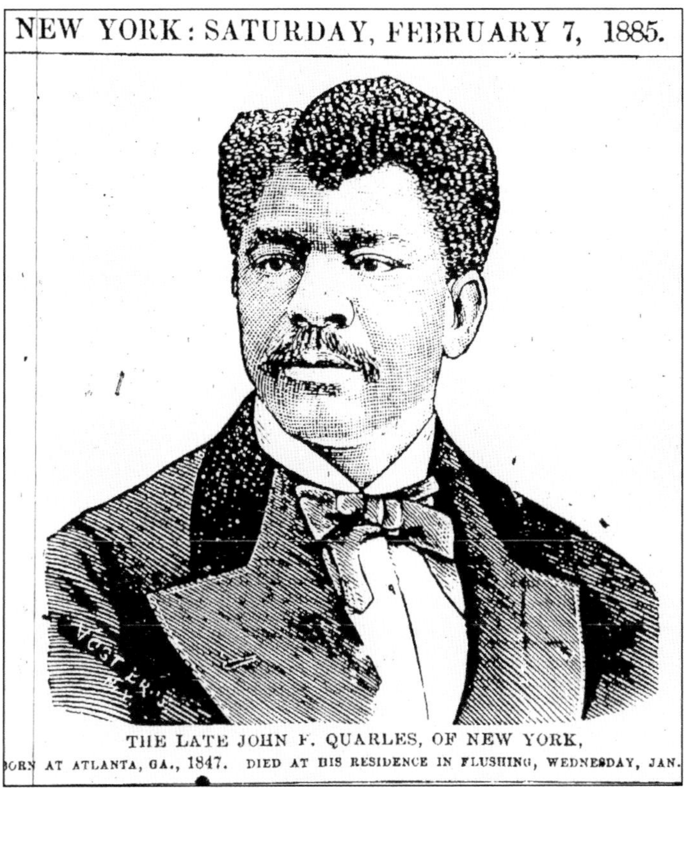

NEW YORK: SATURDAY, FEBRUARY 7, 1885.

THE LATE JOHN F. QUARLES, OF NEW YORK,
ORN AT ATLANTA, GA., 1847. DIED AT HIS RESIDENCE IN FLUSHING, WEDNESDAY, JAN.

Among Westminster's notable early alums was John F. Quarles. Quarles exemplified Westminster's doctrine as one of the first colleges to grant degrees to all qualifying individuals regardless of "color, caste or sex"—a groundbreaking principle in the pre–Civil War era. A native of Atlanta, Georgia, Quarles graduated in 1867 and went on to become one of the most prominent attorneys in the country. His obituary and career were front-page news in New York papers in 1885.

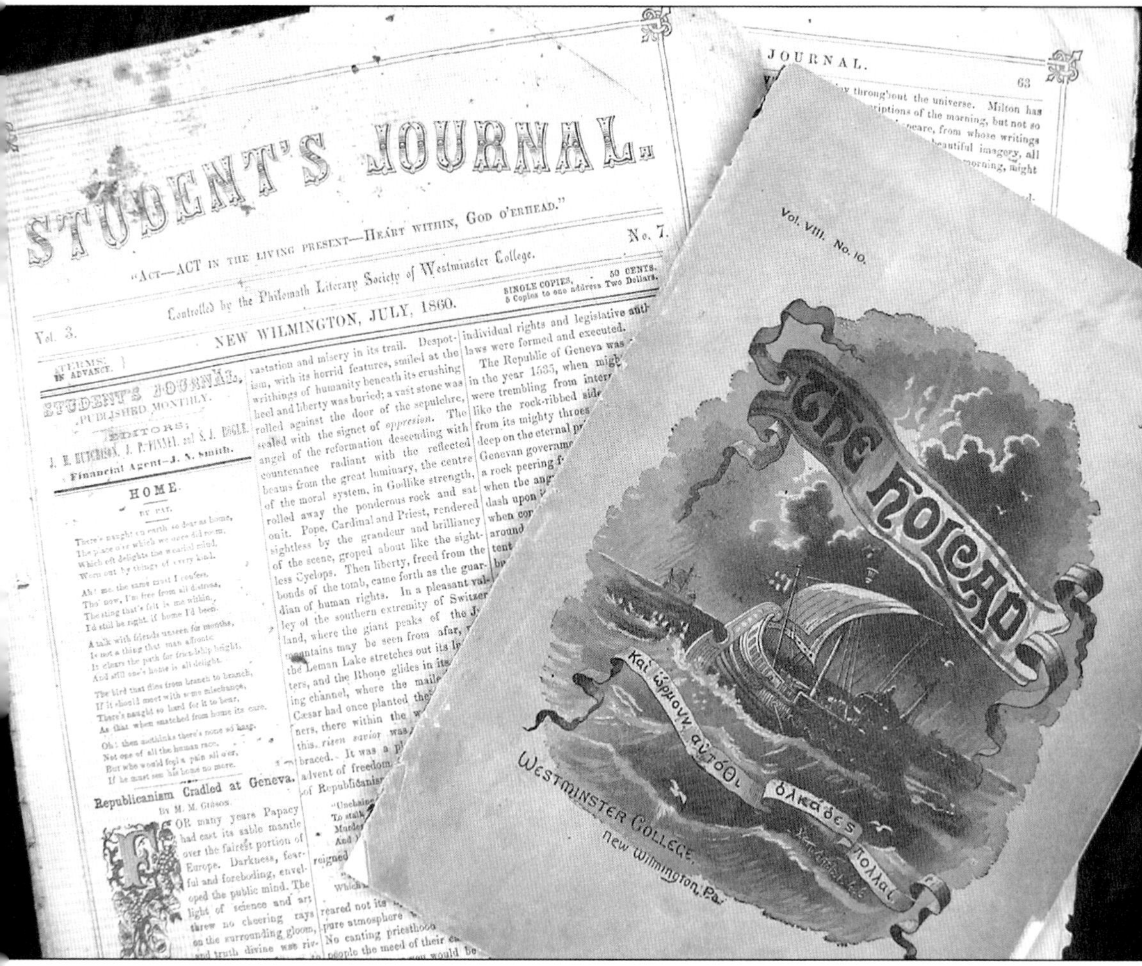

The *Student's Journal* was published in broadsheet format beginning around 1858. Collegians started the *Holcad* in 1884 as a magazine with a literary focus. The publication evolved into a monthly newspaper and became a weekly in 1917. The name comes from the myth "Anabasis," which students were then studying. *Holcad* was a ship and the editors felt that it was their duty, as noted in the March 6, 1928, edition, "to bear the burden of carrying news of Westminster to the students and the outside world."

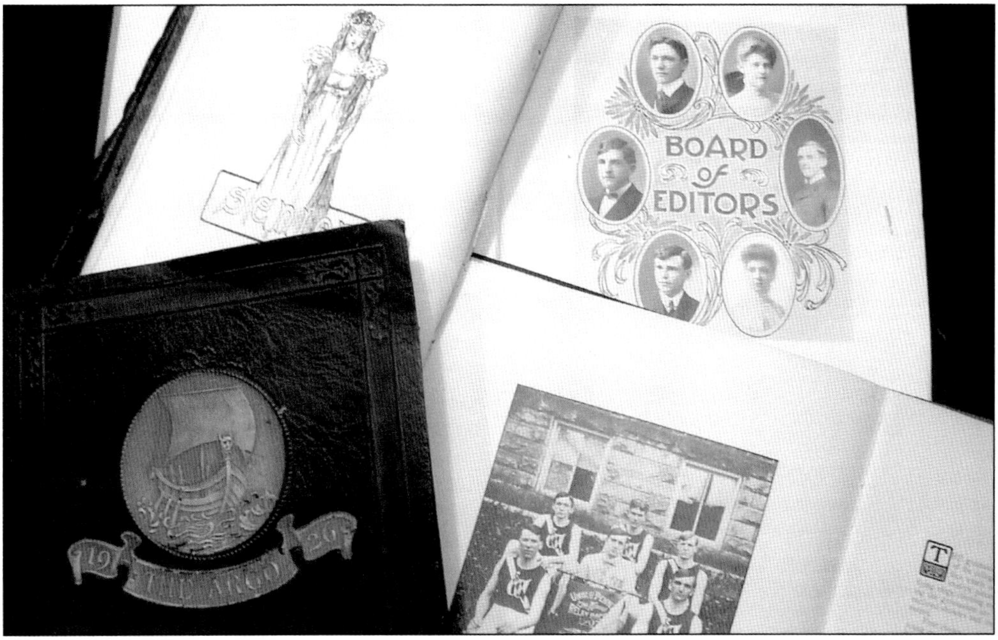

Like its weekly counterpart, the annual student review book was named for a mythological figure. The *Argo* debuted in 1904, and was given the title in homage to the mythic ship with a name, *Argo*, which traveled the Mediterranean with a band of heroes to fetch the golden fleece.

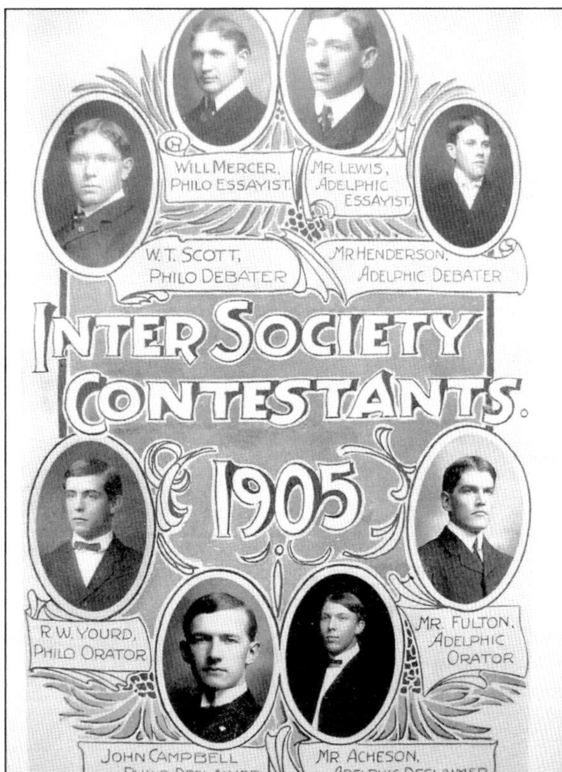

Early publications covered the many literary societies that were popular academic and social clubs at the time. These societies carried such names as Christomath, Philomath, and Legorean. Activities involved forensics and debate. They also had reading rooms (forerunners to the library) and their programs gradually evolved into eating clubs and, finally, fraternities and sororities.

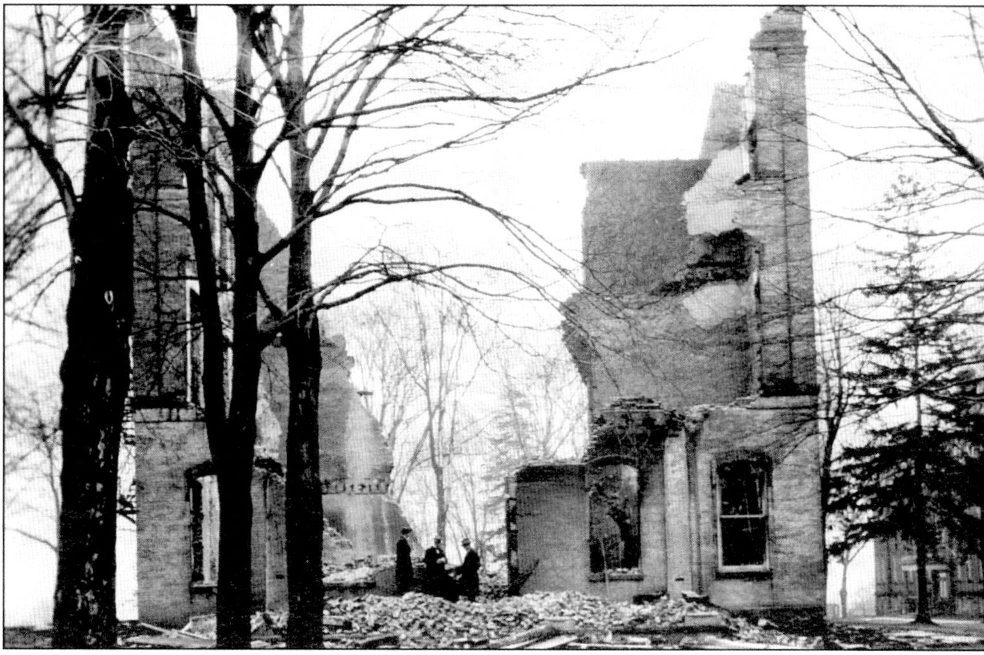

In January 1927, the Old Main building, like its predecessor, was destroyed by a fire. The cause was faulty wiring. Dr. Charles Wallace (center amid the rubble), then president, led an initiative to immediately reschedule classes and to utilize the neighboring United Presbyterian Church. Tuition that year was $200.

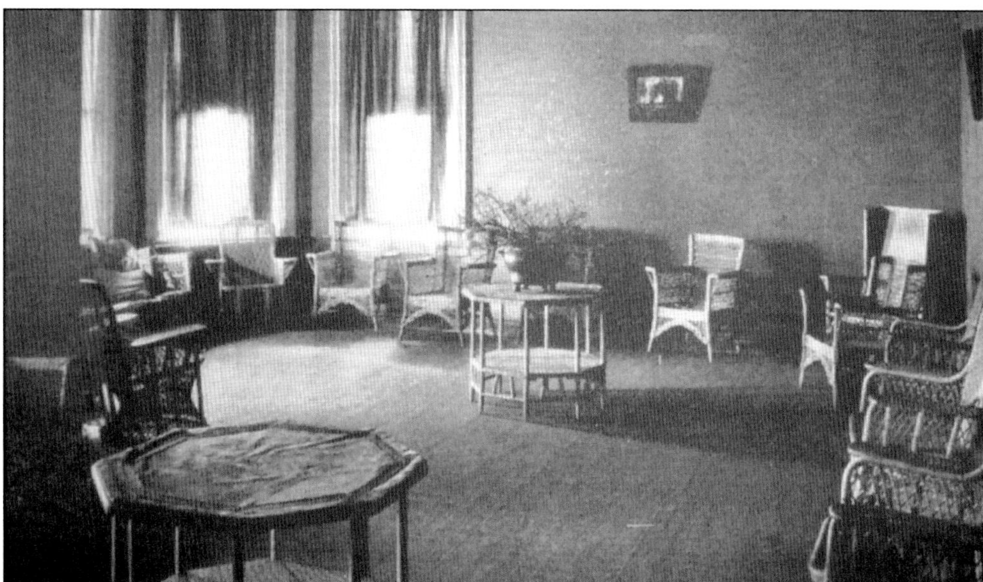

In 1927 the Hillside reception hall was a center of campus social activities. This photograph appeared that year in a 75th anniversary fund-raising booklet. The campaign's goal was to raise $1 million, with half going to an endowment and the rest to a chapel, library, offices, and two dorms. The plan failed for many unpredictable reasons: the Old Main inferno, a competing denominational fund drive by the United Presbyterian Church, and the Great Depression in 1929.

Two

Traditions and Celebrations

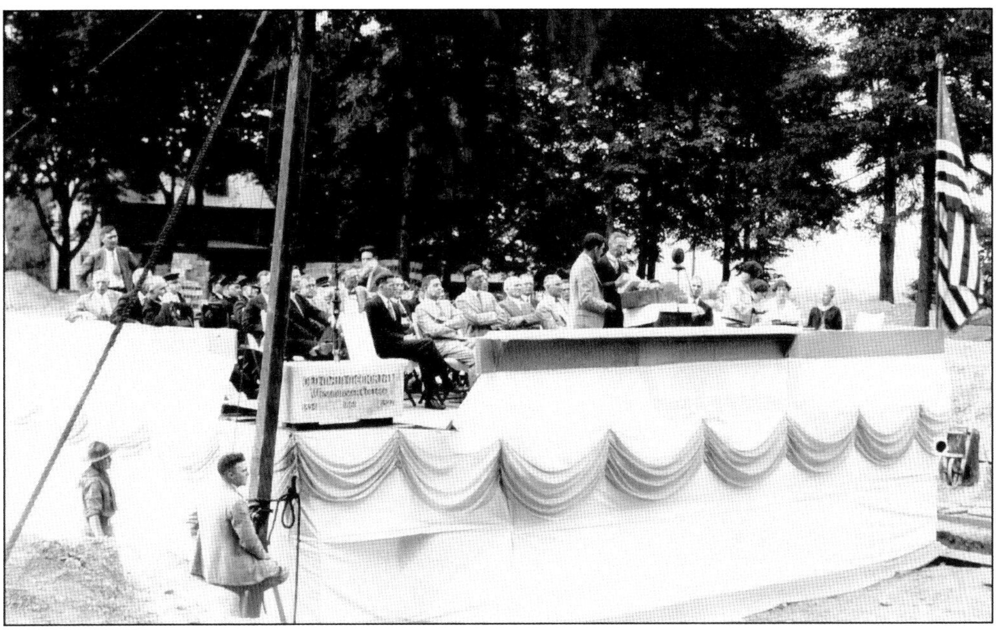

Westminster's present-day campus began taking shape in 1927 with the cornerstone-laying ceremony for Old Main Memorial, which anchors the Collegiate Gothic quadrangle. These early buildings—all constructed prior to World War II—included the gymnasium (later known as Old 77); Jeffers, Ferguson, and Browne dormitories; and McGill Library. During the 1950s and 1960s, Pres. Will W. Orr masterminded a massive campus expansion, which included digging Brittain Lake; constructing Eichenauer, Shaw, Russell, and Galbreath residence halls; opening the Walton-Mayne Student Union; and building the arts and science multiplex.

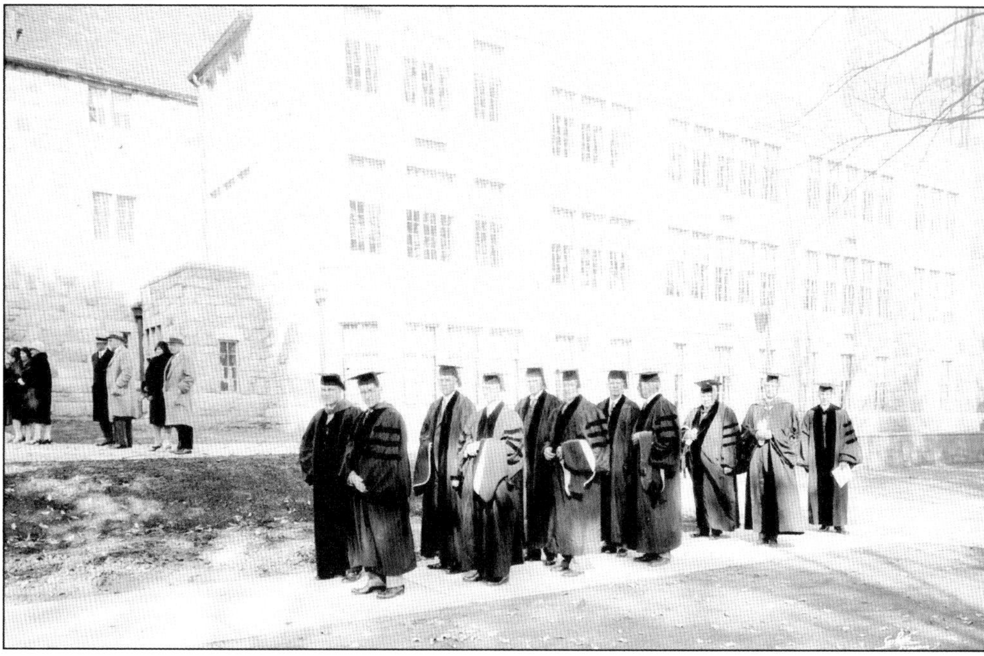

Commencement ceremonies call for a colorful academic gauntlet and a walk across Senior Terrace. The platform party (like the 1930s group above) has always included honorary degree recipients and trustees. Only extreme weather mandates an indoor ceremony at Memorial Field House, as with the *c.* 1950 exercises below.

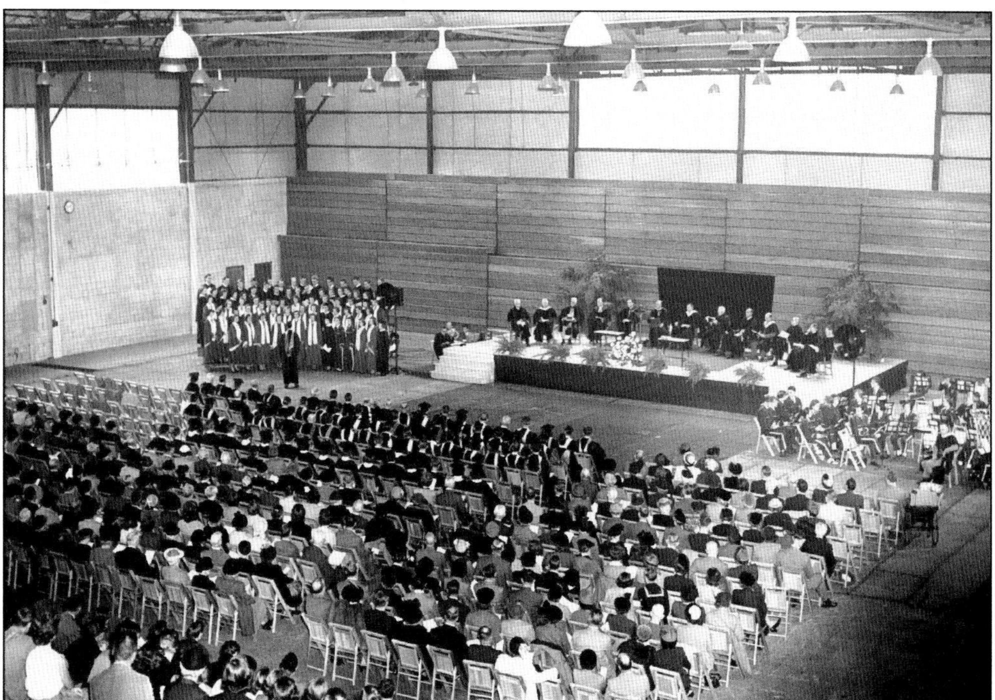

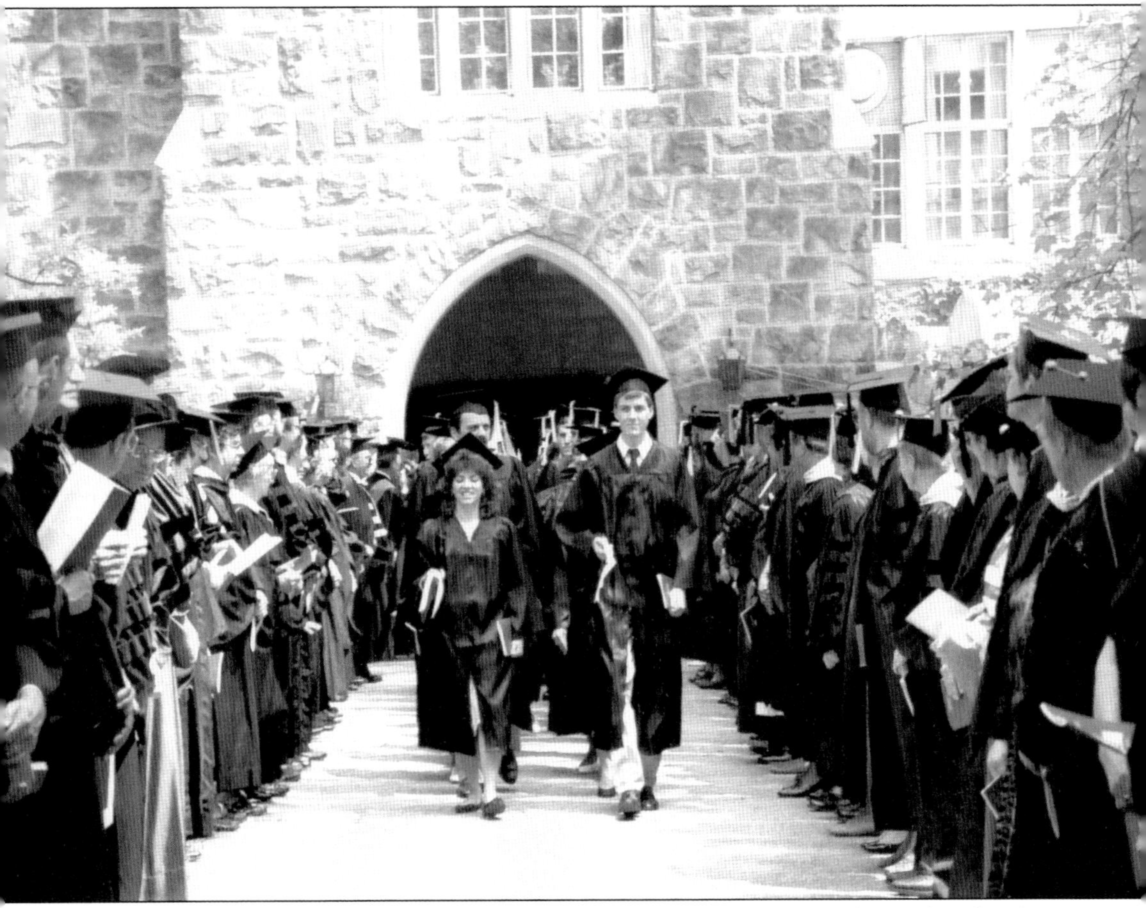

Freshmen year begins with a convocation and walk to the campus through a faculty gauntlet. Following commencement, the students—now alumni—leave via a gauntlet of applauding faculty, administration, and trustees. Graduates in 1988 enjoy the walk.

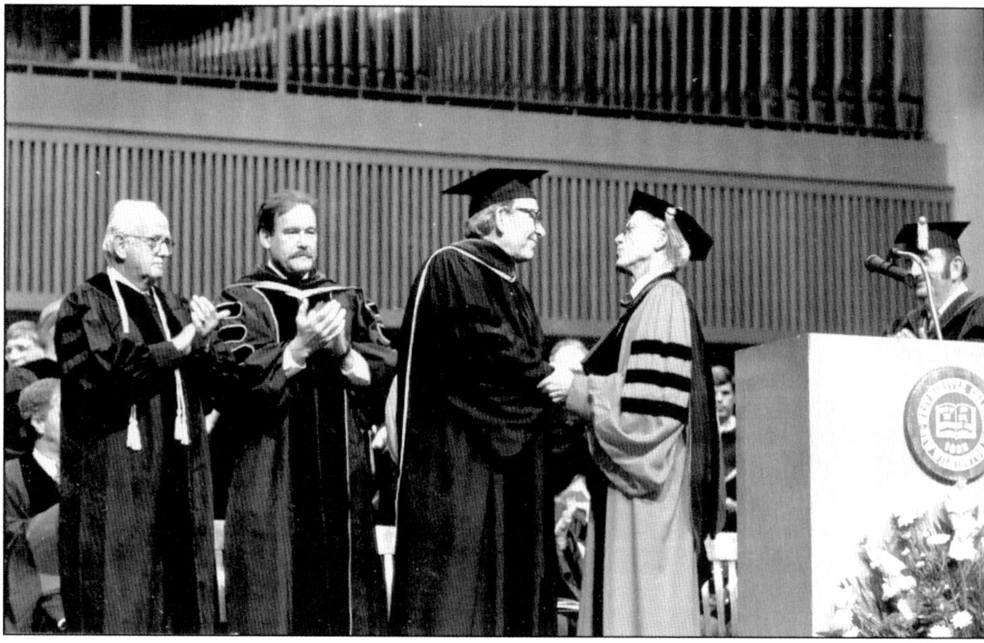

Former Pres. Earland I. Carlson (third from left) received an honorary doctorate from Pres. Oscar Remick during 1992 ceremonies. Joining the applause are trustee Don Wiley (left), Dr. Gary Lilly (second from left), and Dr. Gene Sharkey (right).

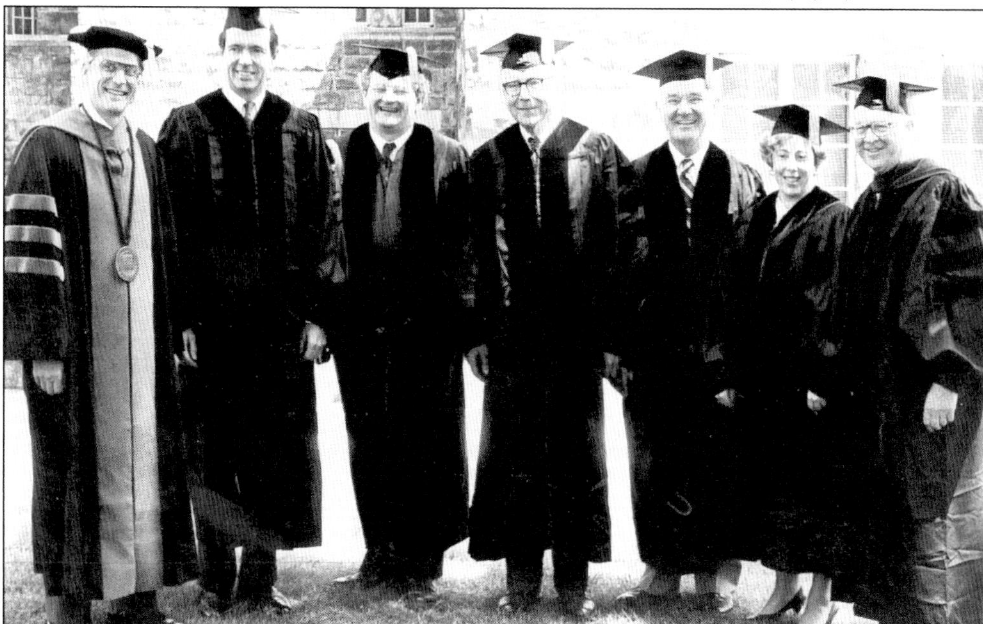

Honorary degree recipients are hooded during each commencement ceremony. Those receiving degrees have ranged from elected officials to clergy, from business executives to philanthropists, and from academicians to celebrities. In 1982, Pres. Alan Splete (left) presented the college's highest honor to, from left to right, U.S. senator H. John Heinz III, Rev. Dr. John W. Stewart, Dr. Arthur S. Link, Dr. Frank P. Piskor, and Dr. Rosabeth Moss Kanter. Also on hand was Robert Lauterbach, then chair of the board of trustees.

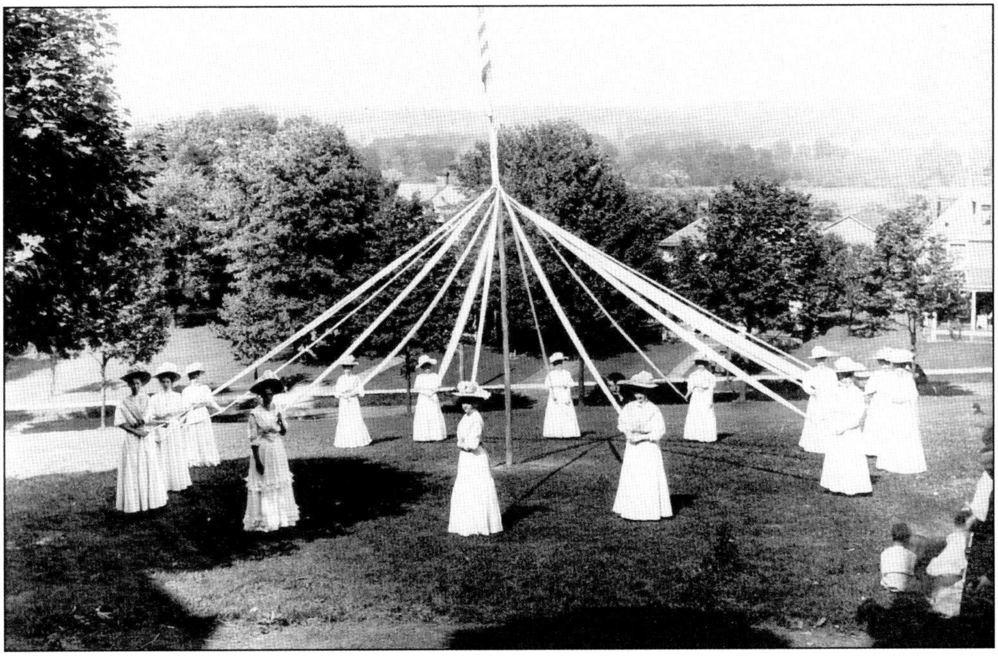

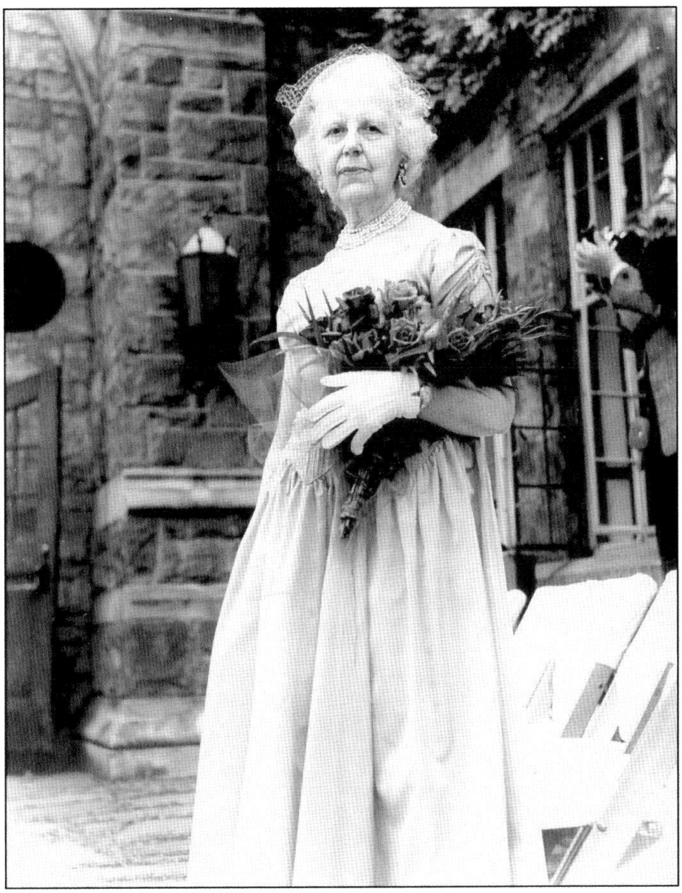

One of Westminster's longest-running traditions was May Day, which began in 1907 at the behest of Caroline (Keech) Russell, wife of the college's fifth president. The first festival featured a maypole dance on the lawn of the Hillside and the crowning of May Queen Irene Galbreath Holminton, who returned to campus five decades later (right) to participate in the 50th celebration.

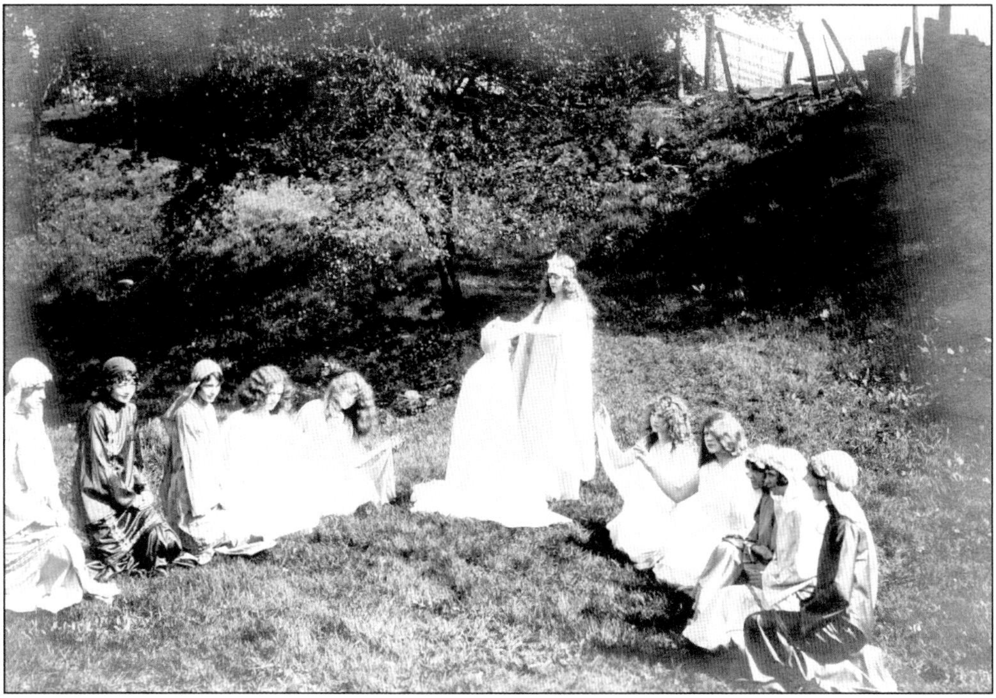

By 1926, May Day had grown in sophistication and ceremony to resemble a scene in a Mary Pickford silent movie, complete with Grecian-style gowns.

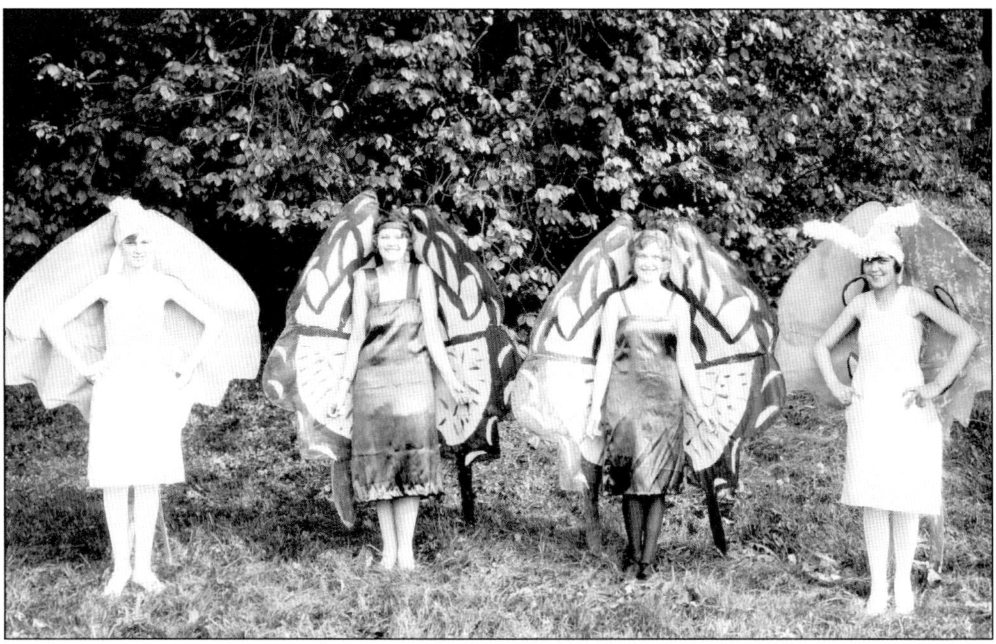

Skits and gymnastic shows, such as this 20th-century version, provided entertainment during the daylong May Day merriment.

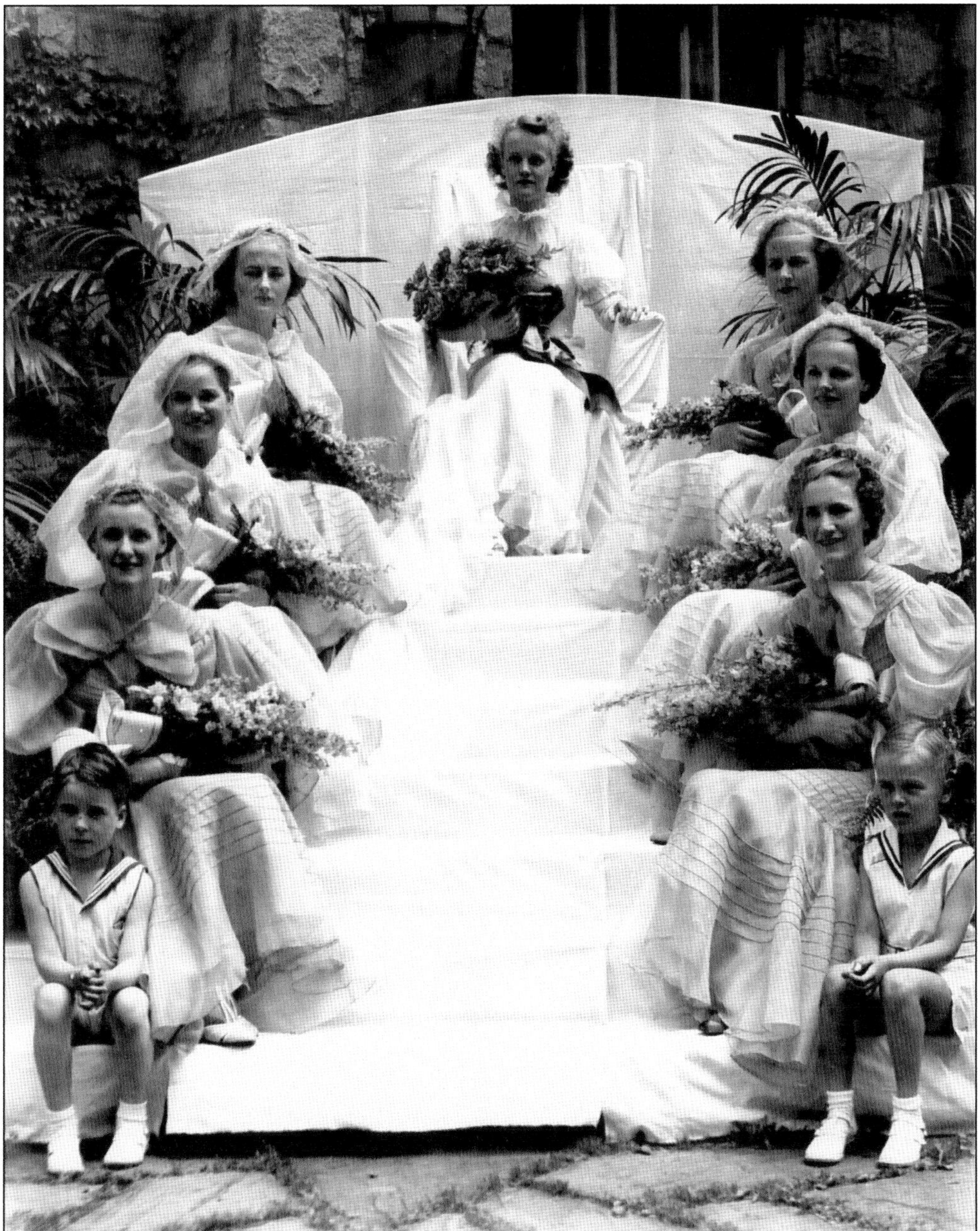

In 1936, May Queen Beverly Blythe reigned during sophisticated rituals that belied the economic hardship of the Great Depression. Throughout much of the 1930s, Westminster's enrollment swelled as young people, most from upper-income families, chose college as an alternative to the exceedingly tight job market.

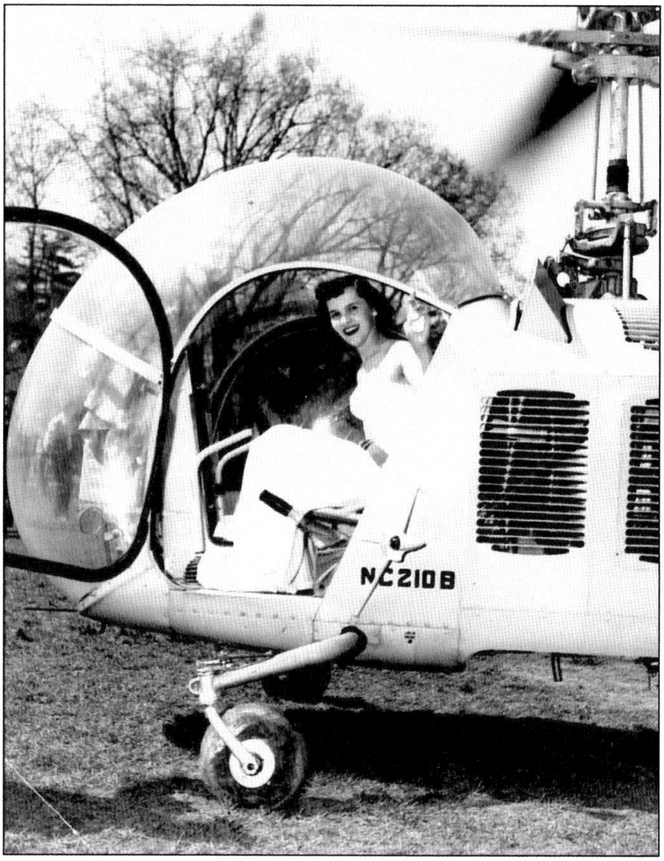

Students declared April 27, 1949, W.O.W. (Will Orr Welcome) Day and May Day. To mark the occasion, May Queen Helen Papazickos arrived via helicopter. Students were so enthused with the selection of the new president that they welcomed Orr and his wife Eloise (in the back seat) with a caravan at the Ohio-Pennsylvania border and continued with a Market Street parade.

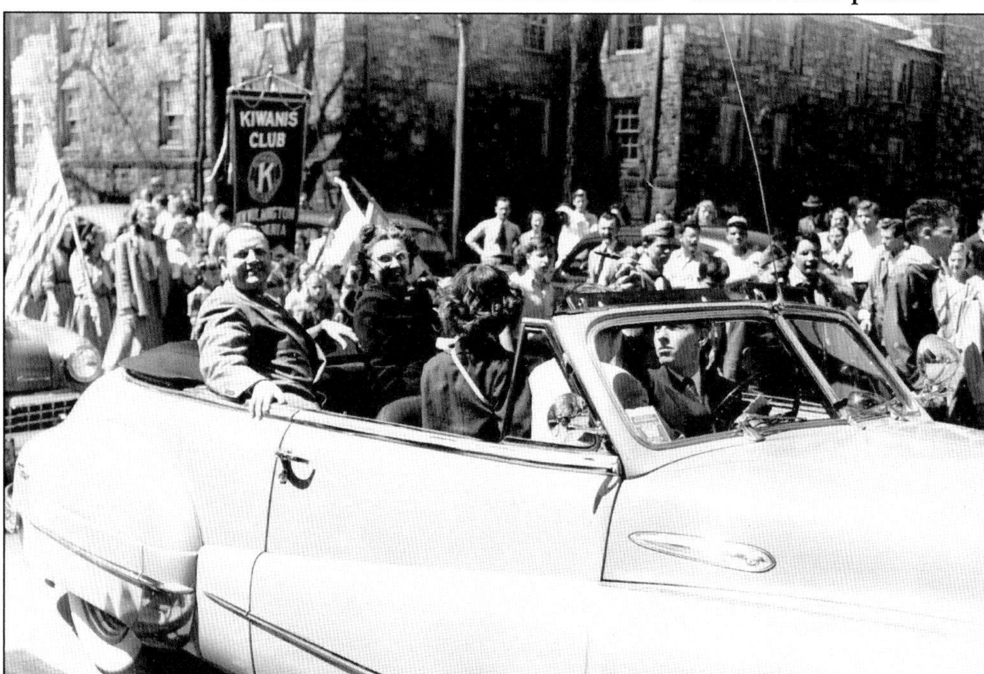

As students created new traditions, May Day parties lost some of their luster and, thus, the annual spring rite ended in the mid-1980s. Amy Klipa (left), the 1983 May Queen, crowned Beth Eck in 1984.

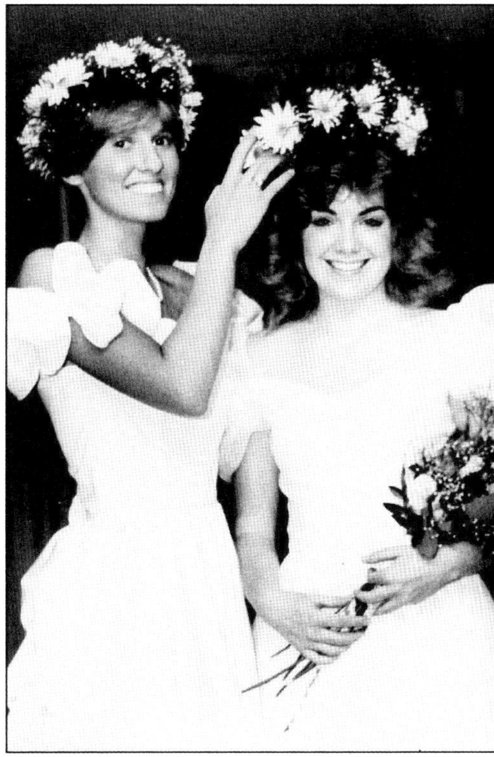

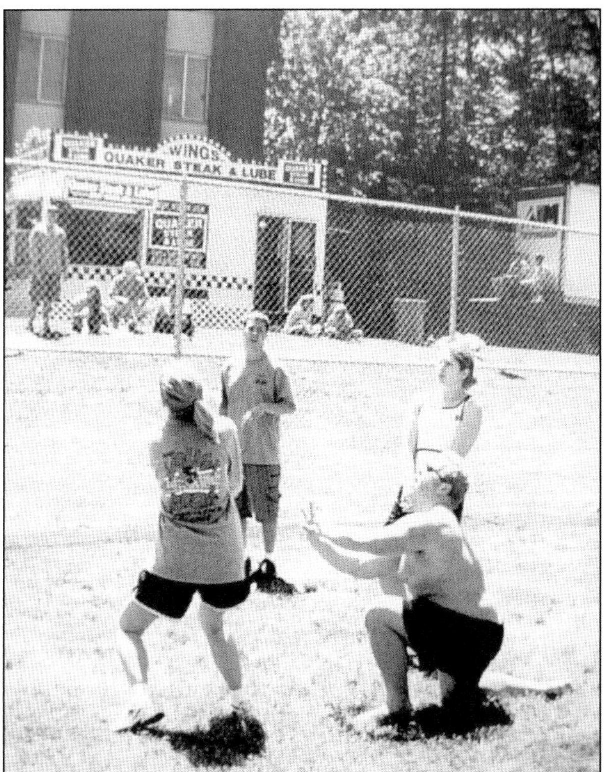

Newly minted traditions include more interactive celebrations, such as Volley Rock, a campus-wide sports event and outdoor festival.

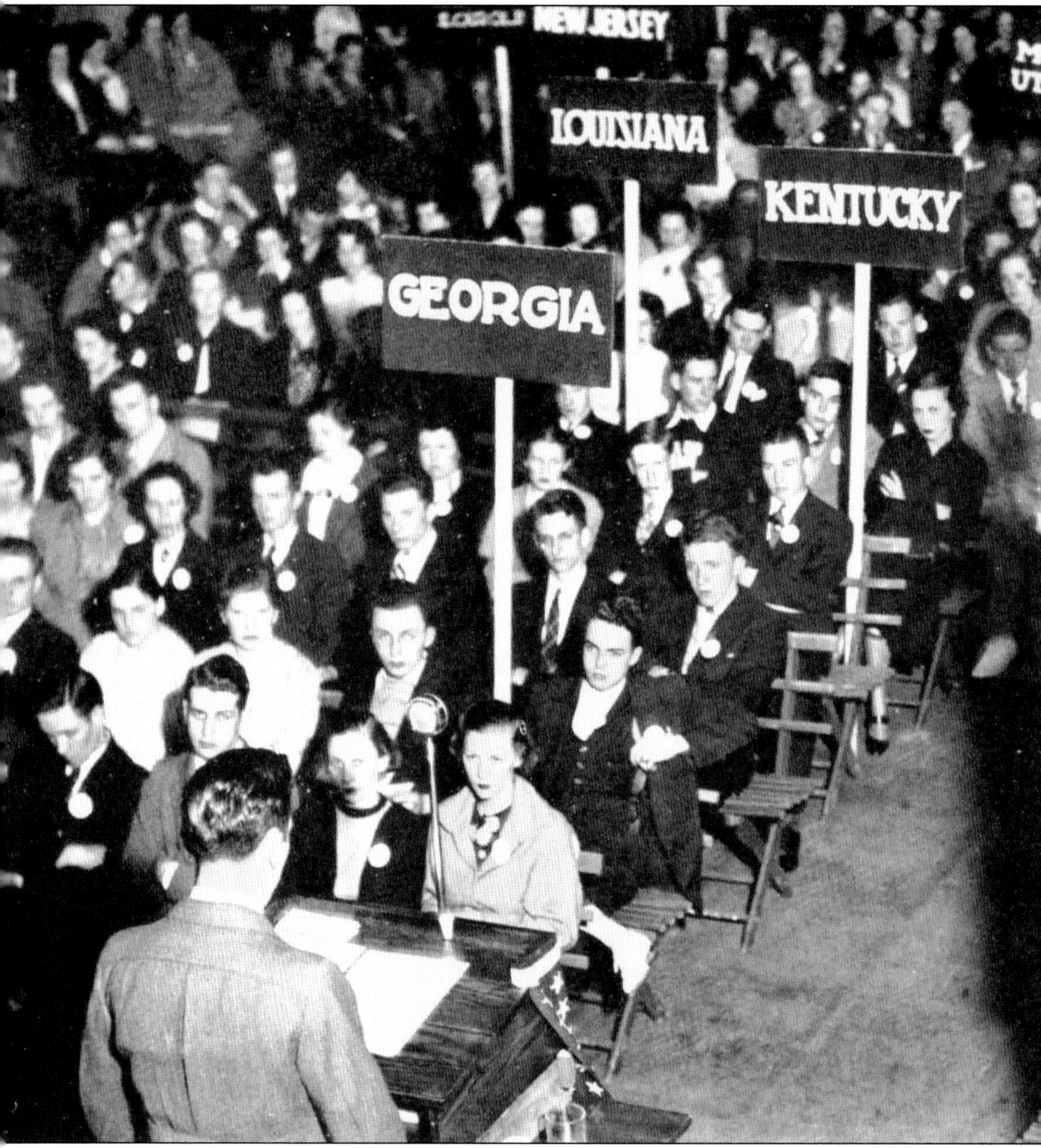

During the 1930s, students nationwide engaged in political discussions about dire economic conditions in the United States and abroad. At Westminster that interest spawned one of the college's most enduring traditions, the Mock Convention. The first convention, held in April 1936, was a large-scale role-playing exercise focused on the pending Republican National Convention. Students convened in the gymnasium to draw up platforms, meet in state caucuses, and conduct convention-floor demonstrations for their favorite candidates. Their presidential nominee was Herbert Hoover. The quadrennial event focuses on the non-incumbent party. The concept came to Westminster with history instructor Thomas V. Mansell '29, who learned of mock conventions during his days at Harvard Law School.

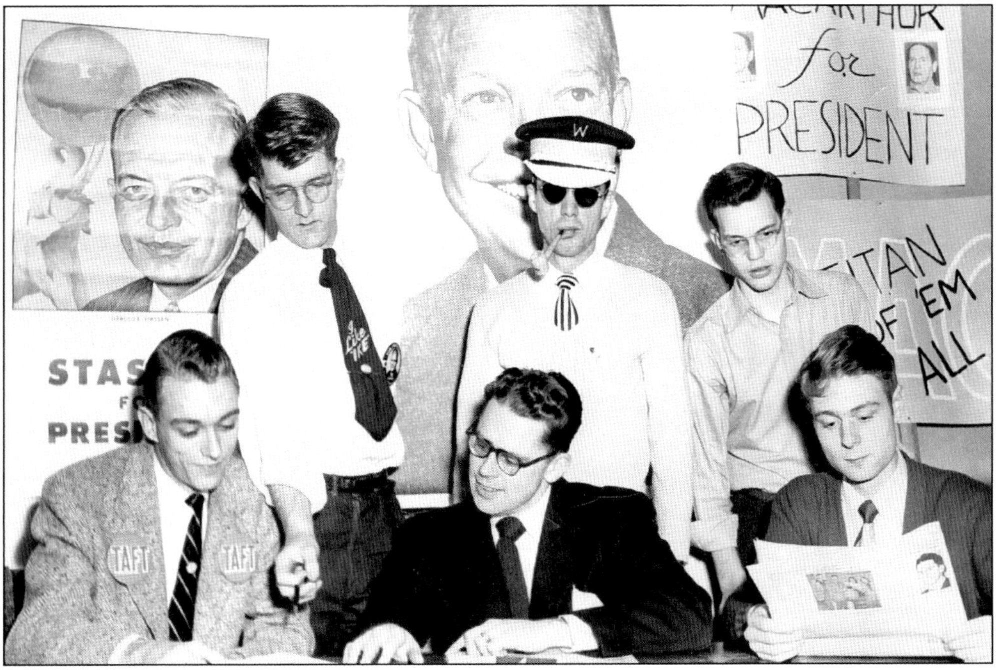

By 1952, the student body embraced politics with vigor and undergrads impersonated various candidates (above), including would-be nominee Gen. Douglas MacArthur. However, the convention's nod went to Gen. Dwight D. Eisenhower. In the ensuing years, Westminster students were prescient in their selections, more often than not, selecting the individual ultimately nominated in the real-life convention. Such accuracy brought national attention to the college from political pundits and the media. The Mock Convention continues to be held quadrennially.

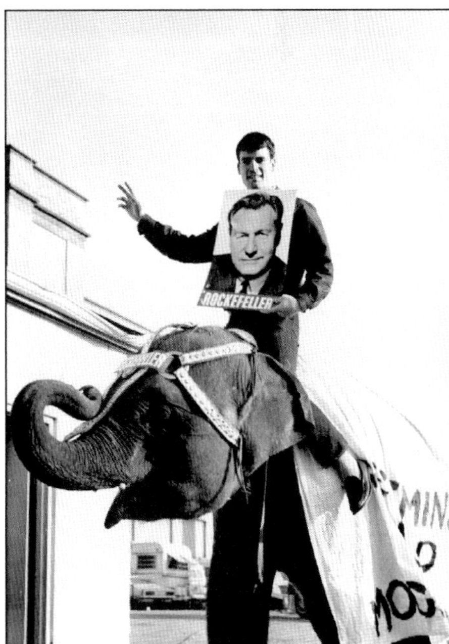

In the 1967 presidential election cycle, students joined in "conventioneering" by wearing buttons, badges, and state-themed costumes. Furthermore, they employed all manner of stunts to promote their political favorites. Despite the hiring of an elephant to bolster votes for Nelson Rockefeller, student delegates nominated Richard Nixon for president and Charles Percy for vice president.

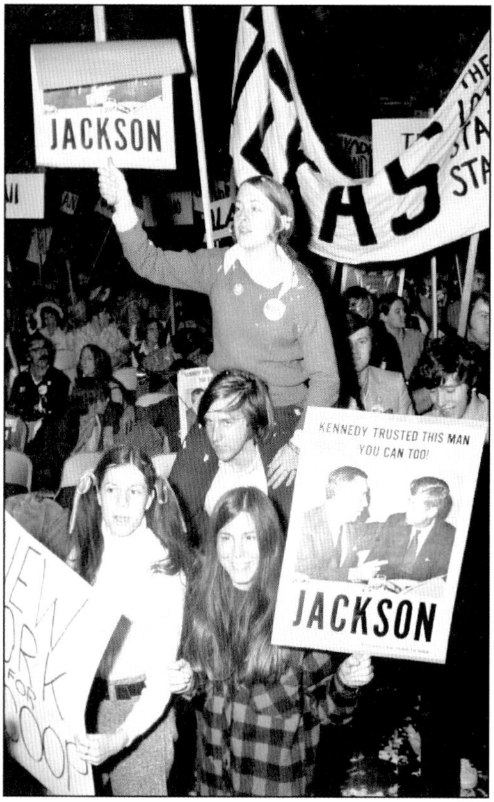

The 1972 floor demonstrations electrified the collegiate delegates.

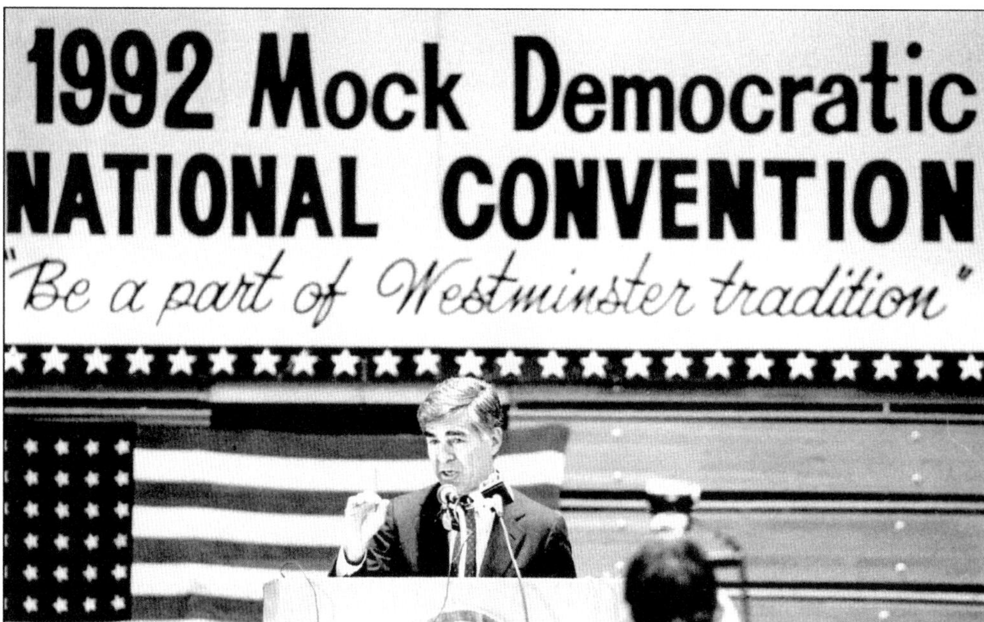

Although Massachusetts governor Michael Dukakis delivered the keynote address in 1992, Westminster students nominated Paul Tsongas for president and Barbara Roberts for vice president.

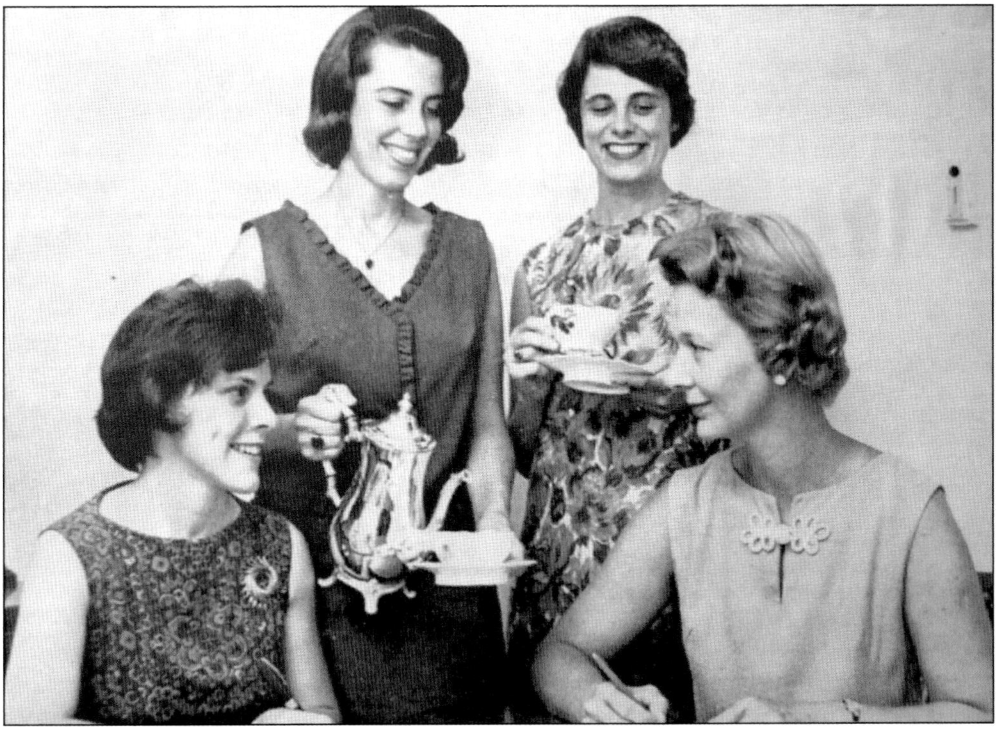

One long-remembered rite of passage for many women remains the freshmen tea. The event was held for Pittsburgh coeds by the Westminster Women's Club and earned regular mention on society pages. Founded in 1906, the club continues to provide fellowship for alumna.

The Westminster College Women's Club
of Pittsburgh

Invites you and your mother to attend the

Annual Freshman Tea

at the College Club

143 North Craig Street

Saturday, September 7, 1963

two o'clock

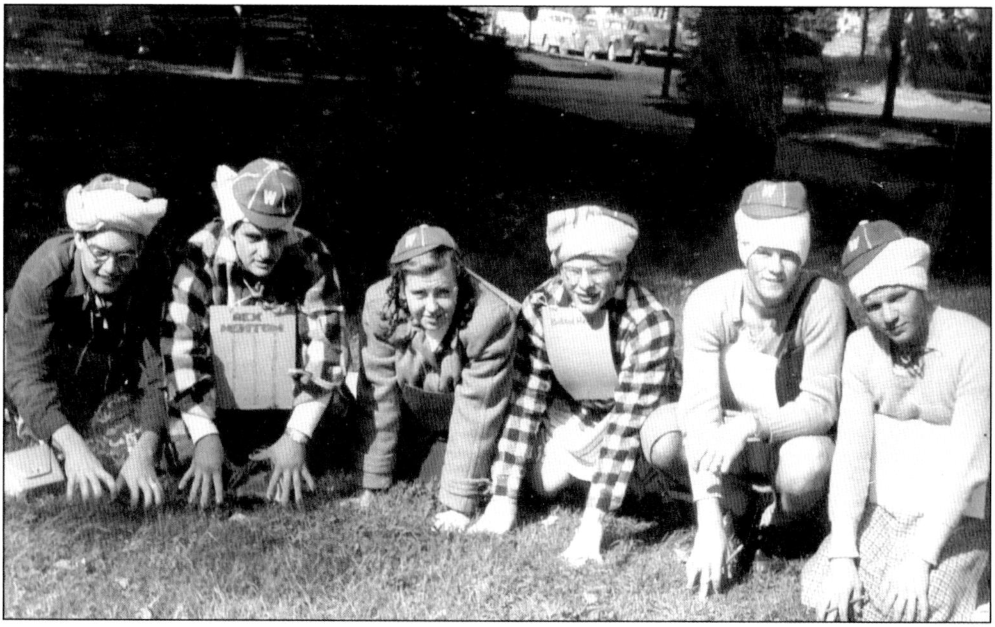

For many decades, freshman hazing was an accepted rite of passage in college life. It included wearing "dinks," as this group did in the 1950s. Freshman week (a 1935 invention) called for participation in various skits. In the 1940s, 1950s, and 1960s, "Hell Week" and the Freshman Tribunal provided fond memories of good-natured teasing and entertainment. During freshmen week, students signed on to various codes of conduct, which included standards of dress (no slacks or shorts for women and required collared shirts for men), compulsory chapel attendance daily, plus dorm sign-in and sign-out rules. Some inventive and determined students generally found creative ways to skip chapel and to escape the prying eyes of dorm "mothers."

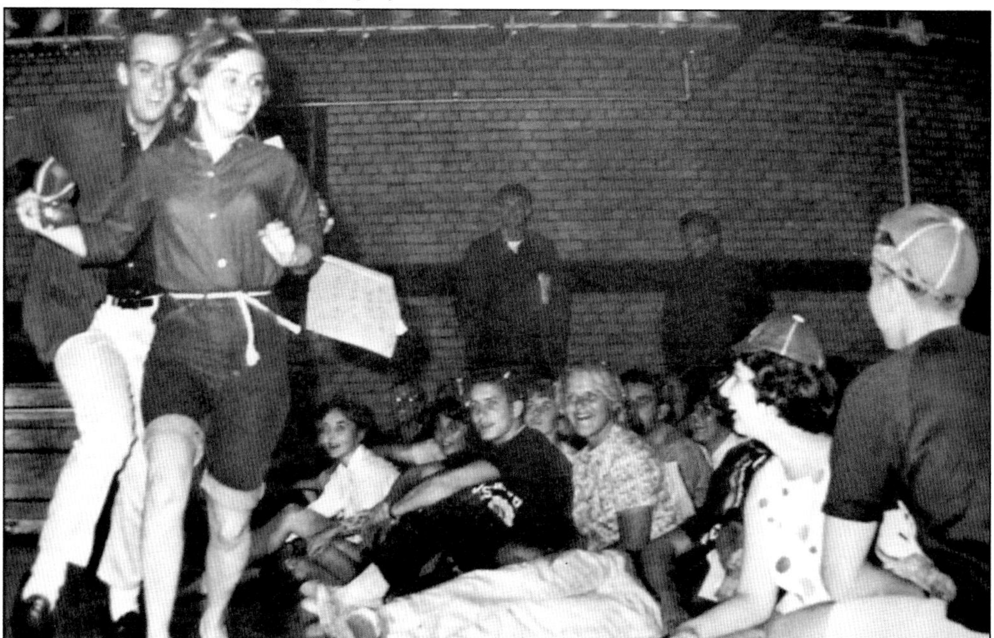

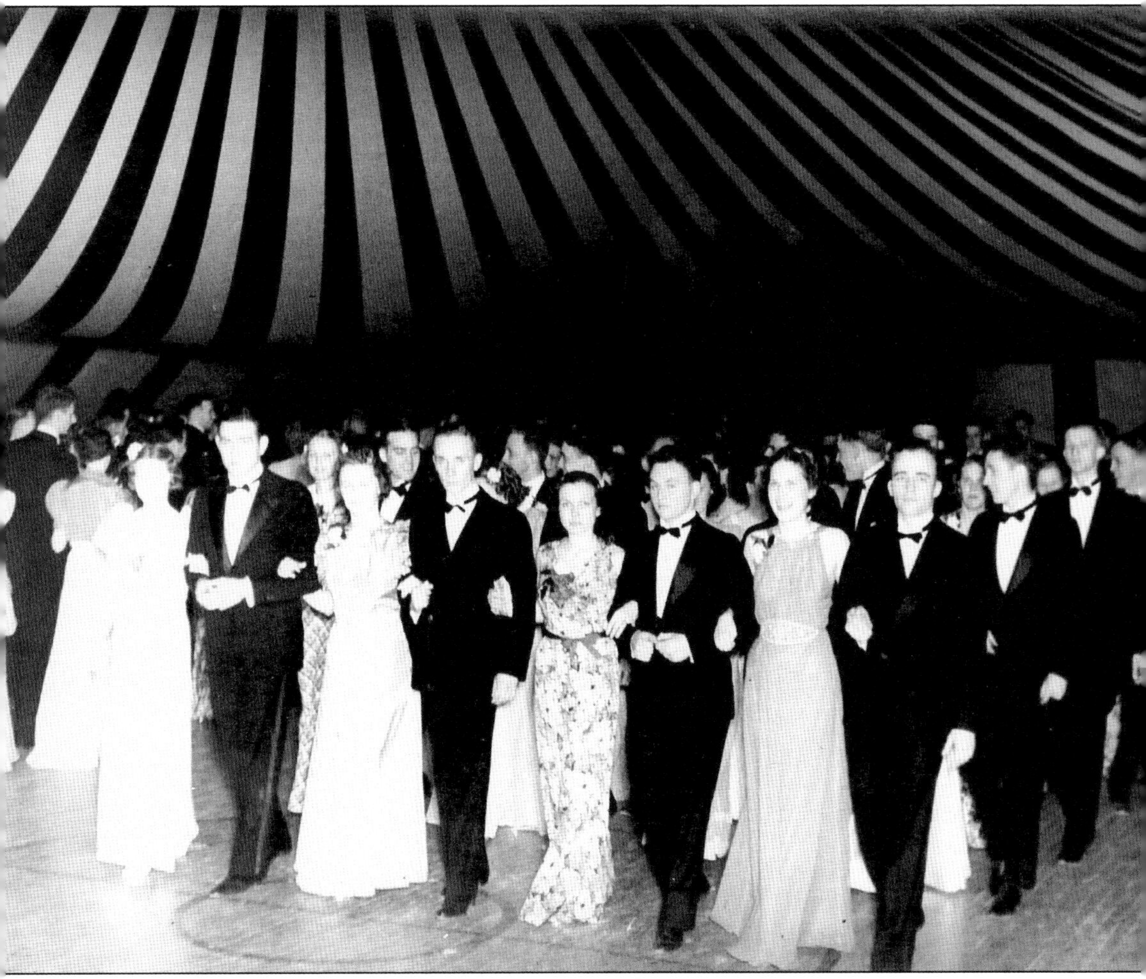

Fall homecoming festivities were first held in 1946. The "Dance of the Year" was often a formal affair in a fully decorated gymnasium. That year Duke Ellington played for the dance at the Cathedral in New Castle. The tradition evolved from the prior Autumn Weekend Festival.

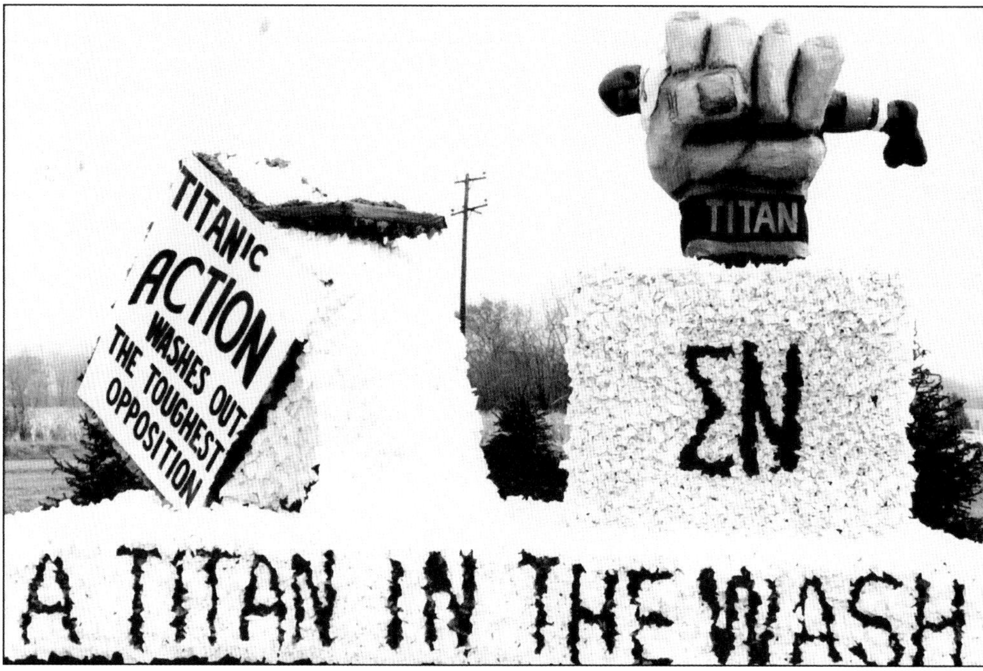

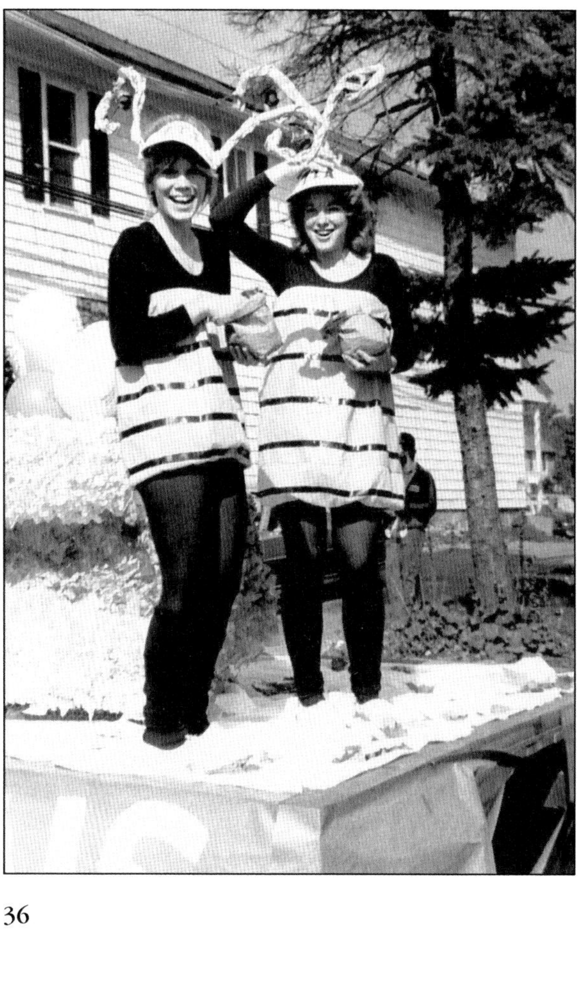

Floats and costumes have been front and center for homecoming parades along Market Street. In 1963, Sigma Nu fraternity snatched a first-place trophy for its entry, and in 1983, Zeta Tau Alpha sorority sisters "went buggy" for the Titans.

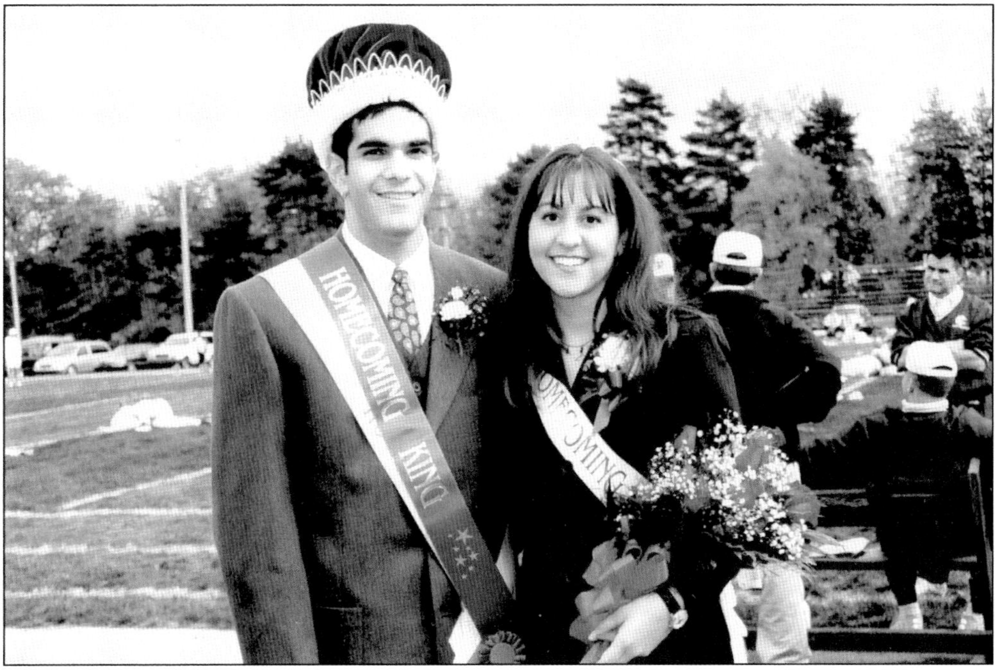

No homecoming football game is complete without the crowning of royalty. Early on, Westminster adopted this fall ritual. Students in 1998 selected Brad Russo and Julie Irvine.

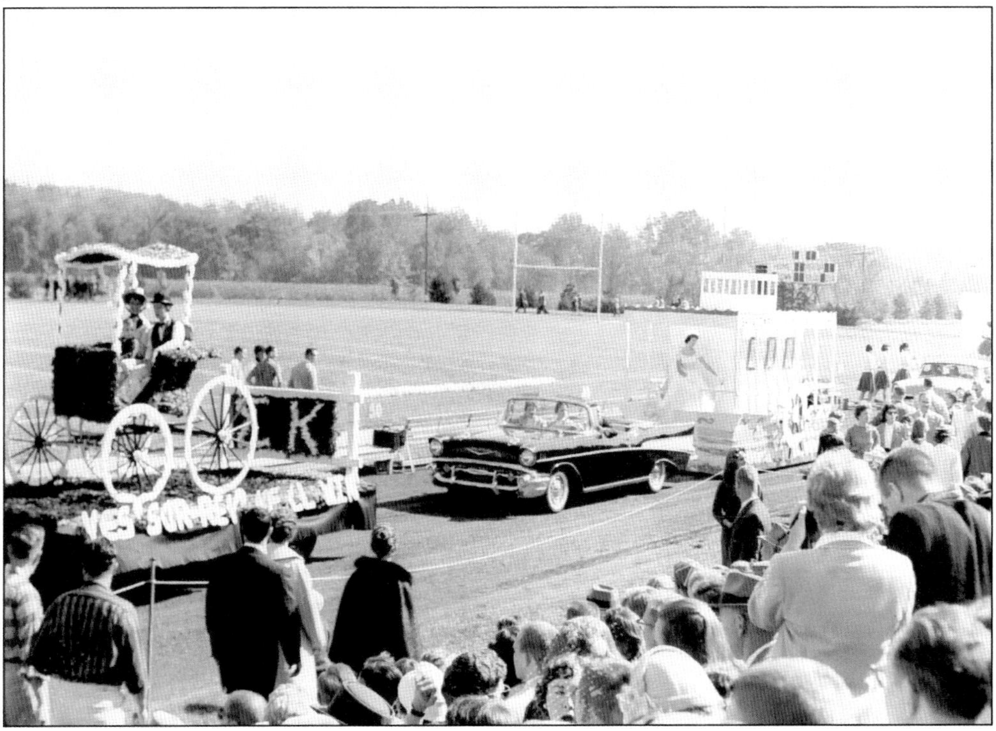

For many years, parade floats passed along the football field prior to the game, just as they did here in the 1950s.

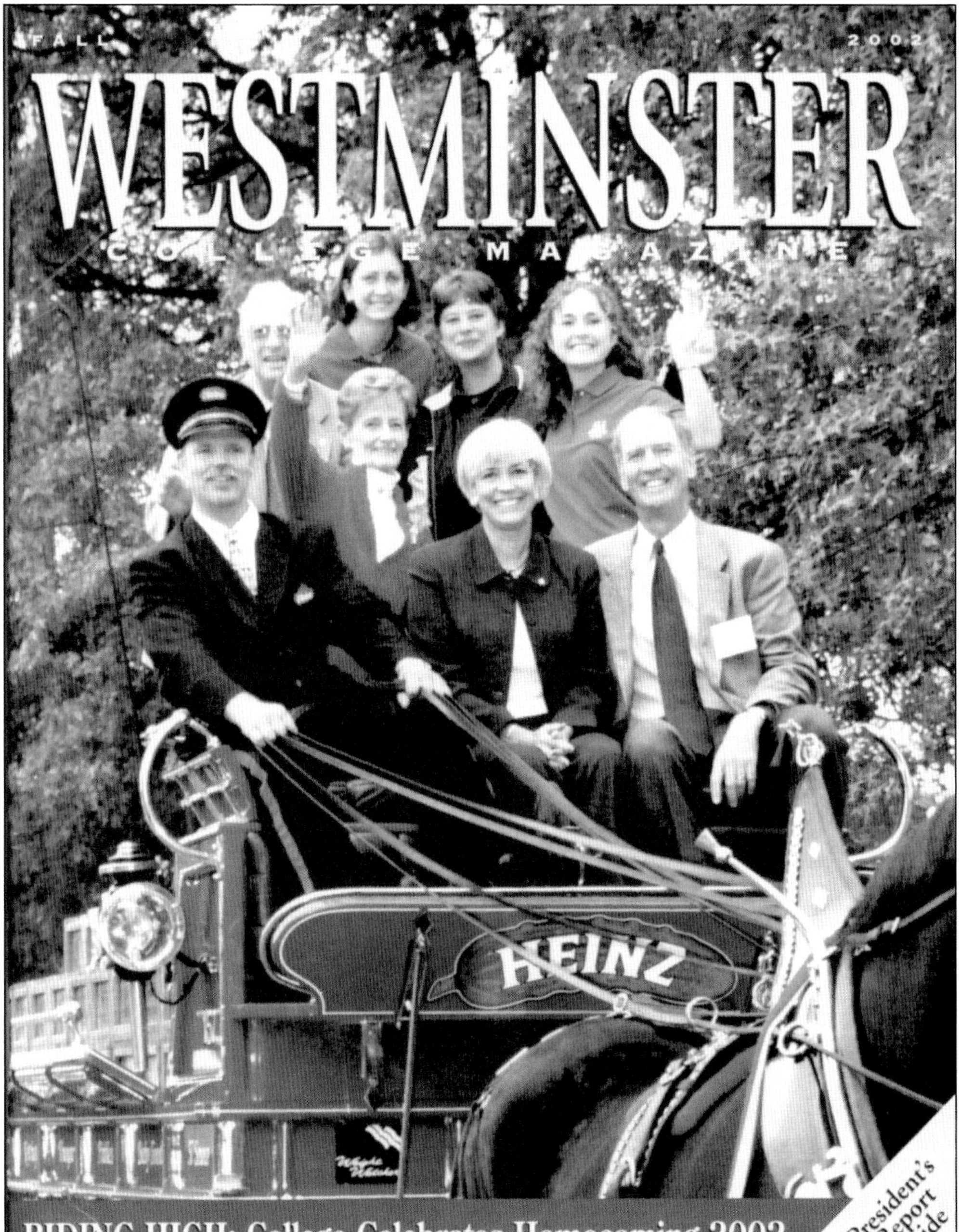

To celebrate its sesquicentennial, Westminster's homecoming parade featured the Heinz Hitch, a delivery wagon drawn by eight matched Percheron horses. The unit was reminiscent of those used at the time of the college's founding. Riding atop the rig were Pres. Tom Williamson and his wife Jean (foreground), New Wilmington mayor Wendell Wagner and his wife Phyllis (both class of 1955), plus student representatives. The ride made the front cover of *Westminster College Magazine*, the alumni quarterly.

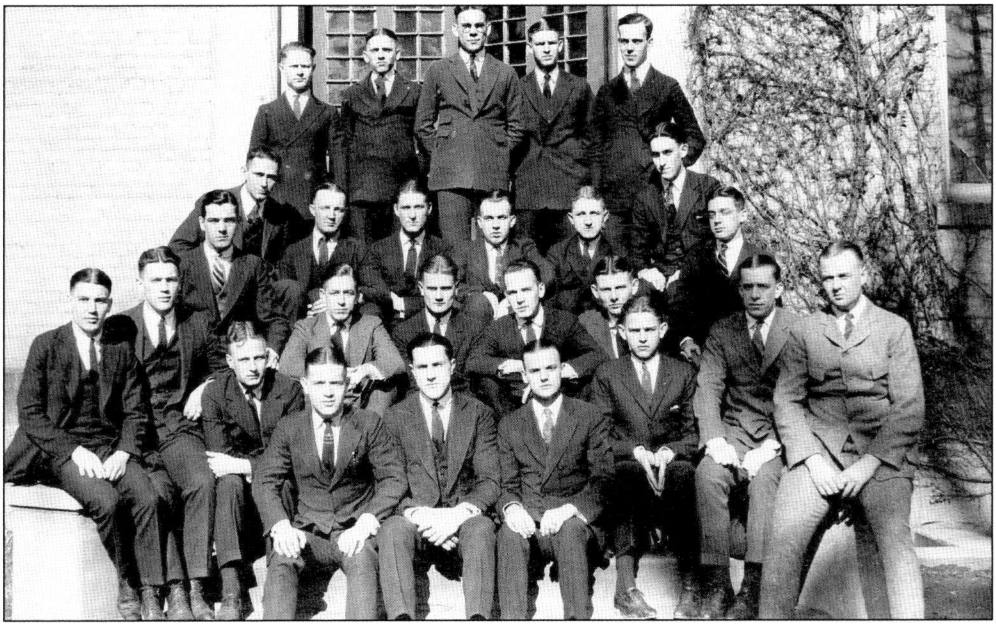

Student organizations, including honorary societies, service clubs, and Greek organizations, have played significant roles in the Westminster experience. Throughout Westminster's first five decades, literary societies—similar to today's forensic and debating teams—were the source of many social activities. Secret societies—such as sororities and fraternities—were banned, and those that did emerge from hiding were quickly stamped out. However, eating clubs grew in popularity not only because they were an economical dining option but also because they were forbidden social outlets. The Van Orsdell eating club (above in 1922) organized as Kappa Phi Lambda, a national fraternity founded two years earlier at Washington and Jefferson College. The Kelly eating club (below) became a chapter of Sigma Phi Epsilon. These were controversial sub rosa organizations until the college reluctantly recognized Greek societies in 1920.

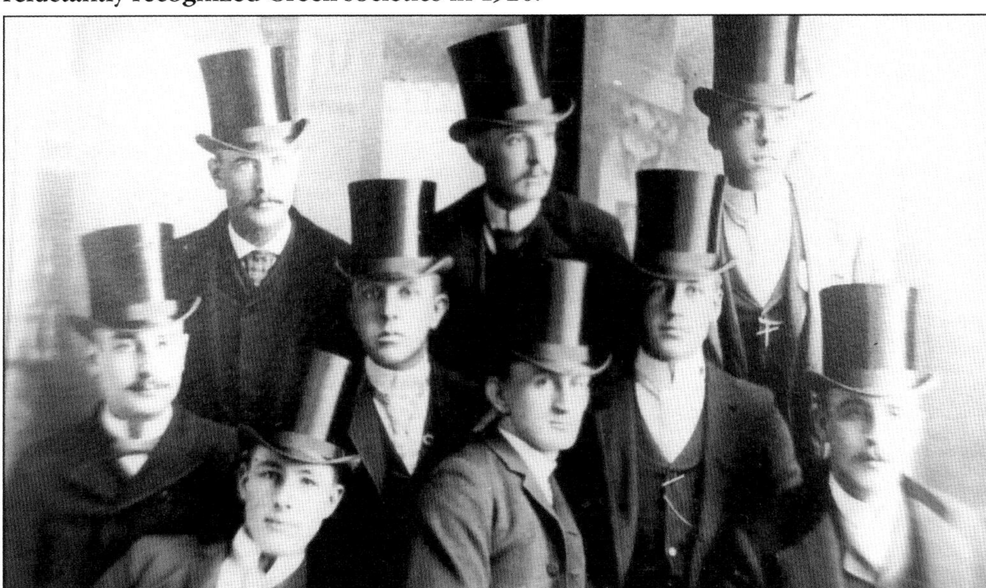

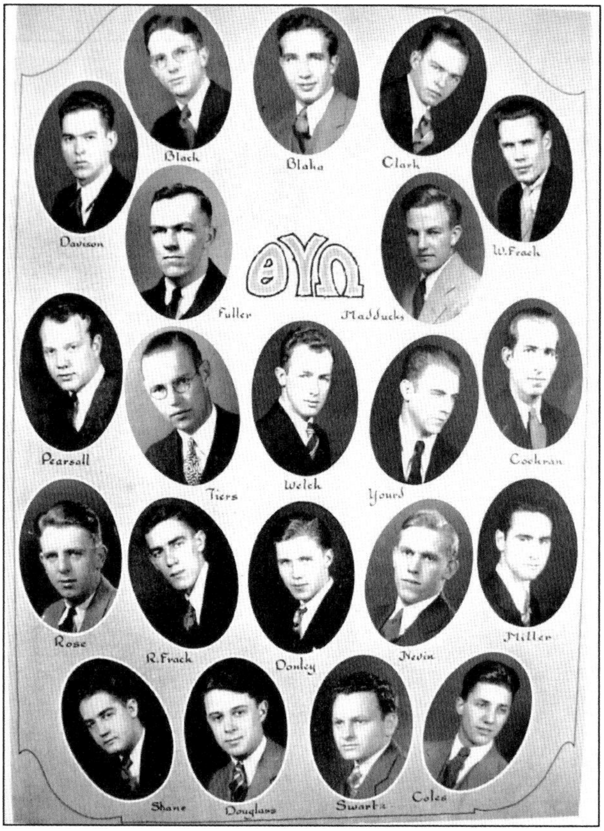

Fraternities began as local organizations, which later joined national fraternal groups. Among the early frats was Theta Upsilon Omega, seen at left in 1933. The Sigma Nu fraternity in 1958 (below) included many top athletes.

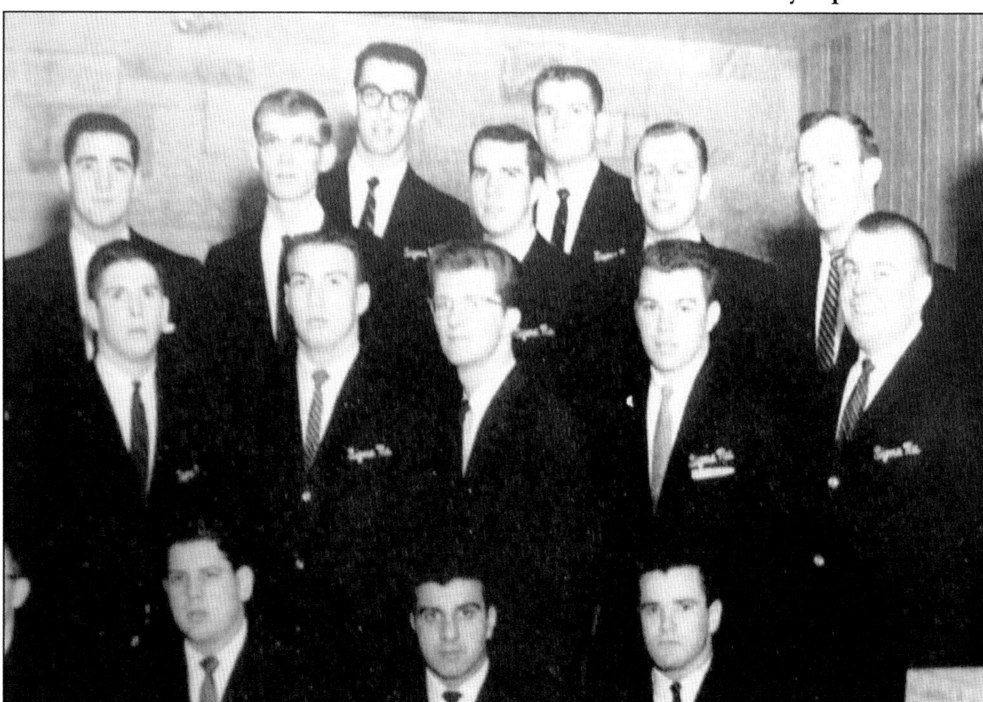

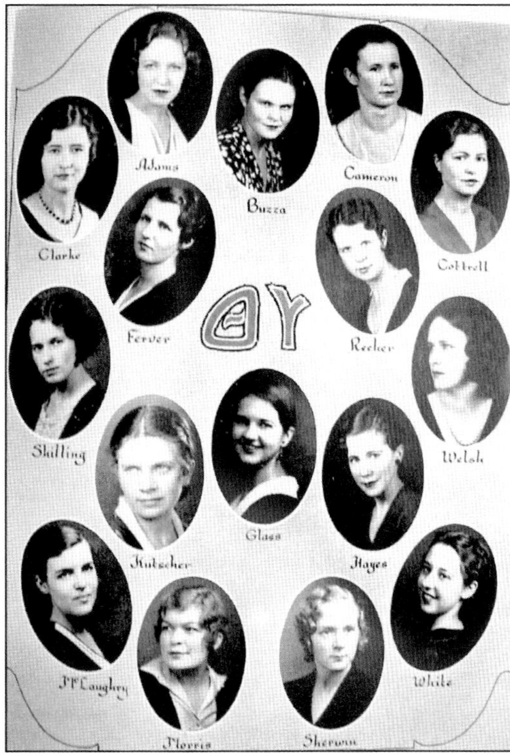

Sororities were often formed by the girls who dated frat boys. Theta Upsilon, seen at right in 1933, is thought to have been an offshoot of the Theta Upsilon Omega. Alpha Gamma Delta members in 1958 looked preppy in their well-tailored blazers (below).

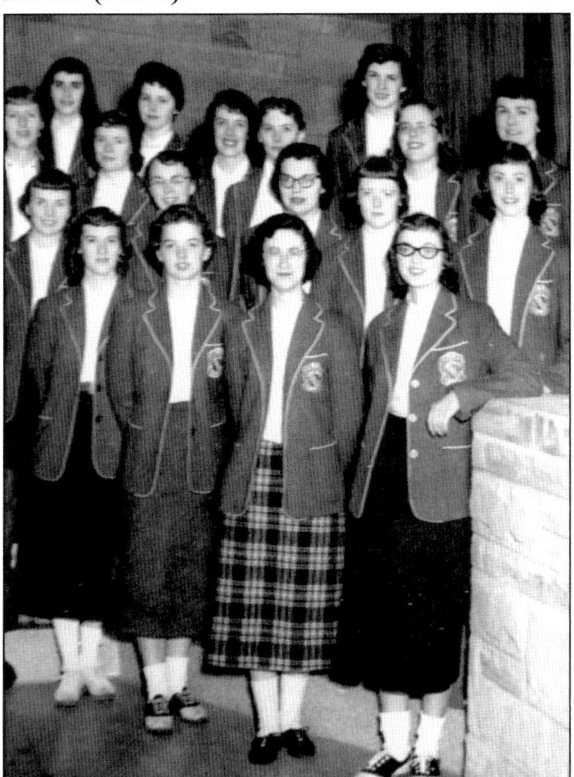

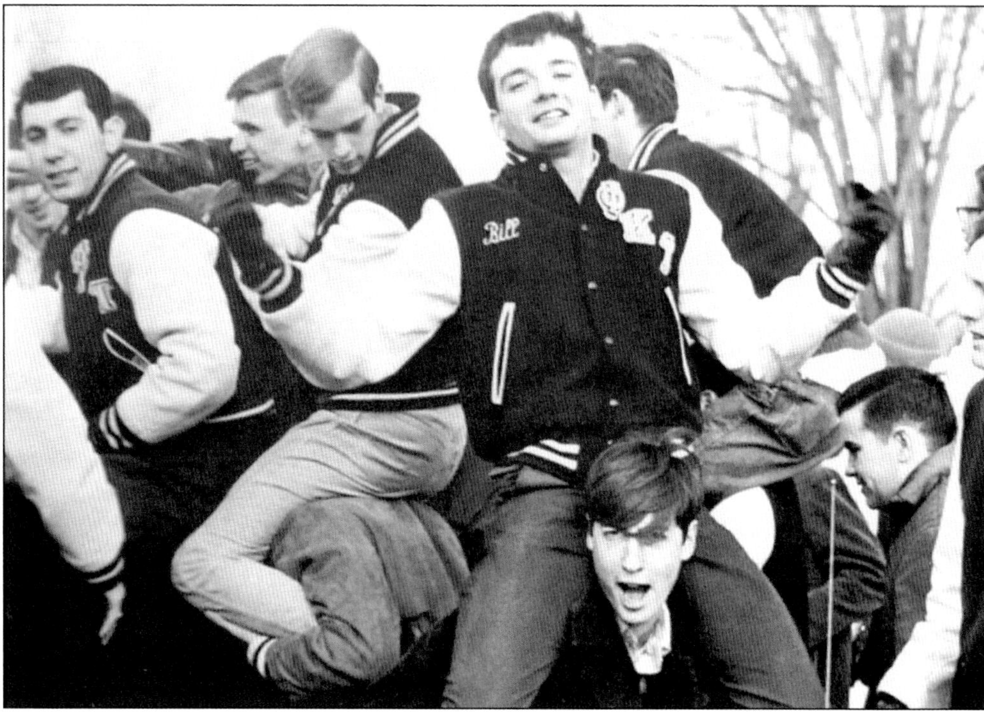

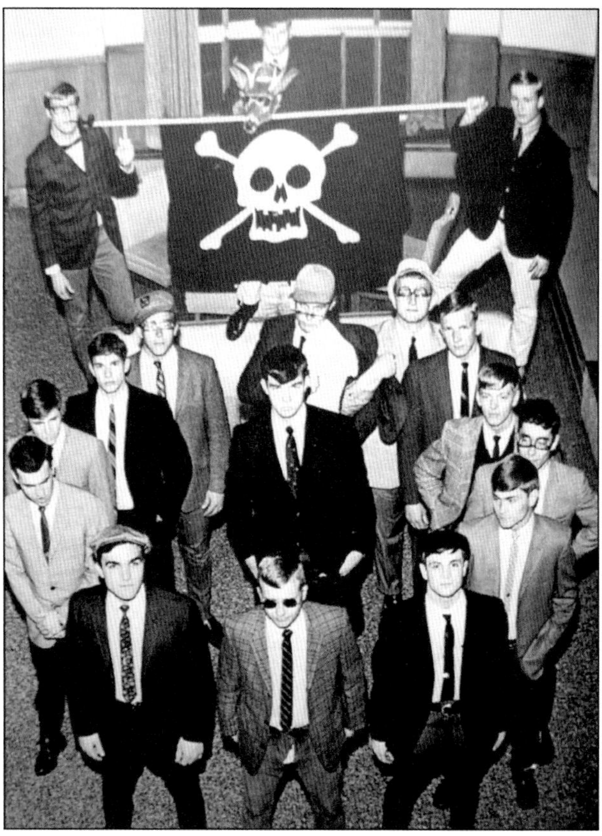

Members of Phi Kappa Tau (above), in 1968, horse around at their house. The same year, the brothers of Sigma Phi Epsilon (left) display their skull-and-crossbones banner.

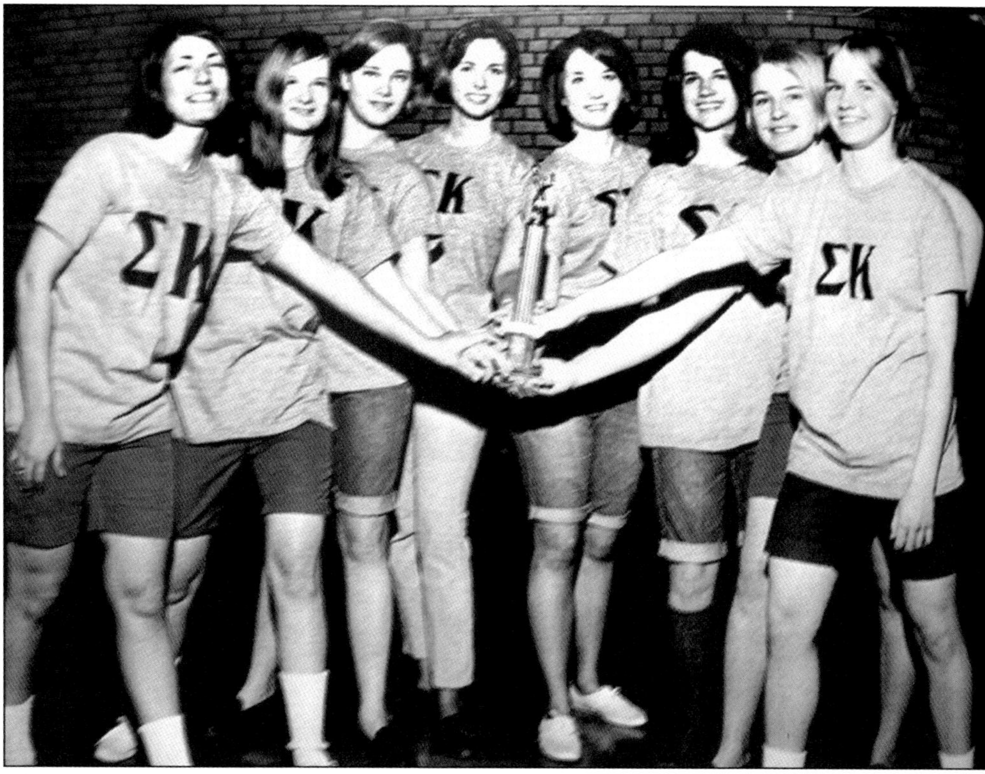

The sisters of Sigma Kappa (1968) warmed up for a basketball game in Old 77. At that time, Phi Mu members lived in their first-floor suite in Galbreath Hall.

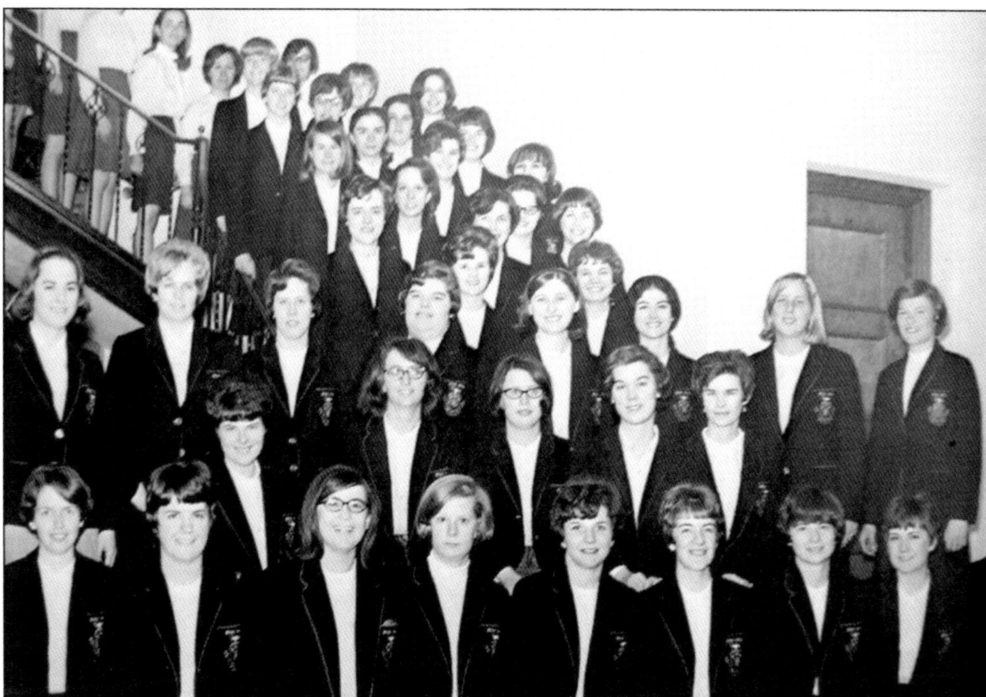

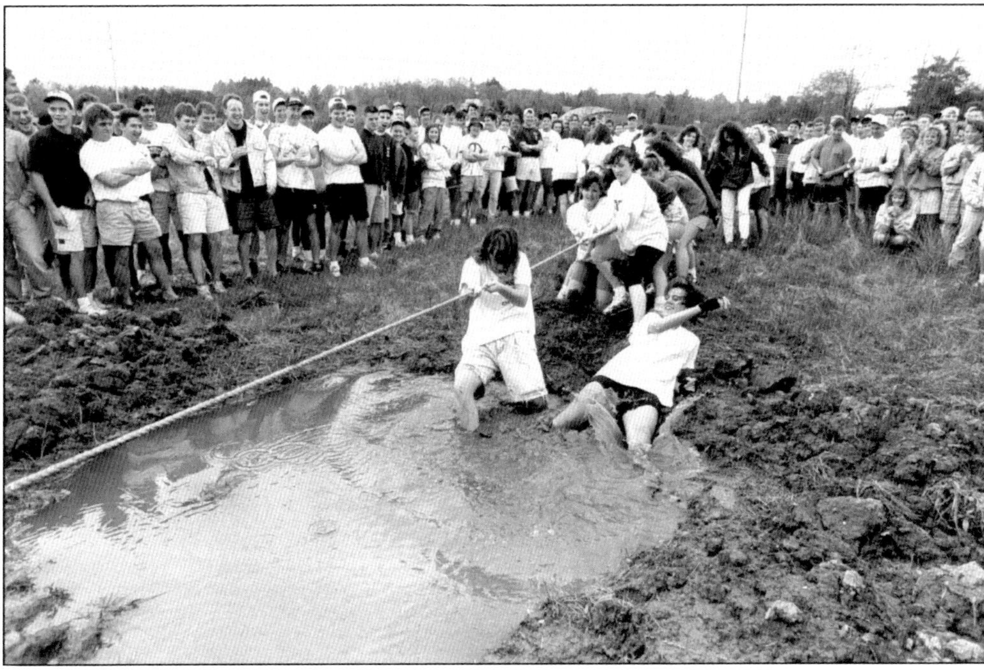

Greek Week, in 1992, gave everyone a chance to enjoy spring weather. Tug of war, a traditional activity, brought fraternities and sororities "together" for a dip in the mud.

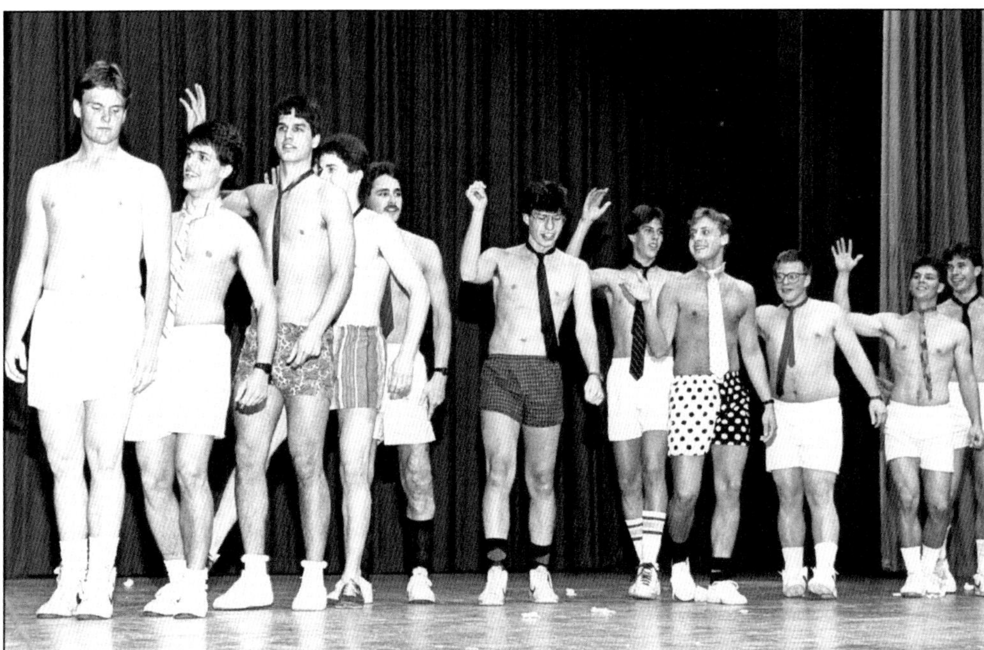

Sororities and fraternities took turns presenting a skit or song at Sing and Swing, held on the final night of Greek Week. The brothers of Phi Kappa Tau nearly "bared it all" in a highly choreographed 1986 routine.

Sorority presidents in 1945 drew lots in the Dean of Women's Office to determine the location of their newly designated houses. Until this time, sororities occupied dorm suites. Minteer House (right) became home to Kappa Delta, Thompson House to Alpha Gamma Delta, McKelvey House to Sigma Kappa, Shafer House to Beta Sigma Omicron, Elliott House to Theta Upsilon, and Mack Lodge to Chi Omega. Sororities reverted to suites around 1960.

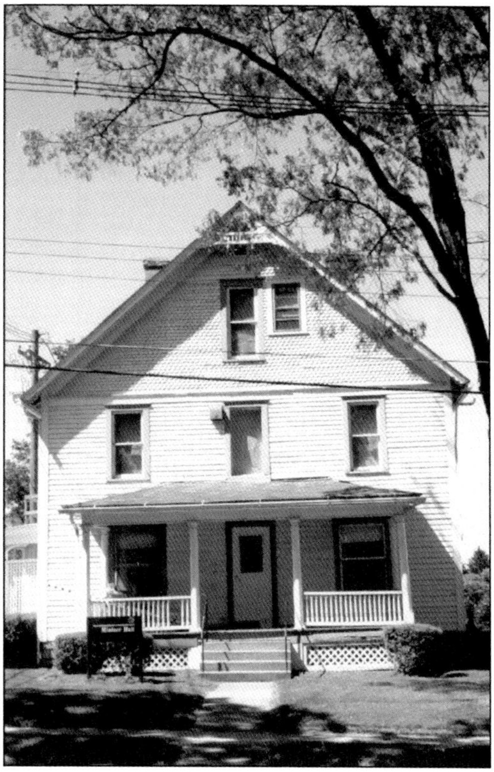

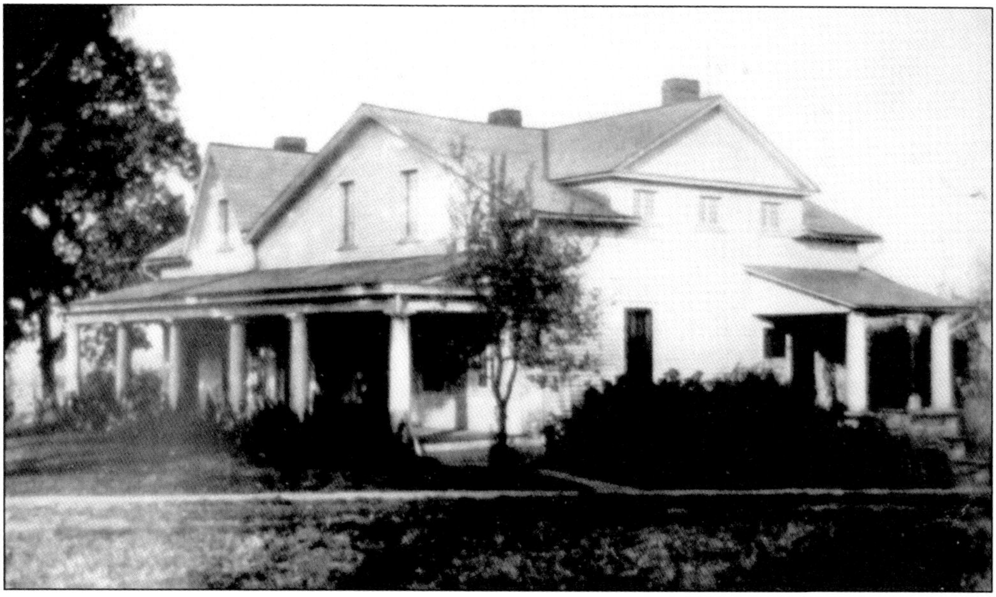

Many memories have been made at fraternity parties and social events. Westminster's five fraternity houses—Sigma Nu, Sigma Phi Epsilon, Theta Chi, Alpha Sigma Phi, and Phi Kappa Tau—all carry their own personalities. The Sigma Nu house once served as the President's Manse (above), Theta Chi's had been the mayor's residence, and Alpha Sigma Phi's remains one of the oldest fraternity houses in the country. Sigma Phi Epsilon's house was used for World War II recruits and Phi Kappa Tau's is the newest on campus.

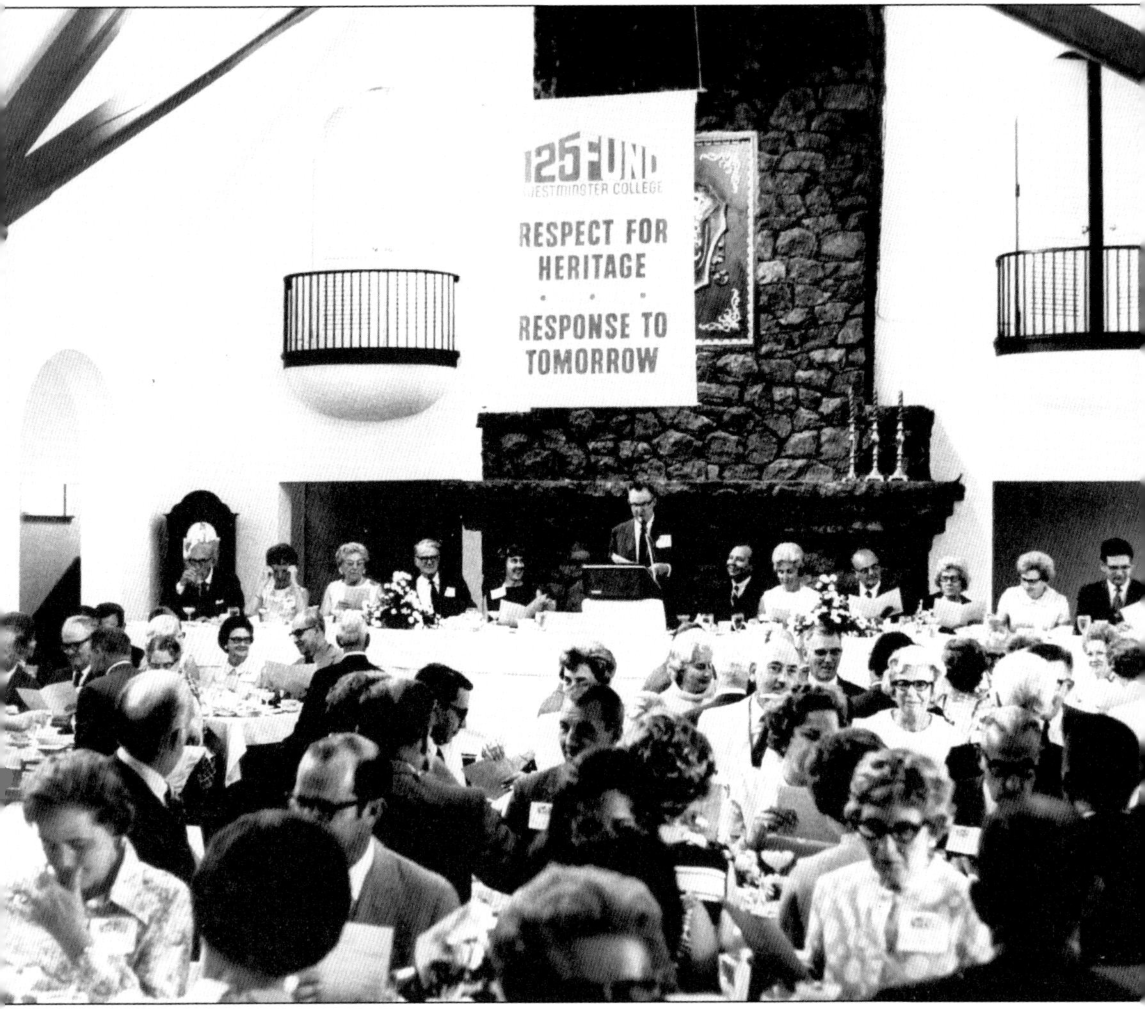

Westminster's 125th anniversary was marked by a major fund-raising campaign. It was led by the board of trustees, who have all been generous in funding buildings, endowments, and scholarships. Additionally, trustees, many of them graduates, have shepherded the college's mission and values throughout its history. Today, 40 trustees represent diverse professions, backgrounds, and interests. Many college events, such as this banquet, have been held at New Castle Country Club.

Three

When Titans Truly Were

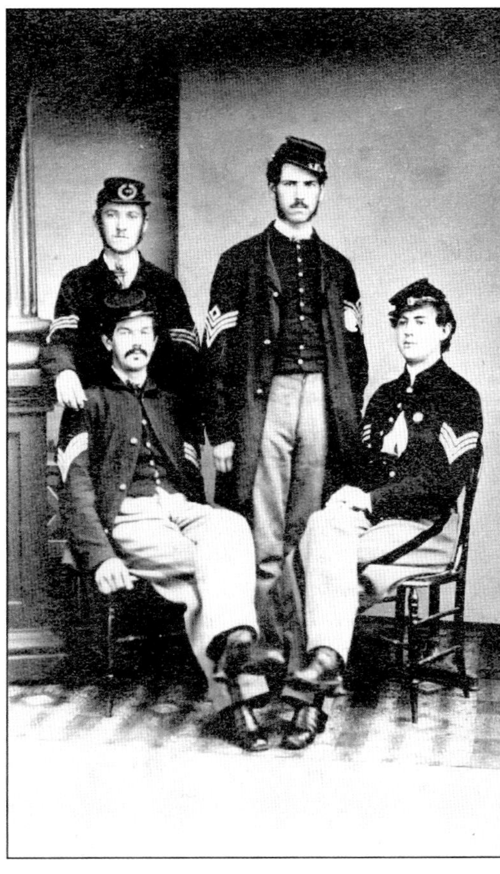

Born on the eve of the Civil War, Westminster College—like its hometown of New Wilmington and its sponsoring church—was decidedly antislavery. The town served as a major stop on the Underground Railroad. Students formed the Westminster Guards, who twice were pressed into active duty. They were led by Rev. George C. Vincent, a college founder and the first "principal." The guard's earliest stint was for two weeks in the fall of 1862 when Confederate general Robert E. Lee's forces threatened the Maryland/Pennsylvania border. In that campaign, Westminster's force camped within a few miles of the bloody battle at Antietam. The following summer, the guards served in July and August near Parkersburg, West Virginia. A quartet representing the Westminster Guards is seen at right.

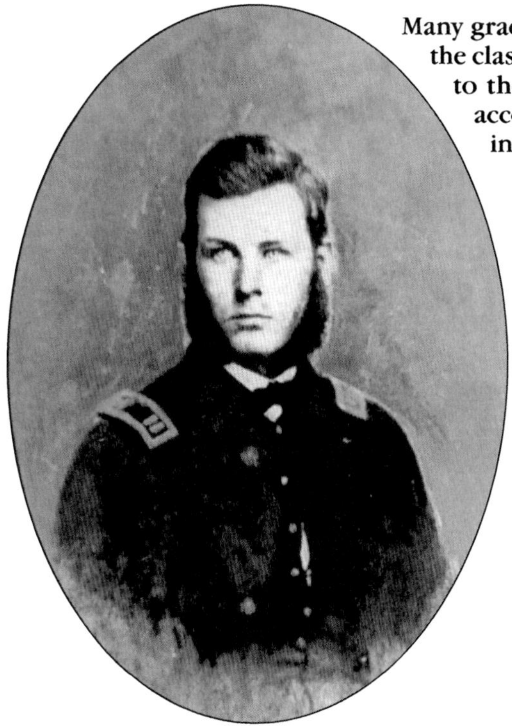

Many graduates enlisted, such as Samuel Taggart of the class of 1862. Taggart died of a gunshot wound to the heart at Petersburg, Virginia. His vivid accounts of fighting are found in letters now in the college archives.

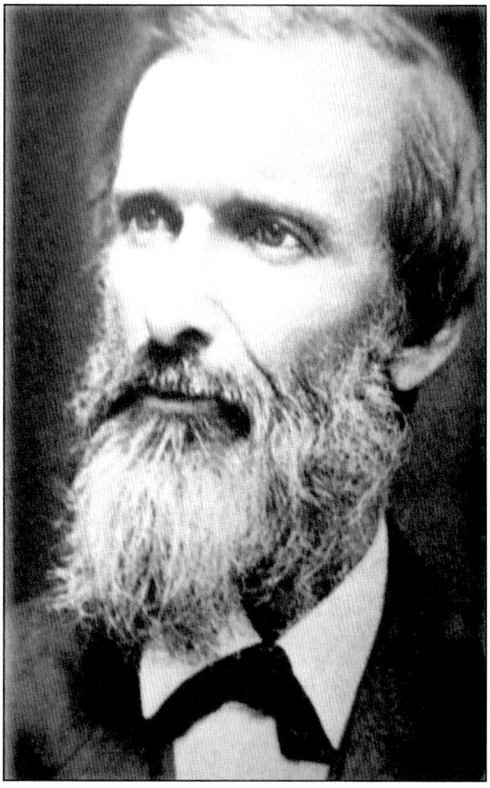

Rev. Dr. Robert Audley Browne served as chaplain of the Roundhead Regiment (100th Pennsylvania volunteers), a group that faced fierce fighting. Browne's wartime experience included deadly battles at Antietam and Vicksburg. Not long after his return, Browne ran for the state senate and served there until he joined Westminster as its second president from 1867 to 1870. He was considered a man of great physical strength and courage and an outstanding pastor.

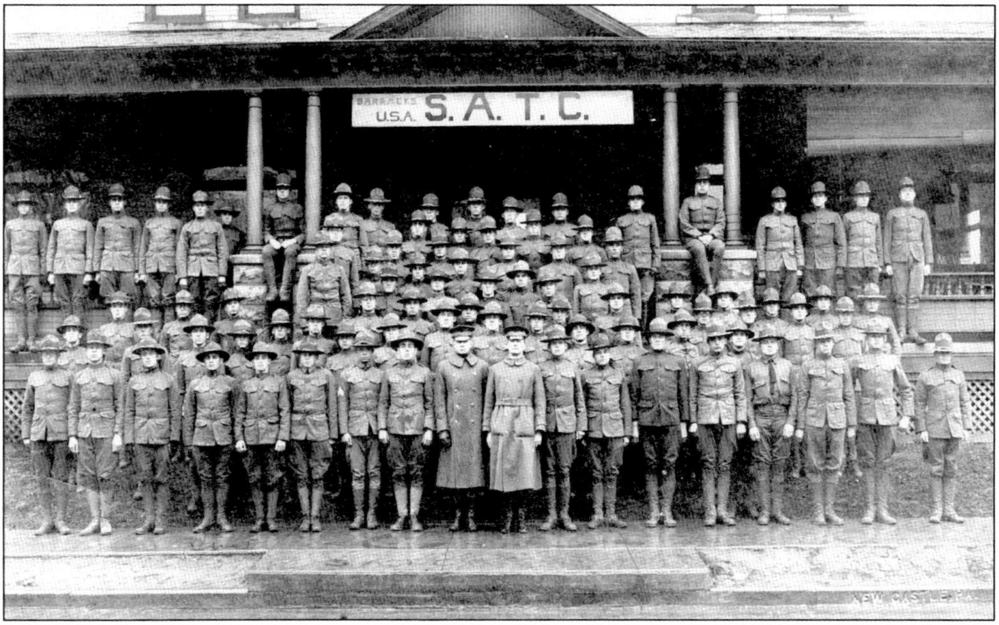

The declaration of war in 1917 prompted the formation of a Red Cross unit on campus. In 1918, more than 100 men were at Westminster—not as students but as part of the Student Army Training Corps for officers training. New Wilmington's Hotel McCreary served as their barracks. By midwinter, the Armistice had been signed and the unit deactivated. Meanwhile, students—primarily women—participated in Red Cross activities in the Hillside.

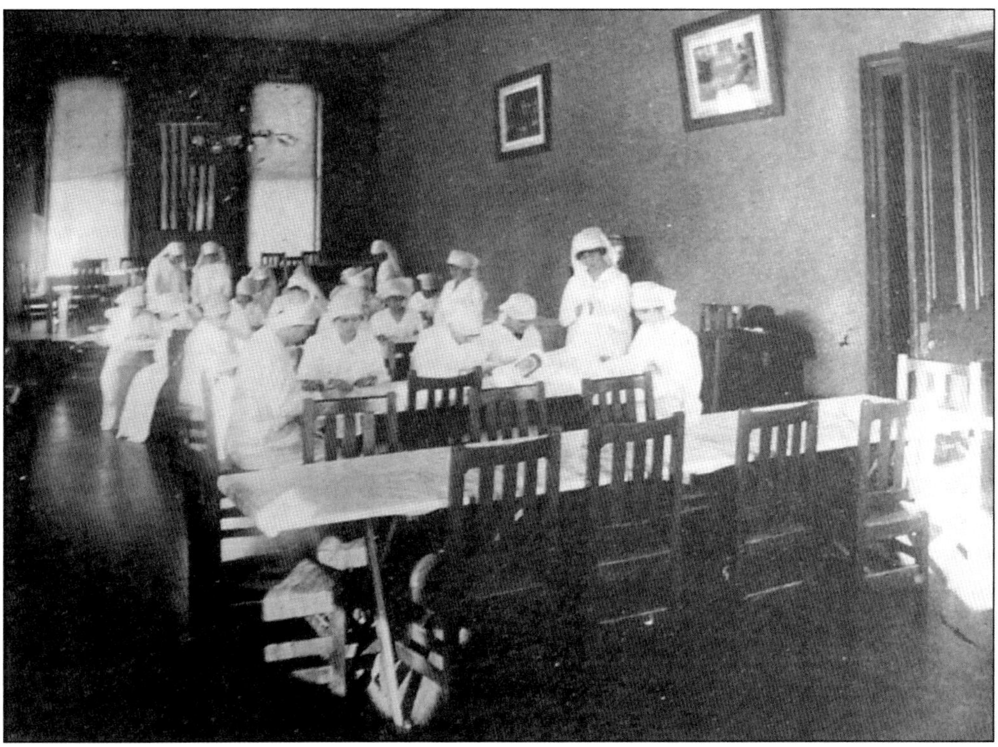

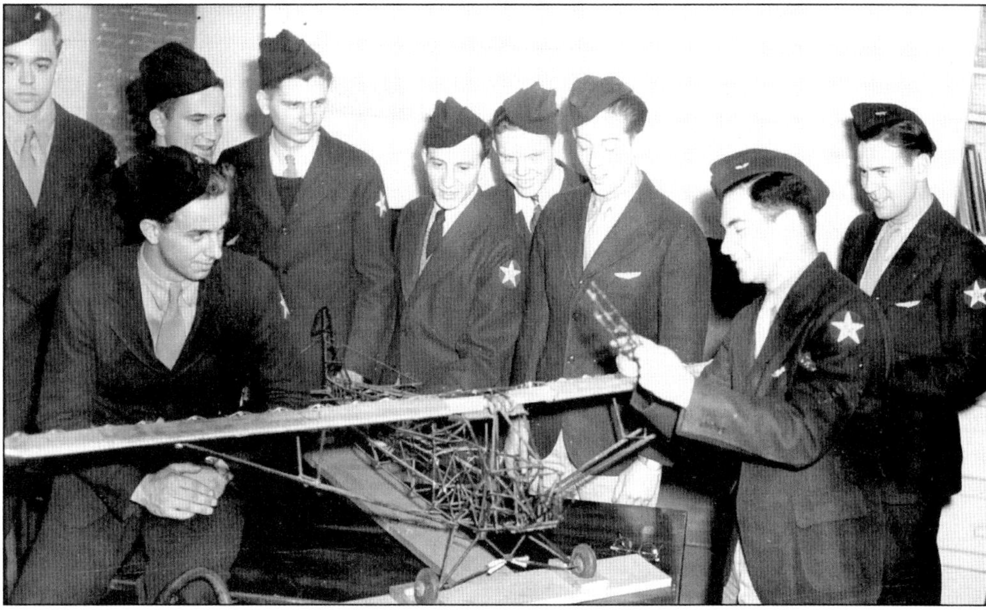

In 1998, Dr. Eugene Sharkey, professor emeritus, wrote and edited a compendium that saluted Westminster College's contribution to the Allied efforts during World War II. *When Titans Truly Were* pays homage to the 44 students and alums who sacrificed their all to the defense of freedom. It also includes firsthand accounts of scores of Westminster men and women who joined the fighting forces. Interestingly, Westminster became heavily involved in preparing aviators under the U.S. Navy's V-5 training program. Cadets arrived, 100 at a time, for short-term intensive training (above and below). The fledgling aviators stayed at "U.S.S. Hillside." More than 1,500 went through the program.

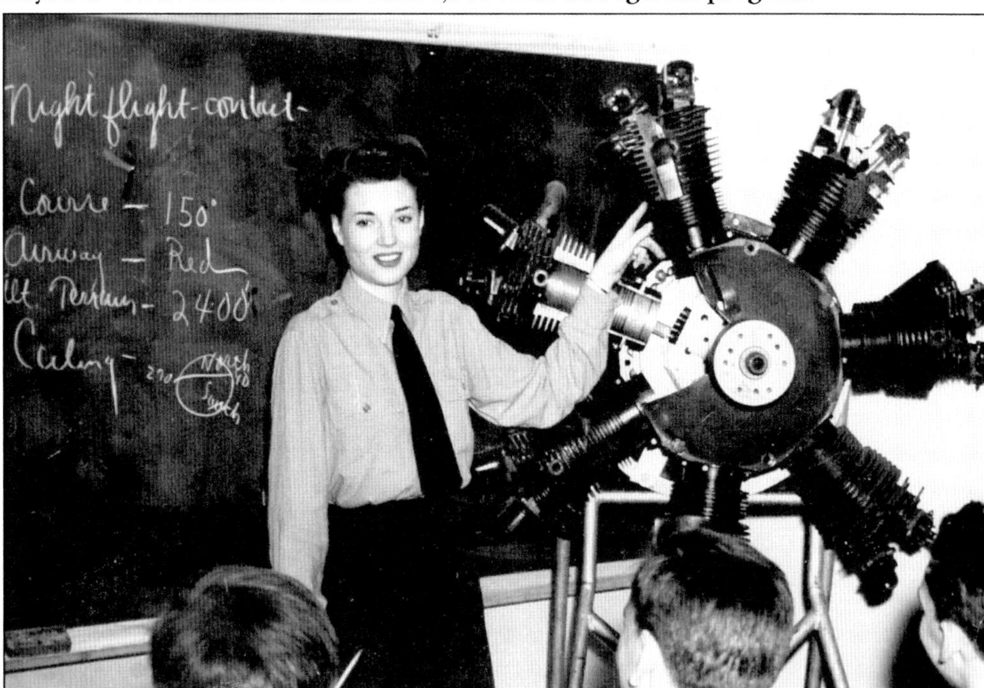

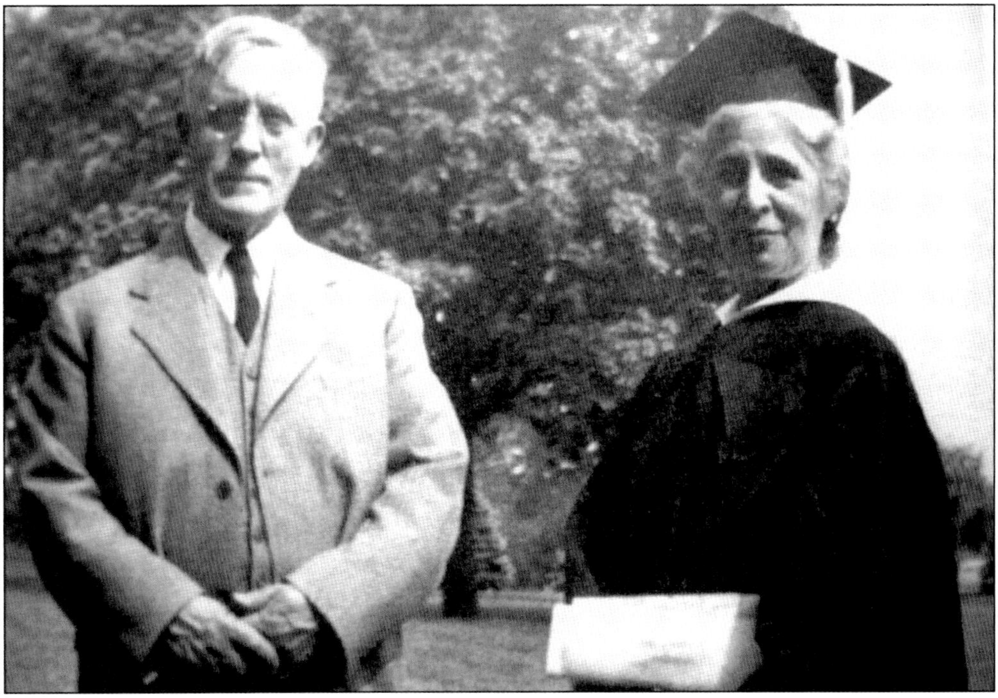

Not long after the declaration of war, scores of Westminster's men entered the armed services. Many remember an emotional 1942 commencement ceremony in which mothers and fathers, including Dr. and Mrs. A. Ray McNeil, accepted degrees for their deployed servicemen sons.

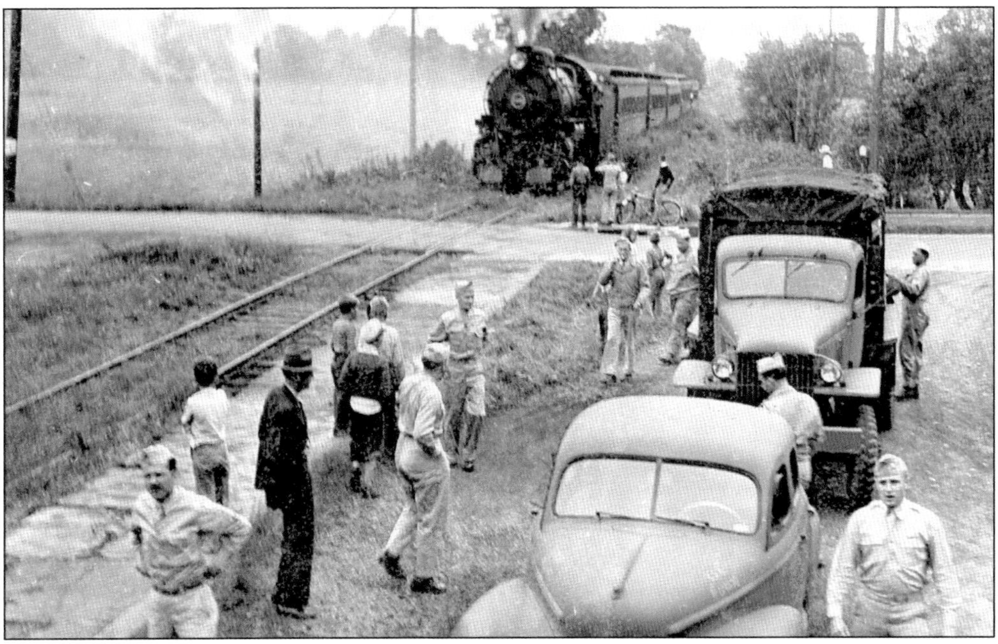

Bound for war, Westminster's soldiers took the "Sharpie" train from Wilmington Junction. According to the 1944 *Argo*, as the troops drove to the station, the college chimes played "Ring out the bells in Old Main Tower again, ring out a song of Victory."

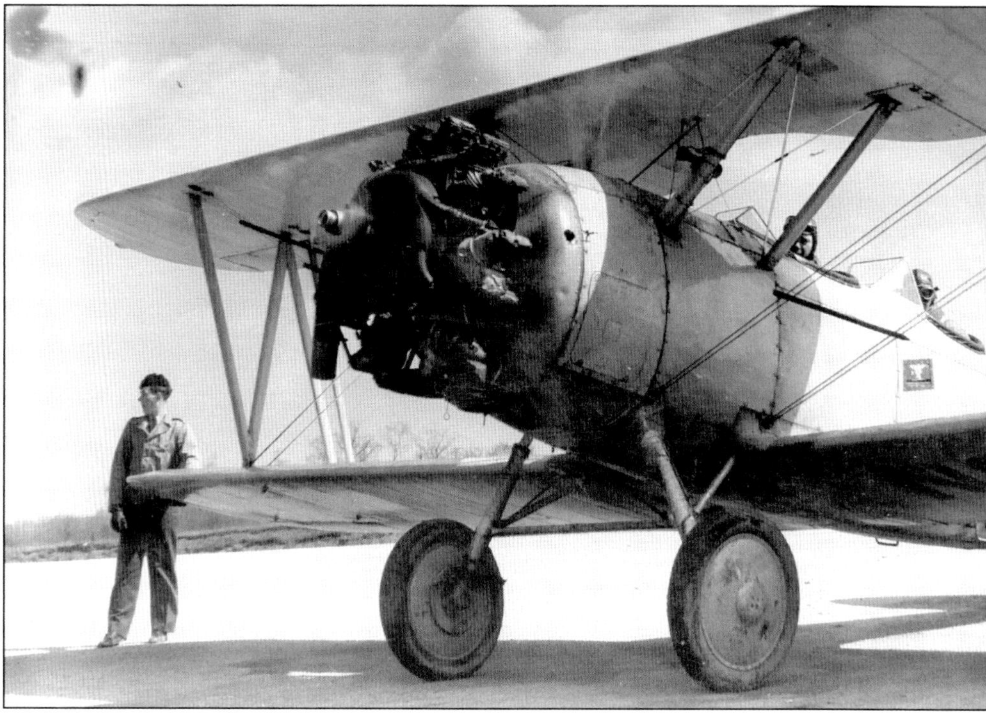

Wilson Airfield in New Castle served as the training ground for the V-5 training program. Concurrently, Westminster offered a civilian pilots program.

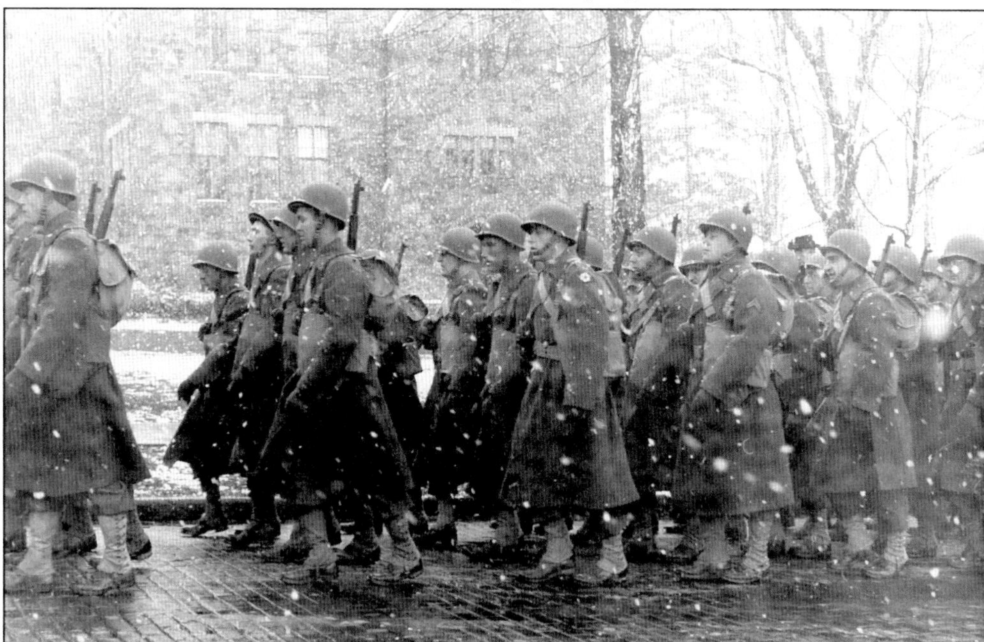

Soldiers in the Army Student Training Program march past Old Main Memorial in an April 15, 1943, snowstorm. At that time, college enrollment had plummeted to 350 women and 63 men. More than 300 soldiers occupied Browne and Jeffers Halls and the Sigma Phi Epsilon house.

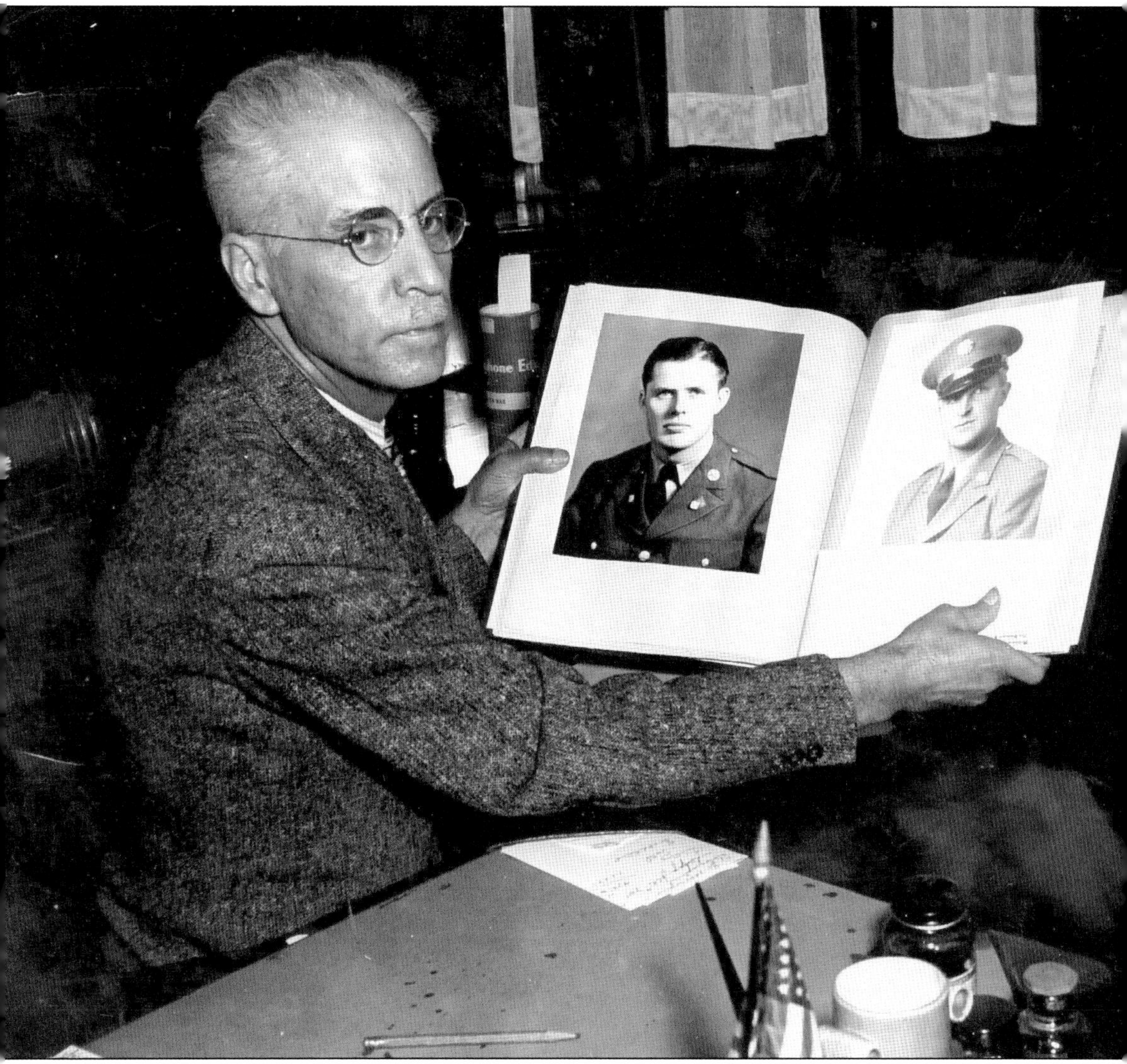

Pres. Robert F. Galbreath wrote personalized letters to each Westminster student serving in the military. "You are all too near to my heart and the heart of Westminster . . . believe me, I just ache with the tragedy of it all and the glory in the splendid morale of all of you," he penned. By the conclusion of World War II, more than 900 Westminster alumni and students had served in the military.

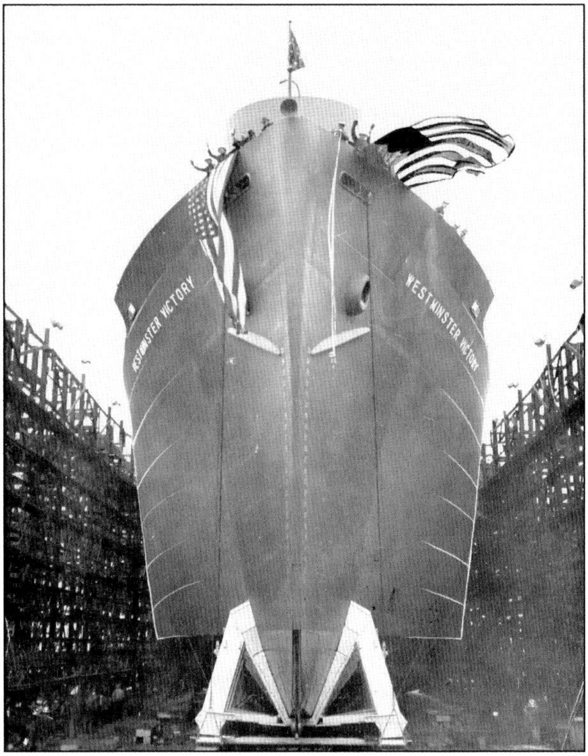

Westminster was one of only 40 schools to be honored with the naming of a victory cargo ship. Colleges were selected based on their contributions to the war effort and their high educational standards. Westminster students and faculty raised sufficient monies to fund the ship's library. The U.S.S. *Westminster Victory* went into commission on March 30, 1945, with a cargo capacity of 10,800 tons. Ultimately the vessel was sold to a Thai shipping company.

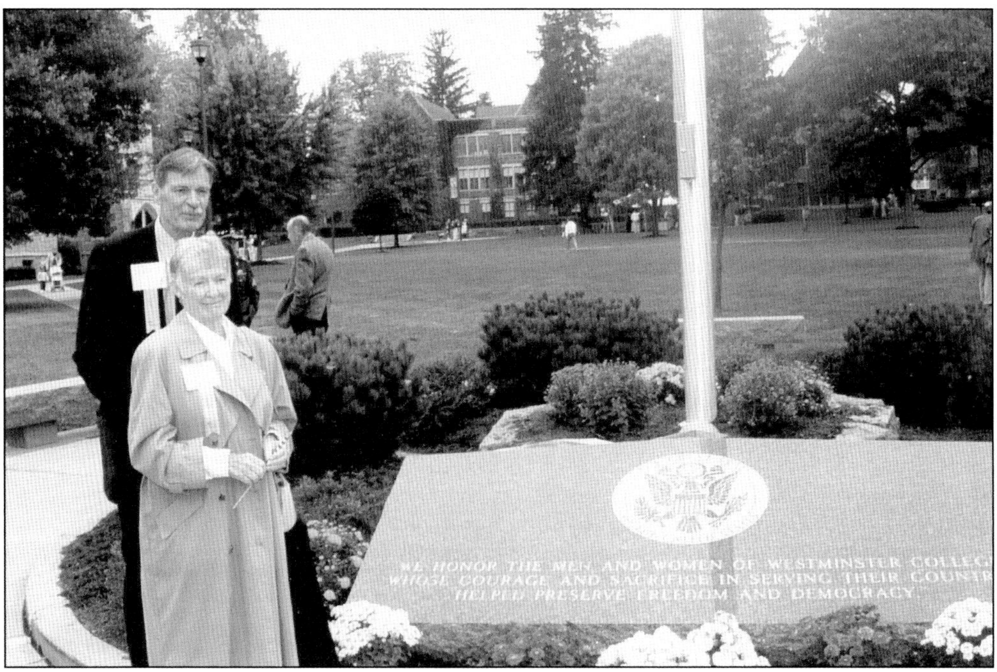

Successive generations of Westminster's men and women have sacrificed to "preserve freedom and democracy." In 1999, Chet and Hidge Clair (both class of 1949) led ceremonies to unveil a monument in the center of the quadrangle. The flagpole and granite monument honor all who served and will serve in the armed forces.

Four

THE ARTS AND THE SCIENCES

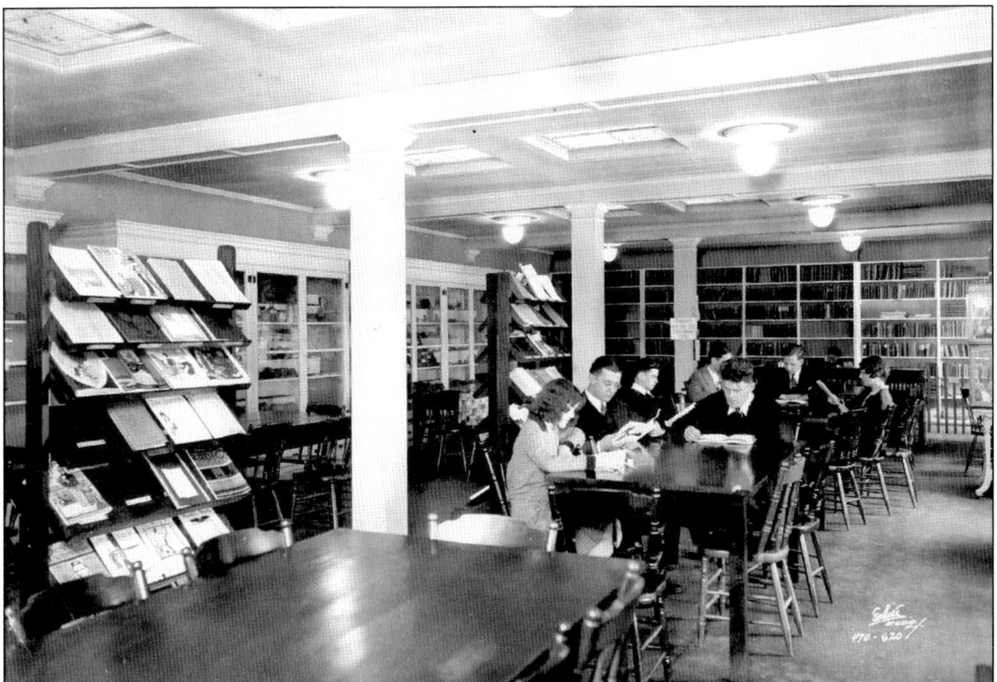

During the late 1920s, students spent many hours studying in the crowded library in Thompson Science Hall. A former laboratory was converted to a library following the 1927 Old Main fire.

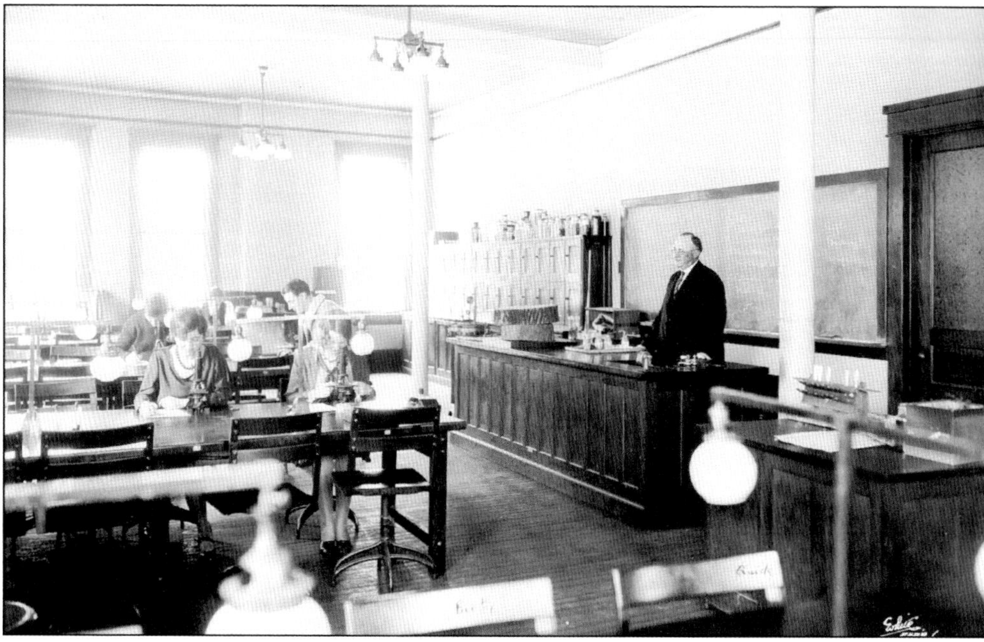

Sartorially attired faculty members conducted courses in laboratory subjects, such as botany and biology. The college was among the first to offer fully equipped classrooms. The early insight of Prof. S. R. Thompson prompted Westminster to be a leader in the field. Dr. Bert Quick (above) taught biology in Mary Thompson Hall (around 1920).

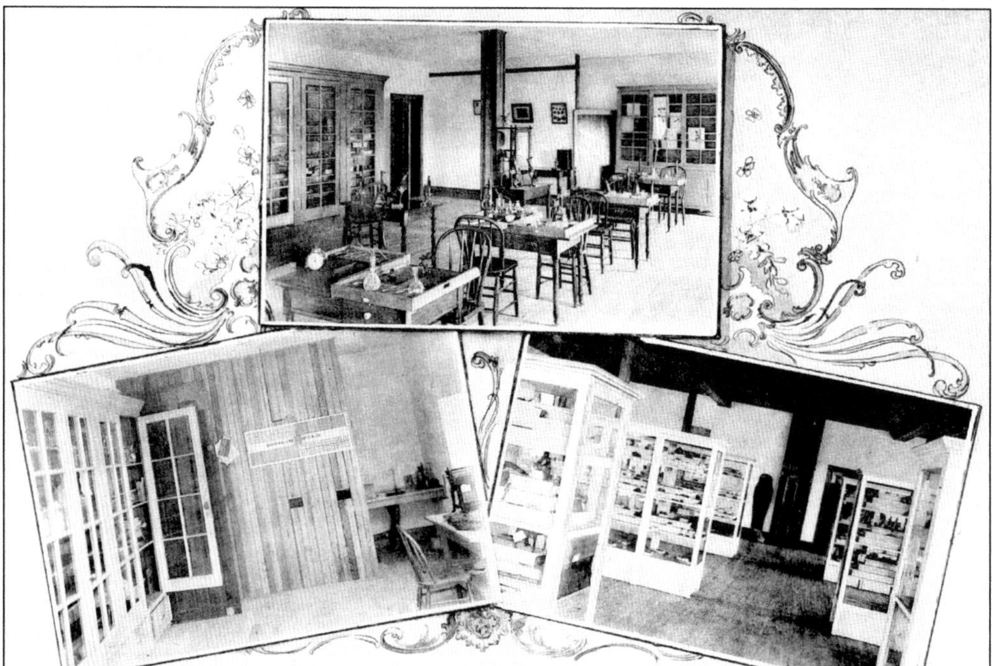

Scientific classrooms in 1896 were well appointed and boasted of the latest styles and approaches to teaching. At that time, Westminster's Egyptology collection resided in the laboratories.

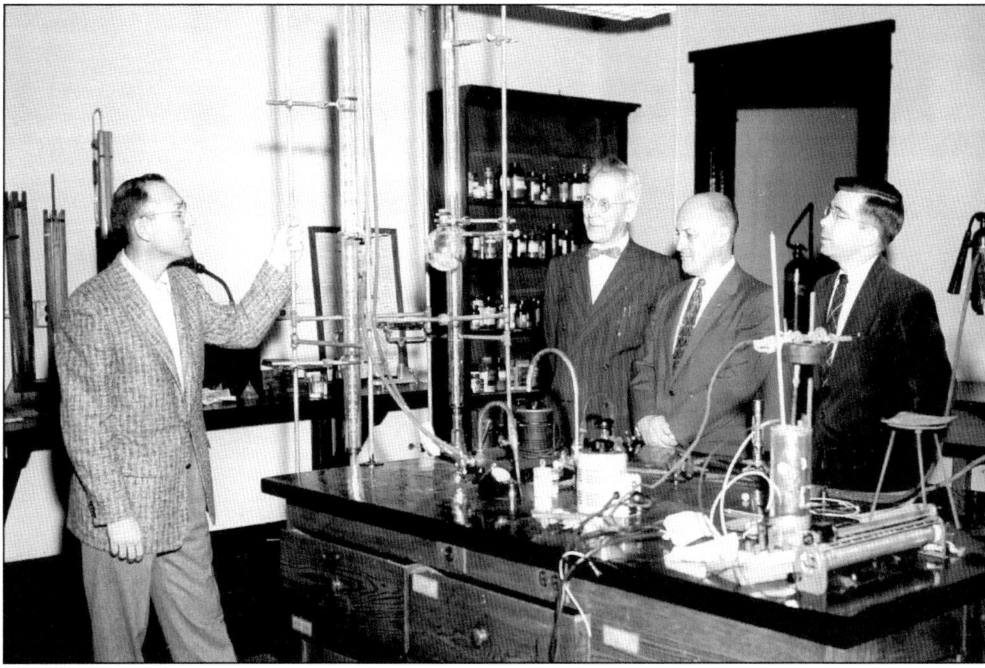

Dr. H. Dewey DeWitt (left) and his colleagues in the chemistry department (seen here in the late 1950s) taught in Thompson Clark Freeman Hall until 1974 when Hoyt Science Resources Center opened. Hoyt offers large and small laboratories for intensive study and collaboration between students and faculty. The center is adjacent to James Patterson Hall and includes the J. S. Mack Science Library.

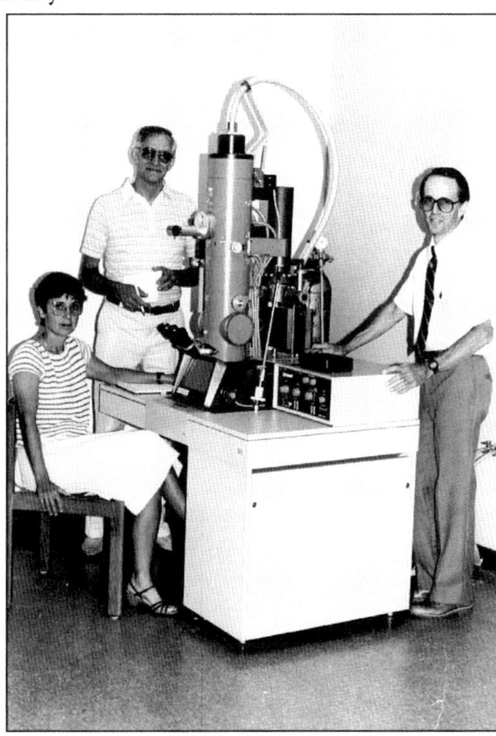

Westminster, unlike some research universities, has made high-end and sophisticated laboratory equipment readily available to students. Such was the case with the installation of a transmission electronic microscope which was first demonstrated in the 1980s by Dr. Clarence Harms (center) and Dr. Monica Becker (left). It was delivered by equipment representative Thomas Burch (right).

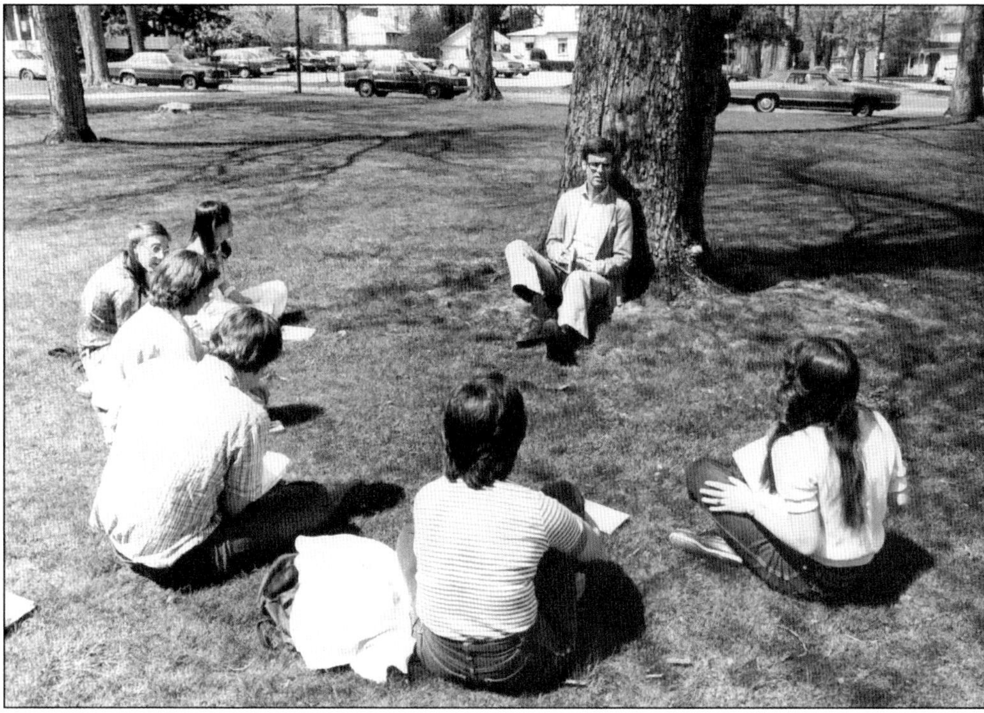

Westminster's picturesque quadrangle has always offered a perfect setting for outdoor classes, such as this 1980s Shakespeare seminar led by Dr. Fritz Horn of the English department.

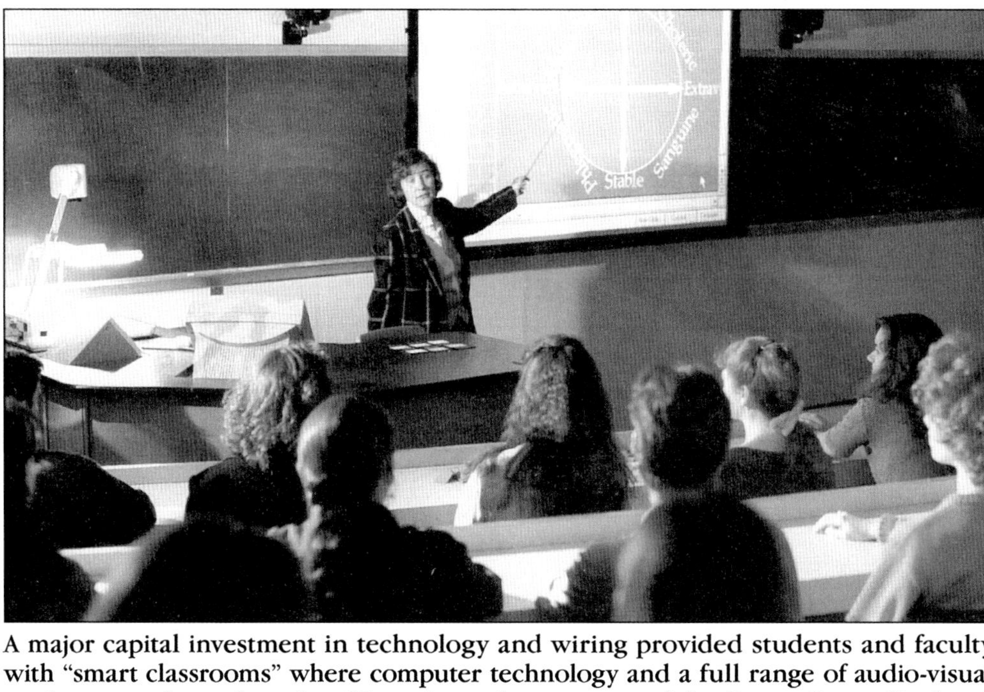

A major capital investment in technology and wiring provided students and faculty with "smart classrooms" where computer technology and a full range of audio-visual equipment enhance learning. Westminster became one of the first to "go online" and was named, in 2000, as one of America's Most Wired Colleges by *Yahoo! Internet Life*. Dr. Sandra K. Webster taught in one of the first smart classrooms.

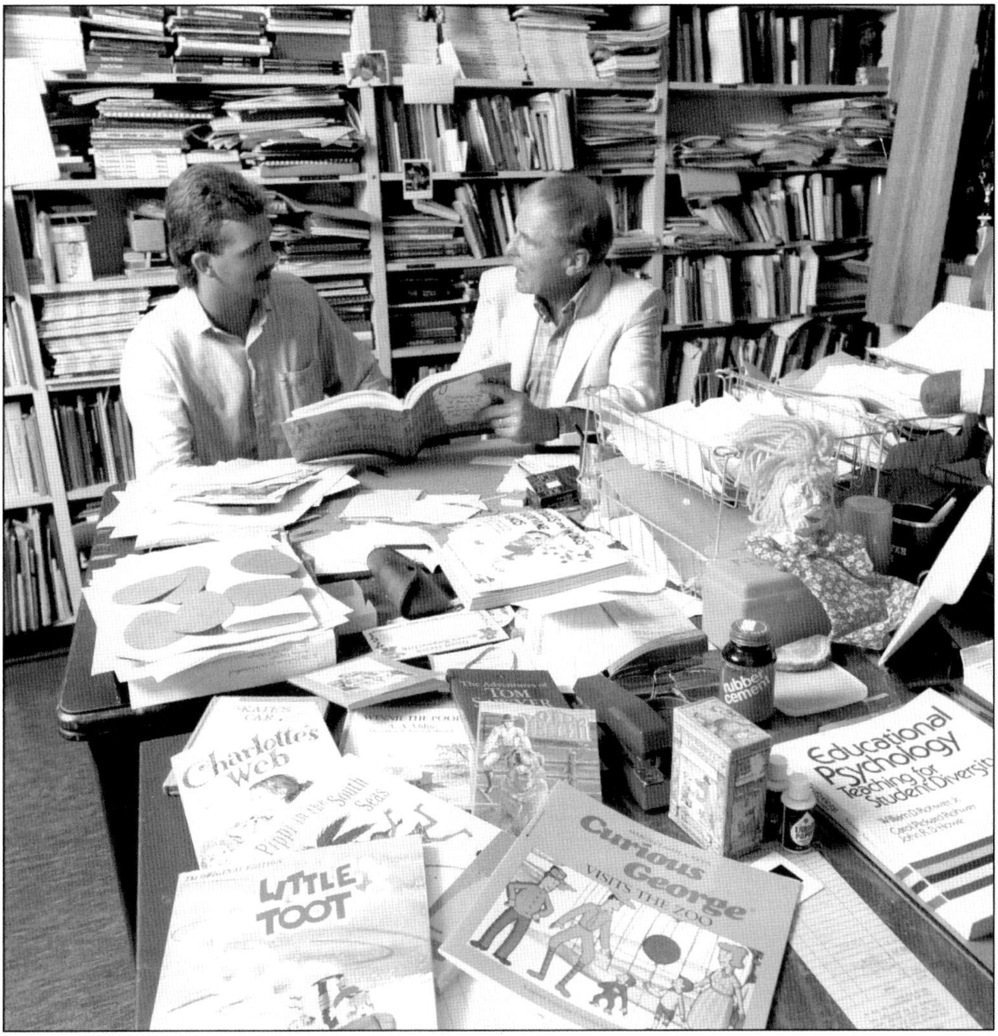

Westminster College has long been recognized for a commitment to teaching and learning. The Westminster Plan curriculum puts the liberal arts into action. The college, with 1,600 students, offers 41 majors. It has been honored as one of "The Best 361 Colleges" by the *Princeton Review* and recognized by the *Templeton Guide* as a "Character-Building College." This well-earned reputation stems from a dedicated faculty in all disciplines from the performing arts to laboratory sciences. Since its founding, the college has dedicated resources to premiere facilities and scholarships. Dr. Jerb Miller (right) has been memorialized with the Jerb Miller Scholarship, a much-sought-after academic grant. Westminster alums working in the field of education are eligible to nominate one high school senior each year for the recognition. Miller joined the faculty in 1968 and served in the department of education. He was an influential authority on children's literature and shared a boundless enthusiasm for the subject.

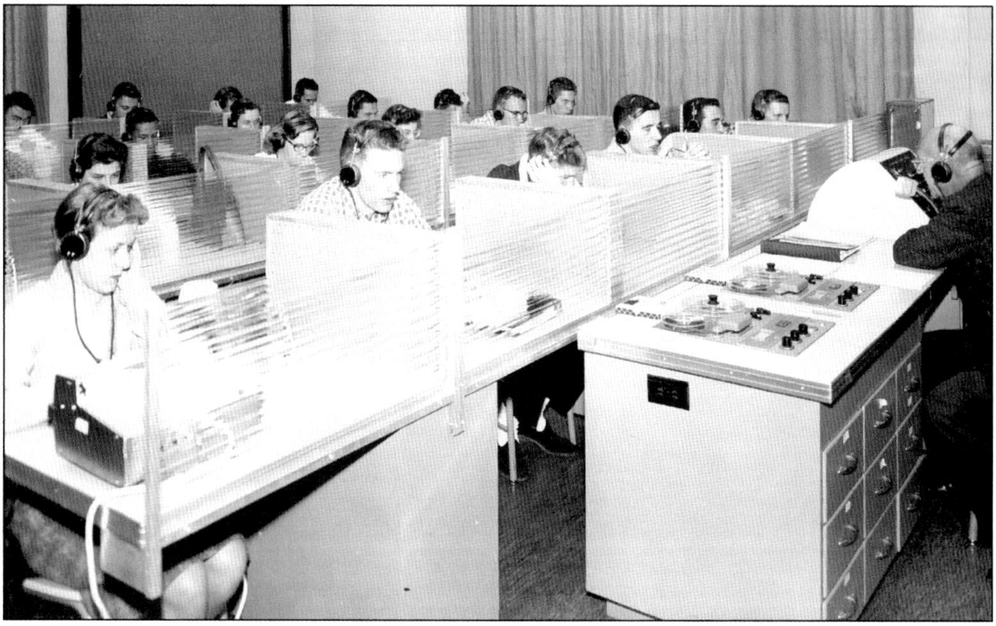

Education in modern languages received a boost with the 1961 opening of the Arts and Sciences building and the rollout of the language laboratory. *Wie geht es Ihnen*? Bing!

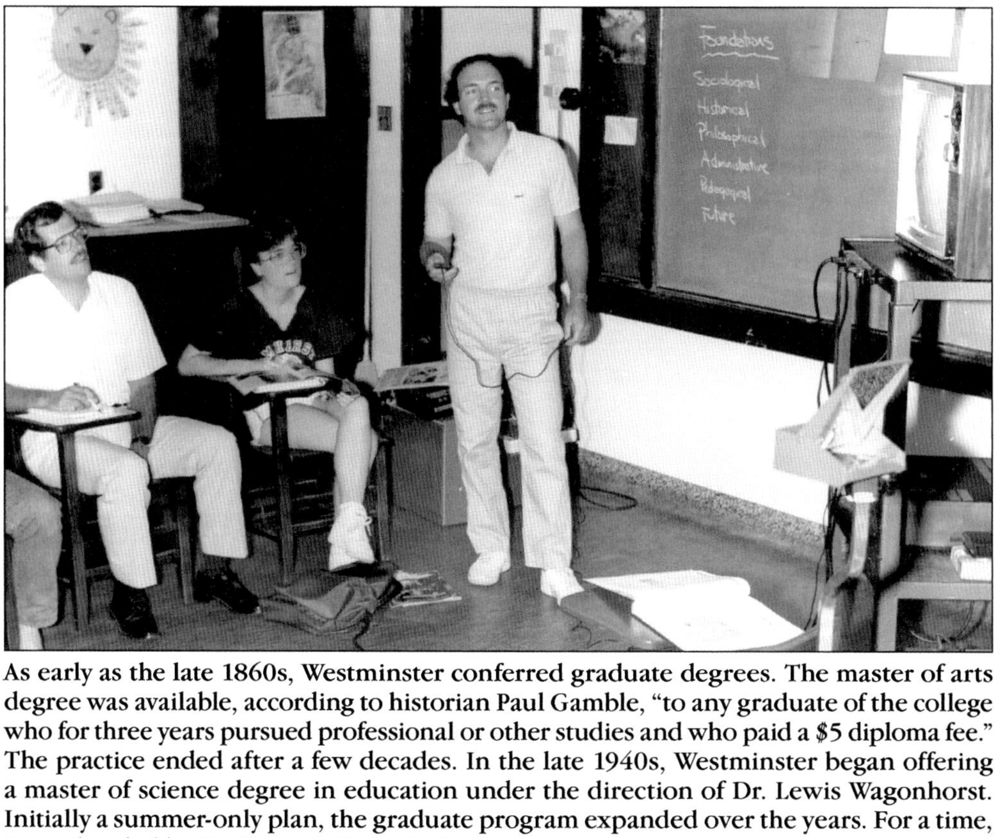

As early as the late 1860s, Westminster conferred graduate degrees. The master of arts degree was available, according to historian Paul Gamble, "to any graduate of the college who for three years pursued professional or other studies and who paid a $5 diploma fee." The practice ended after a few decades. In the late 1940s, Westminster began offering a master of science degree in education under the direction of Dr. Lewis Wagonhorst. Initially a summer-only plan, the graduate program expanded over the years. For a time, it was headed by Dr. Darwin Huey (right).

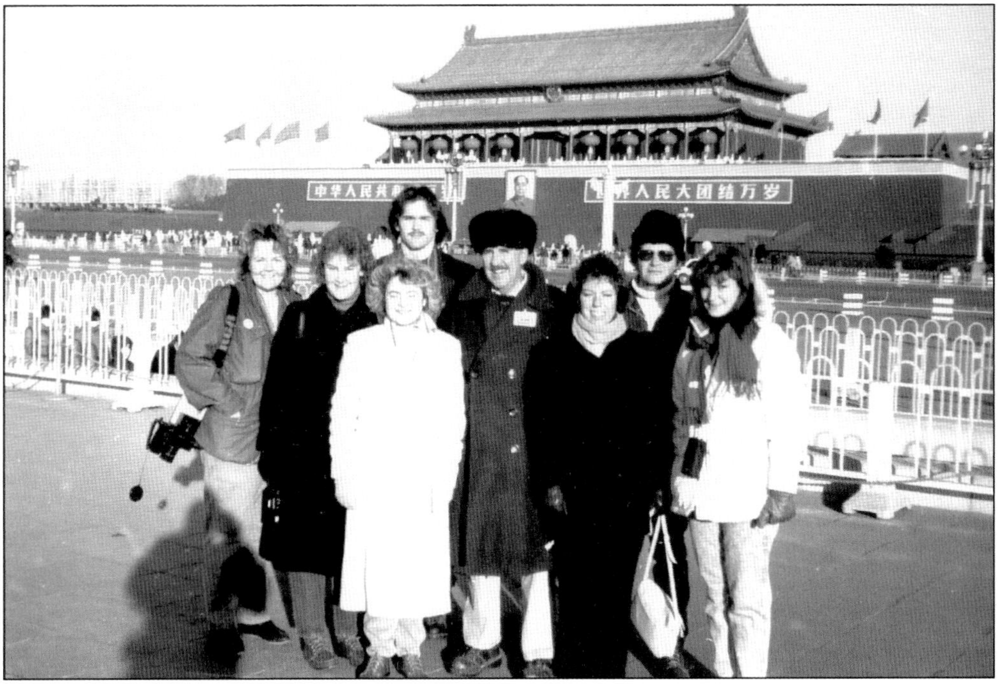

Academic year 1970–1971 saw great innovation in the college's calendar. A 4-1-4 plan permitted students to take four classes in each of the fall and spring terms and one intensive specialized course in January. Known as "J-Term," the time permitted students to take internships or travel studies, such as this group did to Beijing in 1989. Westminster returned to a more traditional calendar in the early 1990s.

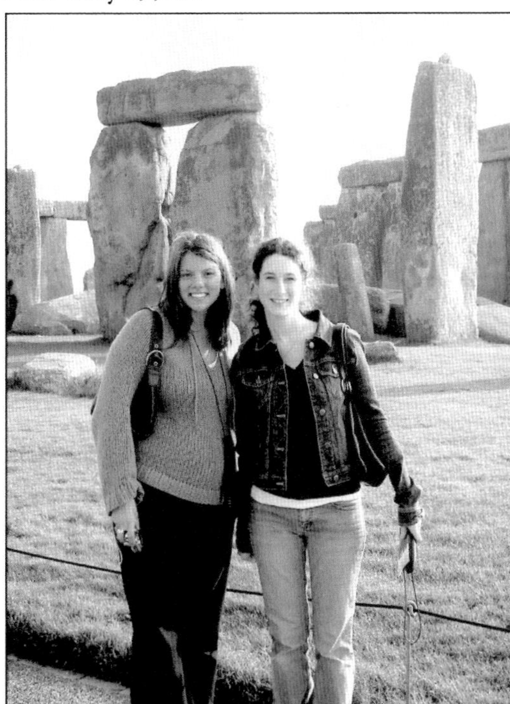

"Westminster at Oxford" stands as the latest innovation in academic programming. It started in 2004. A small group of students, along with Westminster faculty leaders, attended classes at Oxford, England. The semester-long experience permits additional travel throughout the British Isles and the Continent. Many have enjoyed Stonehenge and other Old World venues.

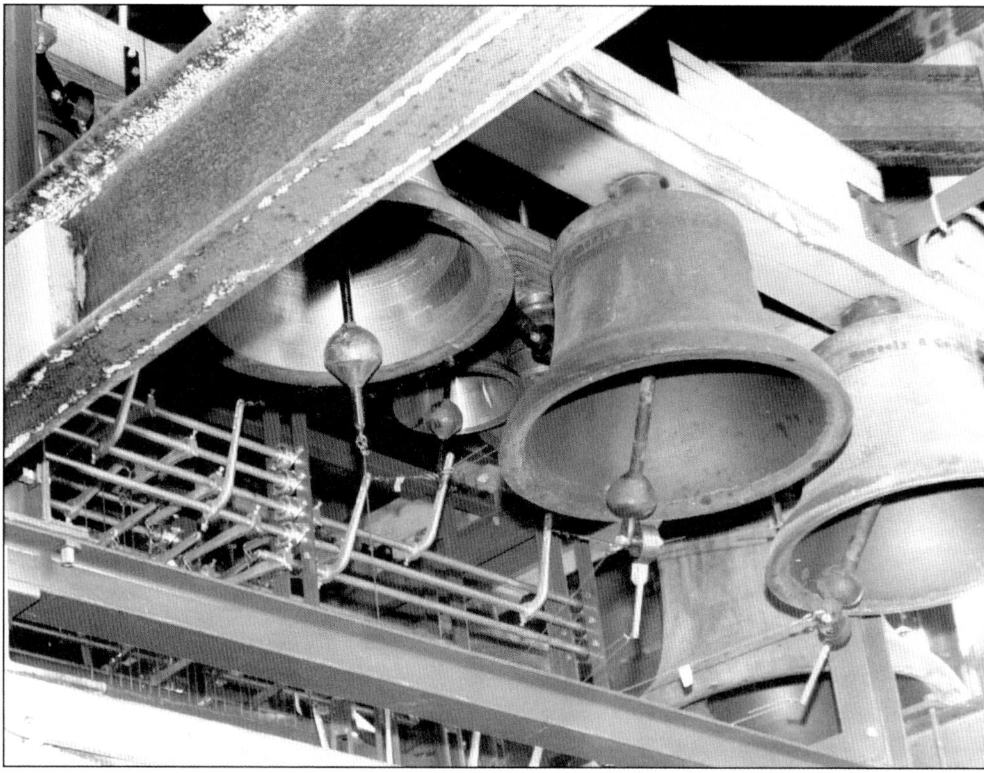

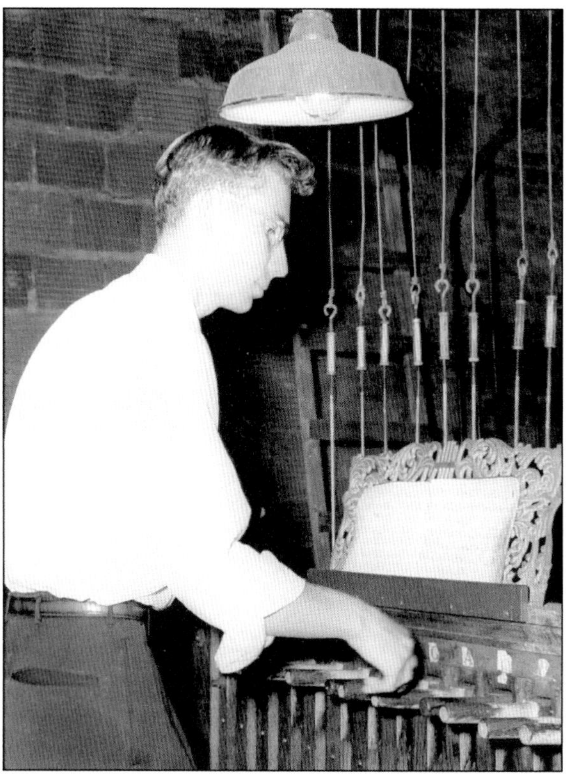

For all who visit New Wilmington, Old Main Memorial's bells and carillon remain among the most memorable hallmarks. Installed in 1935, the chimes strike the iconic Westminster tune of 4 notes on the quarter hour, 8 notes on the half-hour, and 12 notes on the three-quarter hour. On the hour, chimes ring 16 notes and strike the hour. The tune was first written in the 1790s for bells in a church tower at Cambridge University and later adapted for London's Big Ben. The notes were taken from the fifth bar of Handel's *Messiah*—"I know that my Redeemer liveth." The carillon is played often for special occasions from a console in the bell tower. Carillon bells were first installed in 1935 with additional ones added in 1978 and 2006. Rev. Dr. Paul M. Musser '45 learned to play the carillon as a student and continues to do so today.

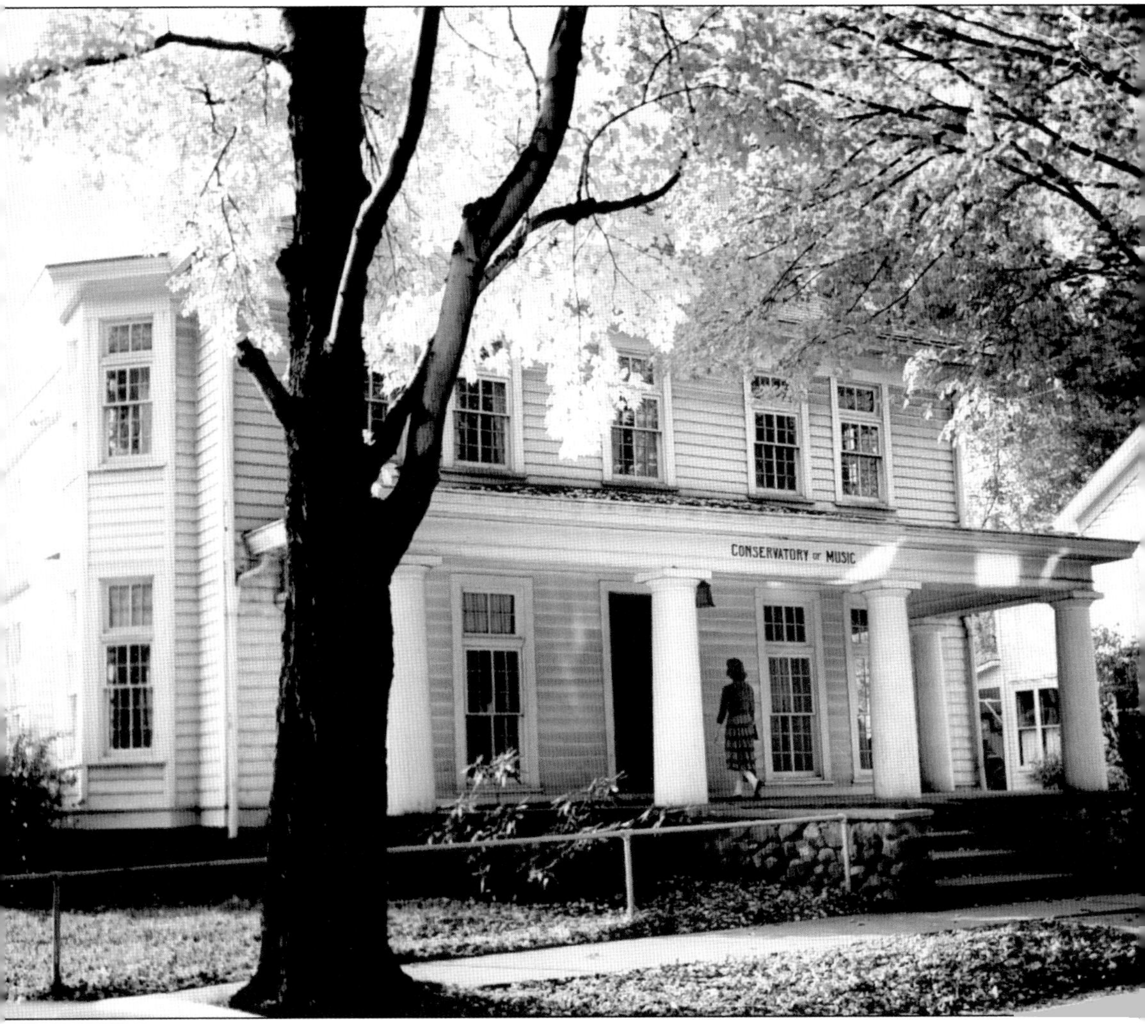

Westminster has long been a leader in music. The original conservatory was in the Hillside, the campus's oldest building. During 1907, in a push led by Prof. W. W. Campbell, a musicologist and music teacher, the college built the outstanding Conservatory of Music. It housed classrooms, a recital hall, and 28 practice rooms. Later the music department moved to quarters near Orr Auditorium. The building then became the Annex. Finally it was known as West Hall and housed the English department. The structure burned in 1998.

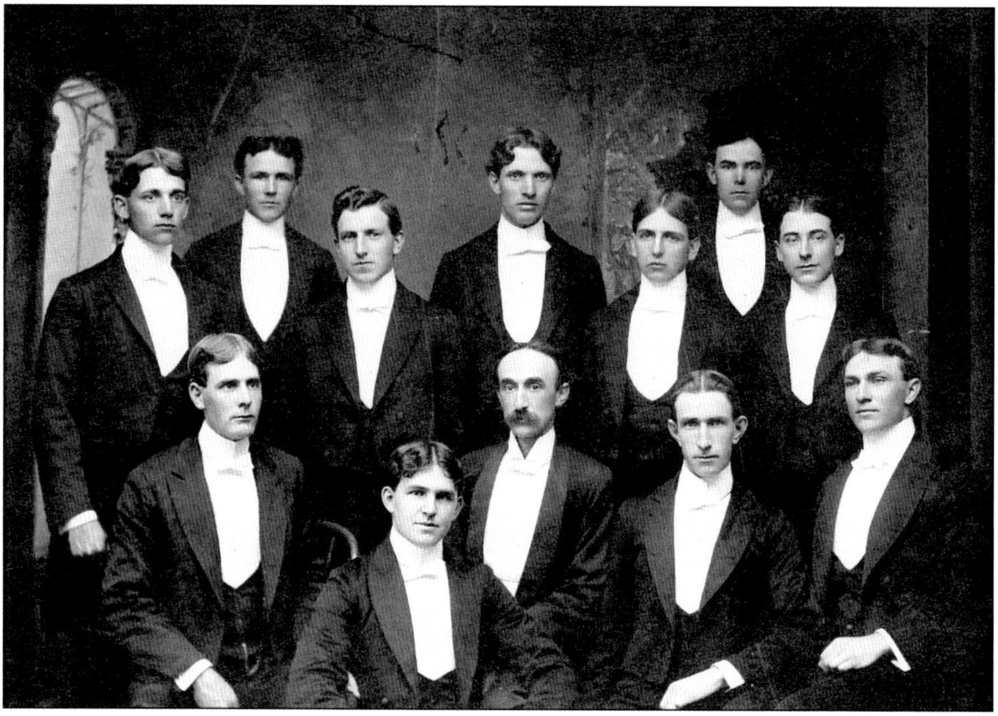

Westminster's 1901 glee club toured concert halls under the tutelage of Prof. Martin Luther Peterson (seated center). In a March concert, the club debuted "The Westminster Hymn," now referred to as the alma mater. The song was written by Dr. Morgan Barnes, Westminster's Greek—not music—professor, who adapted a tune from Giancomo Meyerbeer's opera *Les Huguenots*.

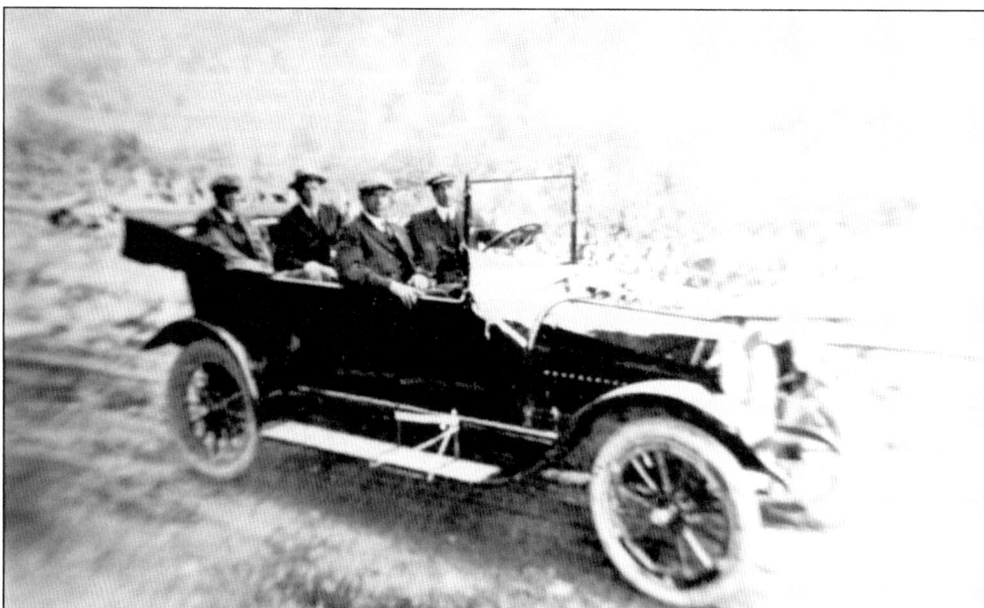

The Studebaker Six, a 1915 campus quartet, traveled the country and offered 70 separate concerts. The foursome was so named because of its flashy convertible.

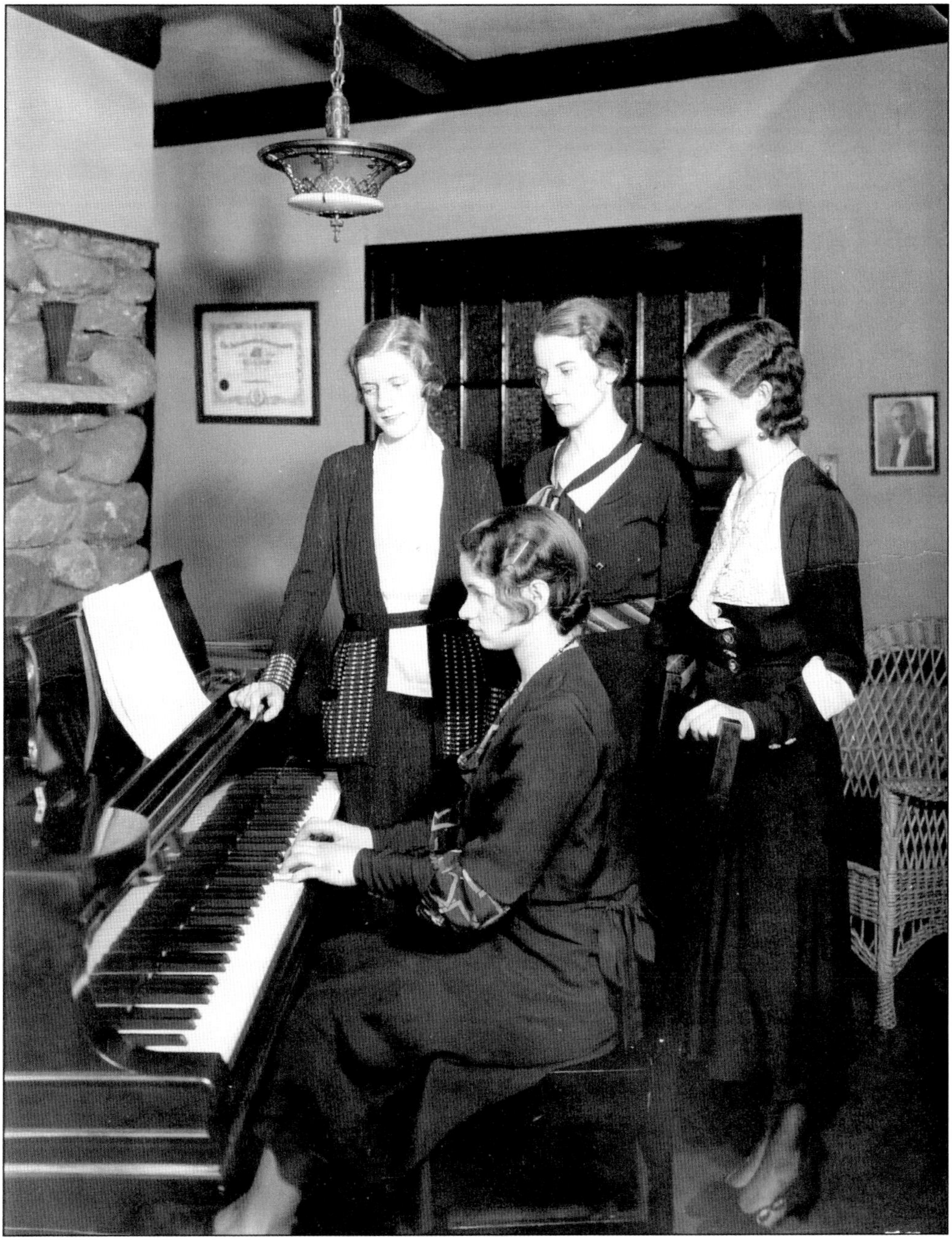

The original Conservatory of Music in the Hillside was well appointed and offered young ladies an opportunity to study pianoforte and voice in a pleasant and cozy atmosphere.

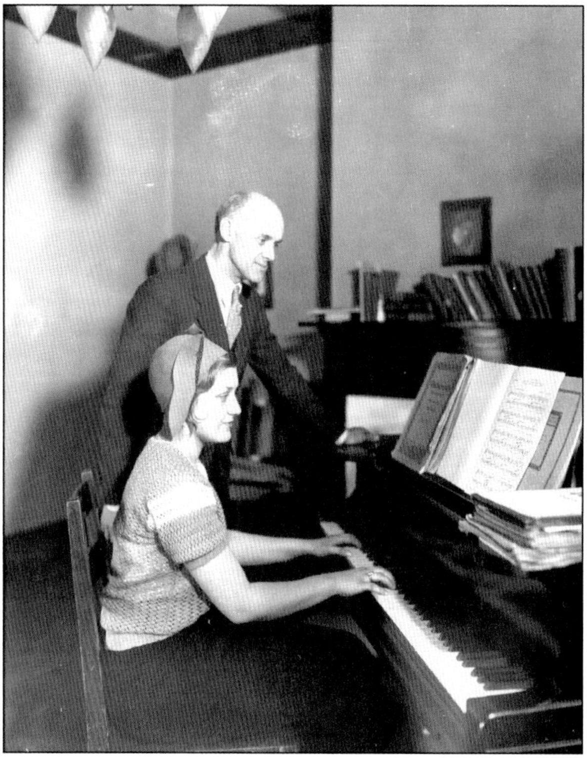

Although Westminster has continued to upgrade practice and recital spaces, the dynamic of student and teacher remains largely unchanged. Practice rooms were similar in 1928 (left) and 1980 (below).

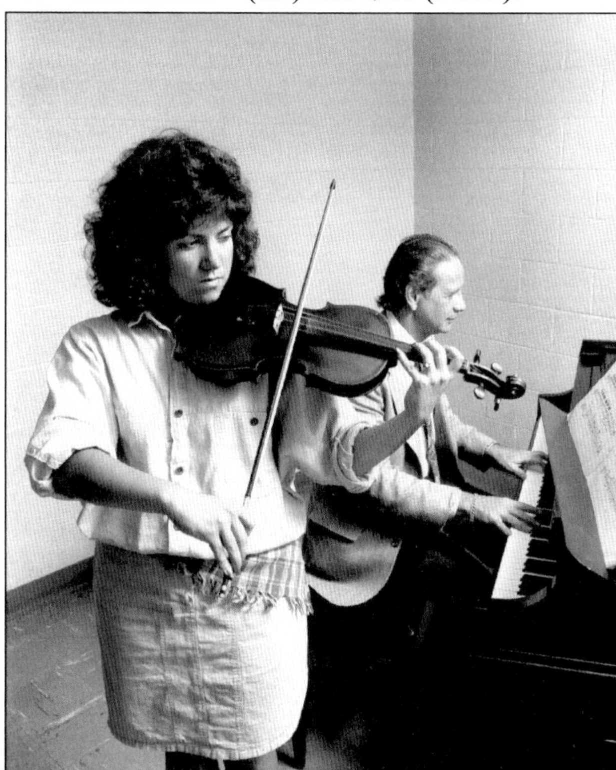

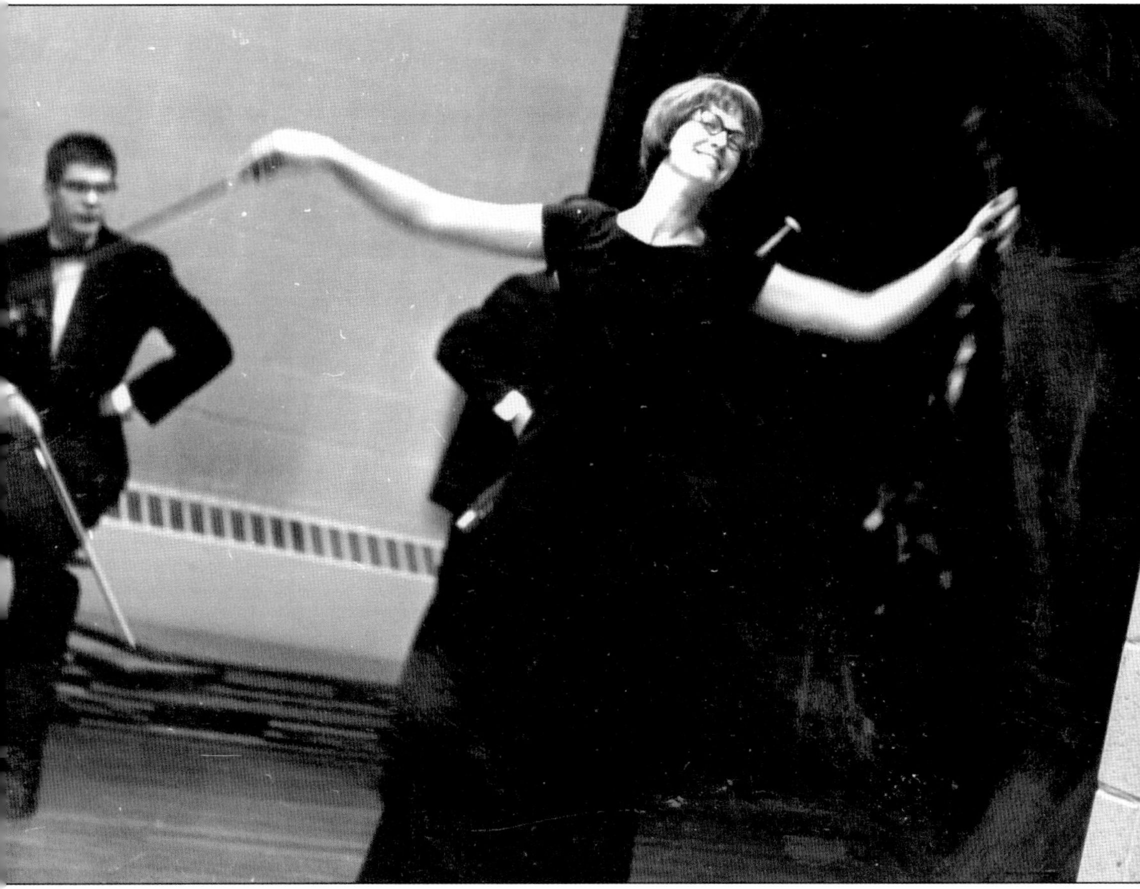

Senior recitals have been a required rite for students majoring in music. An exuberant Annette Rowley prepares for her big event in 1970.

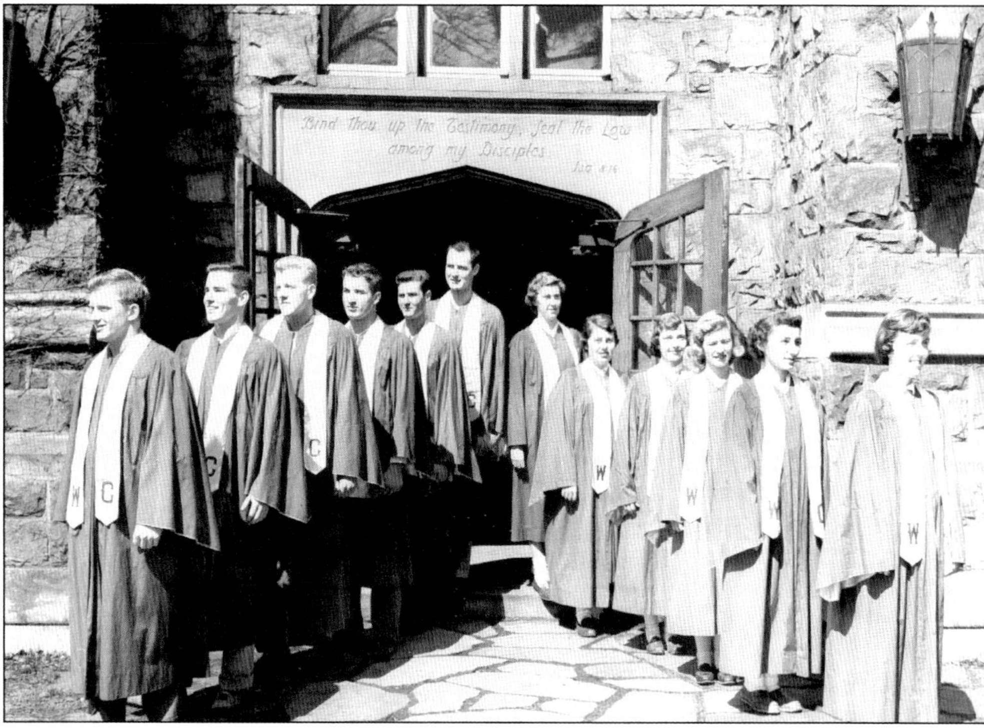

Choirs in the 1960s (above) presented recitals and concerts at chapel and special celebrations and gatherings. Starting in 1920, May Day festivities began with Senior Sing on the terrace of Old Main Memorial. Members of the class of 1932 (below) tuned up in cap and gown.

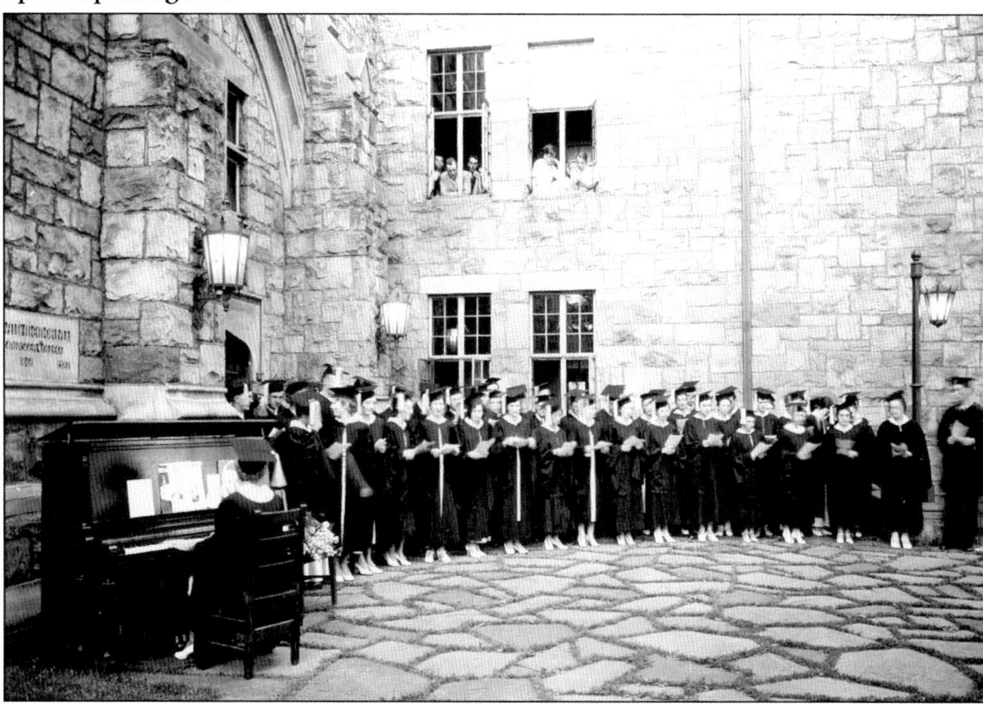

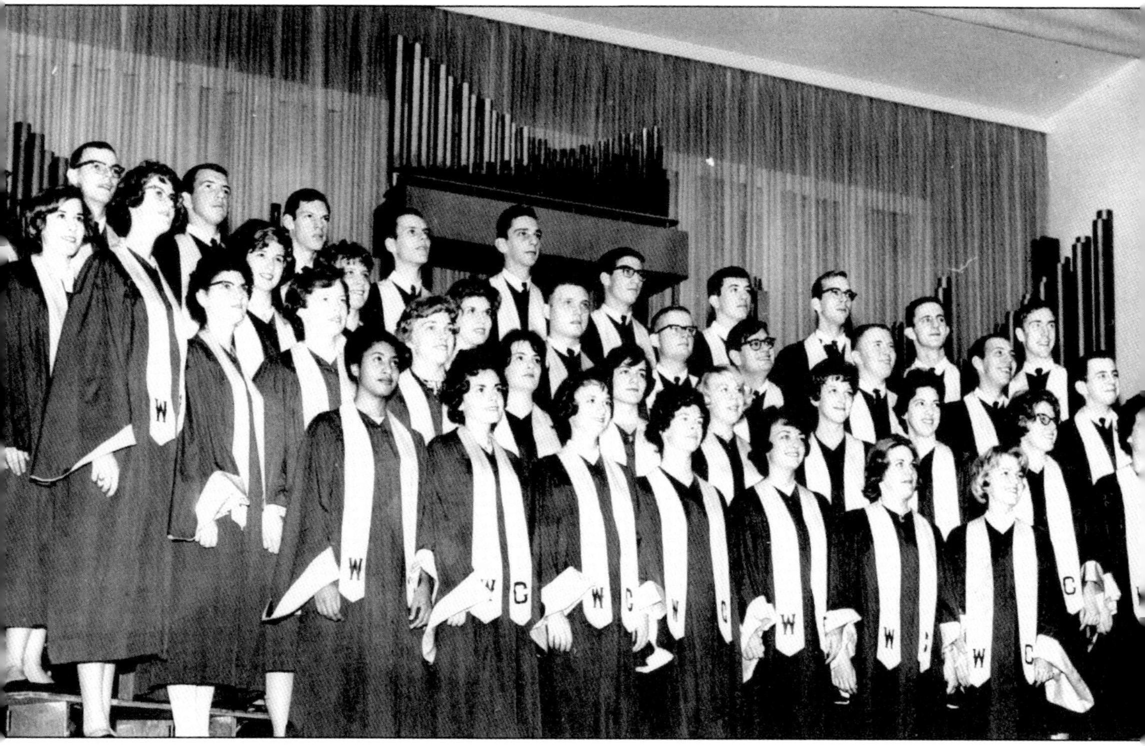

In 1963, the Westminster Concert Choir toured America's South. June Singleton (first row, far left) joined as a talented soprano and soloist and was the choir's sole African American member. Because of southern customs at the time, the bus tour was carefully planned so that Singleton would be graciously accommodated at all stops. Acts of discrimination were minor, but did occur. In Savannah, Georgia, director Clarence Martin accepted a last-minute invitation to perform. It turned out to be the high point of the tour. Singleton, during a tribute to Broadway's *West Side Story*, sang "There's a Place for Us." It was an emotional and memorable performance.

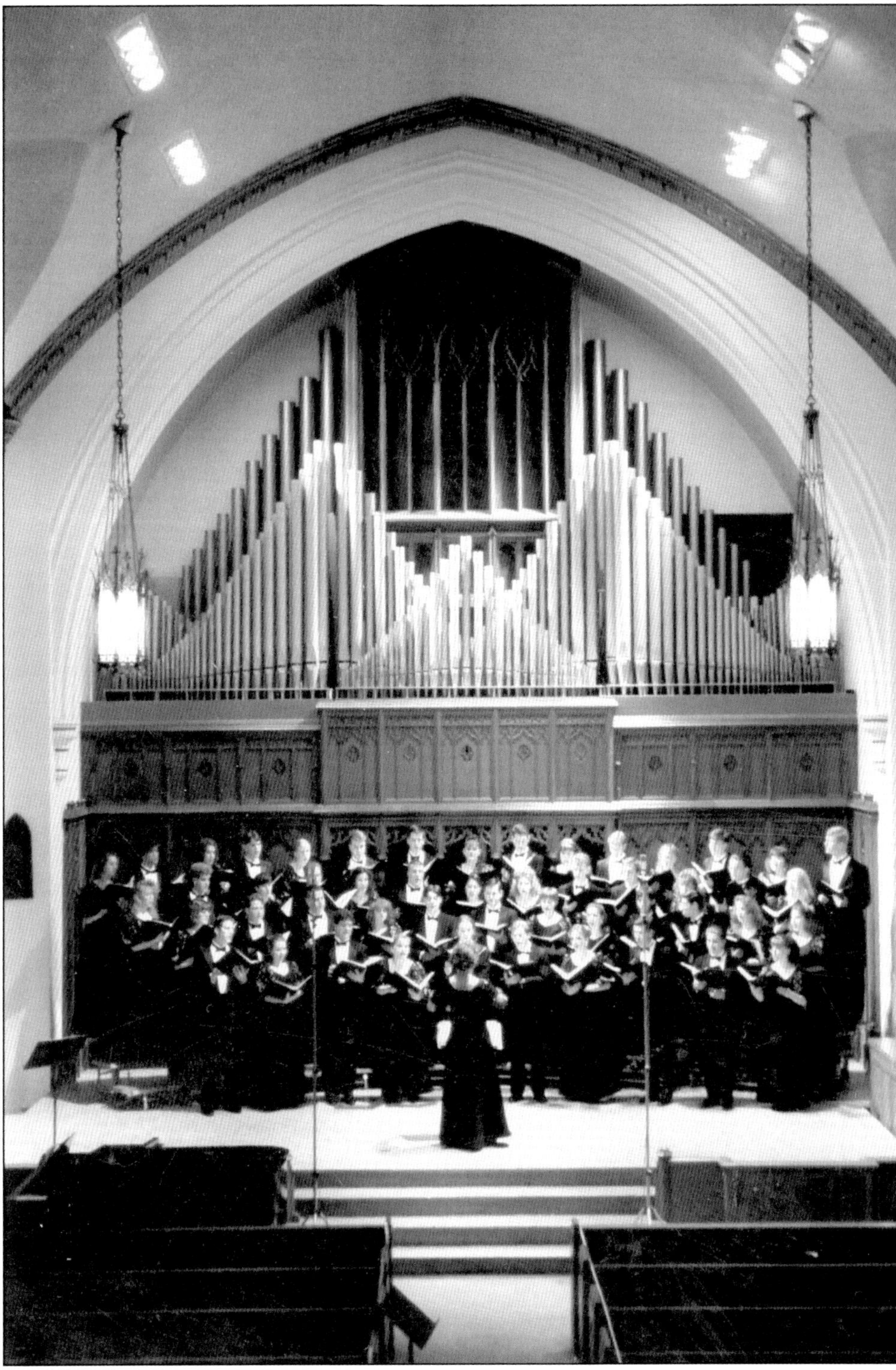

The Westminster Chapel Choir (seen here in the late 1990s) performed for chapel services, which had been required daily until 1969. Thereafter, services became a voluntary activity, but the choir continues to offer inspiration.

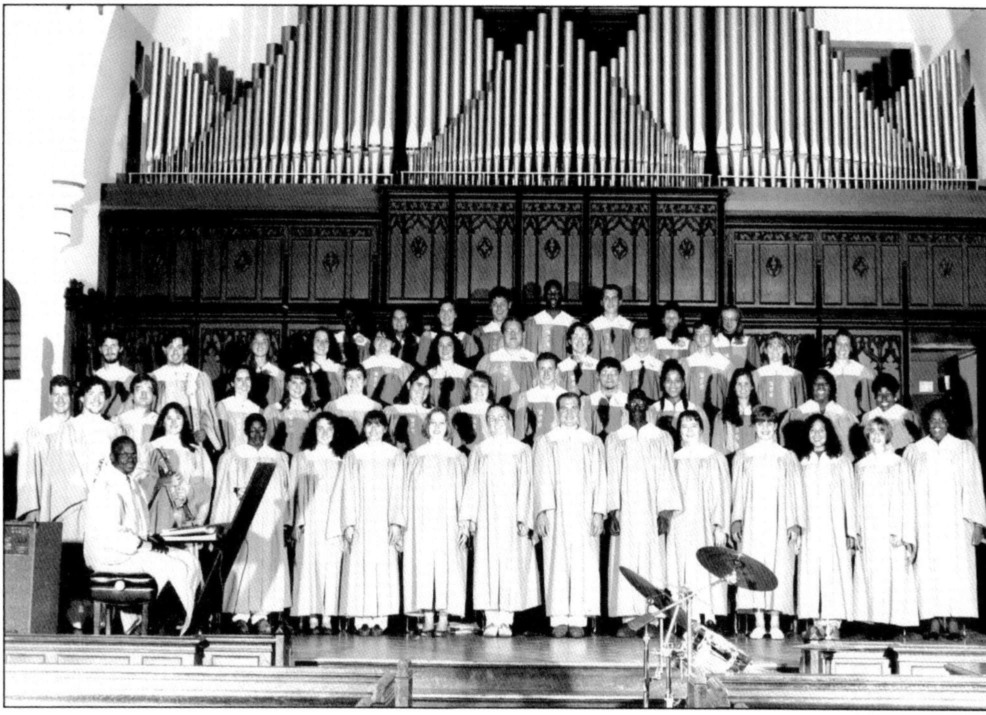

Opportunities for musical performance expanded with the Westminster Gospel Choir.

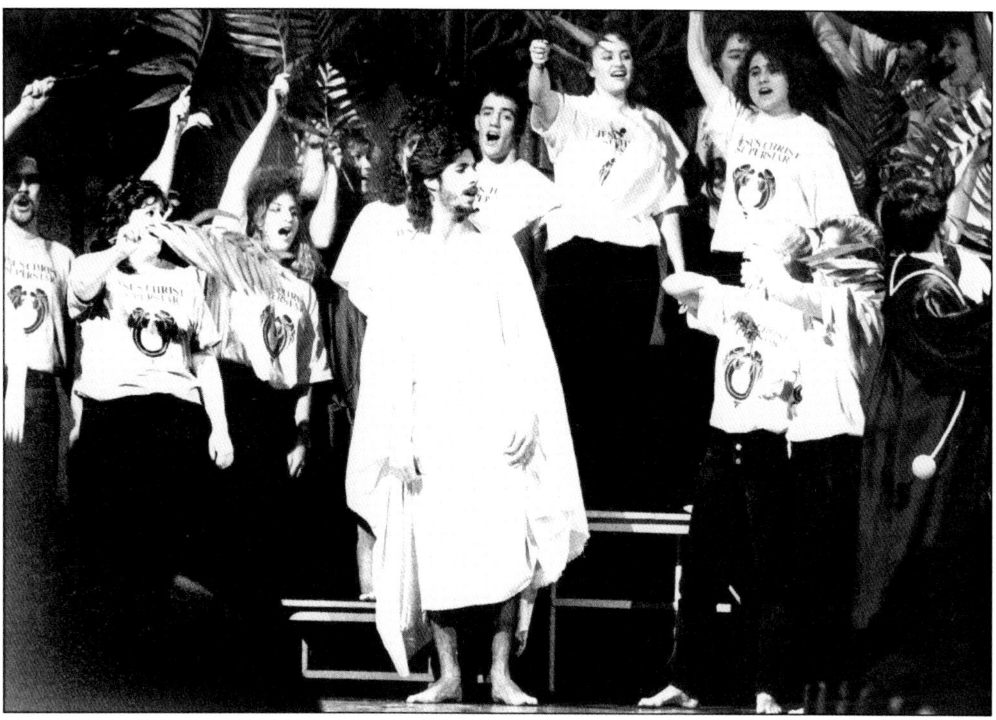

Chapel services have presented a broad range of worship events, including this 1990s rendition of the musical *Jesus Christ Superstar*.

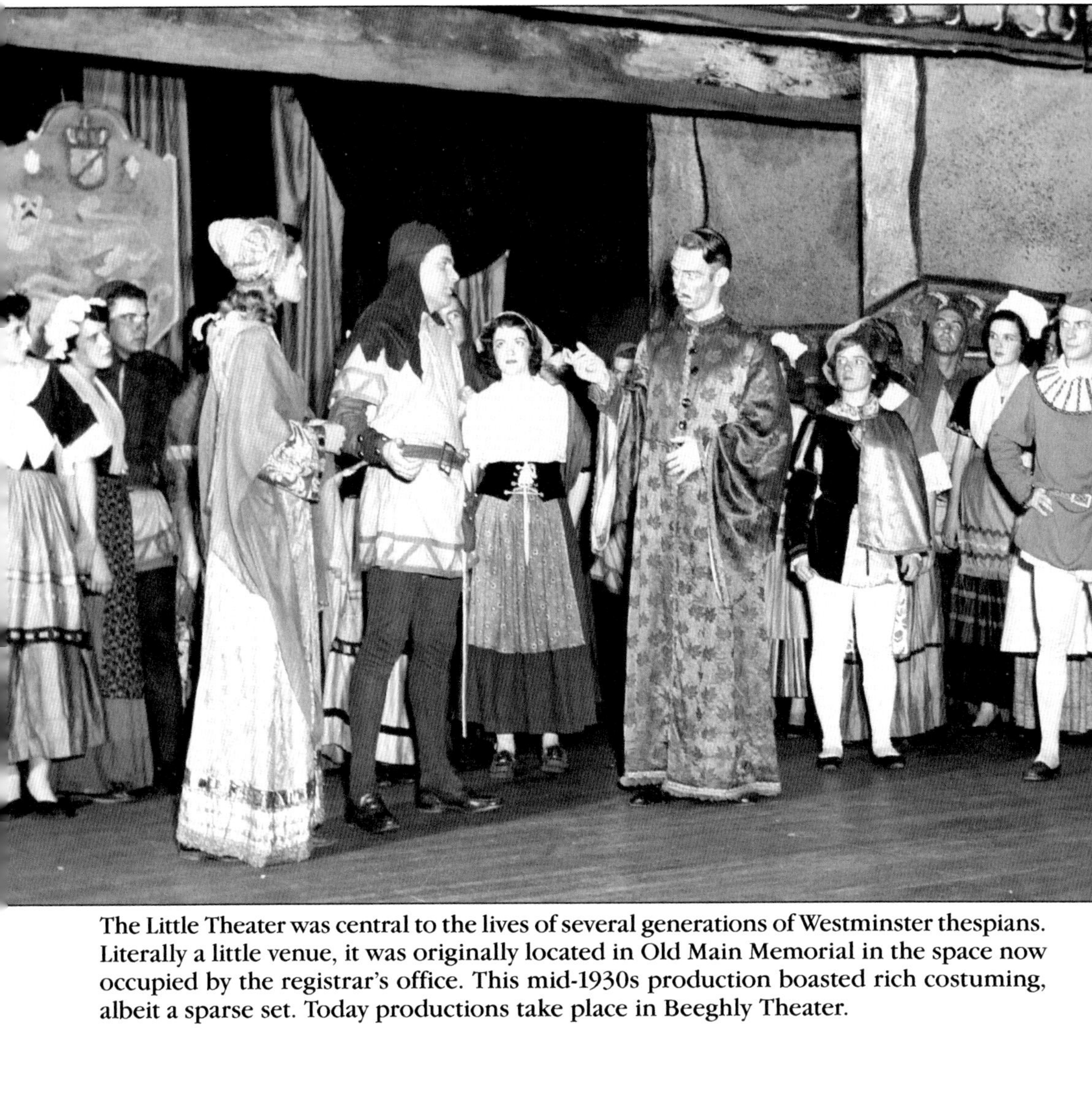

The Little Theater was central to the lives of several generations of Westminster thespians. Literally a little venue, it was originally located in Old Main Memorial in the space now occupied by the registrar's office. This mid-1930s production boasted rich costuming, albeit a sparse set. Today productions take place in Beeghly Theater.

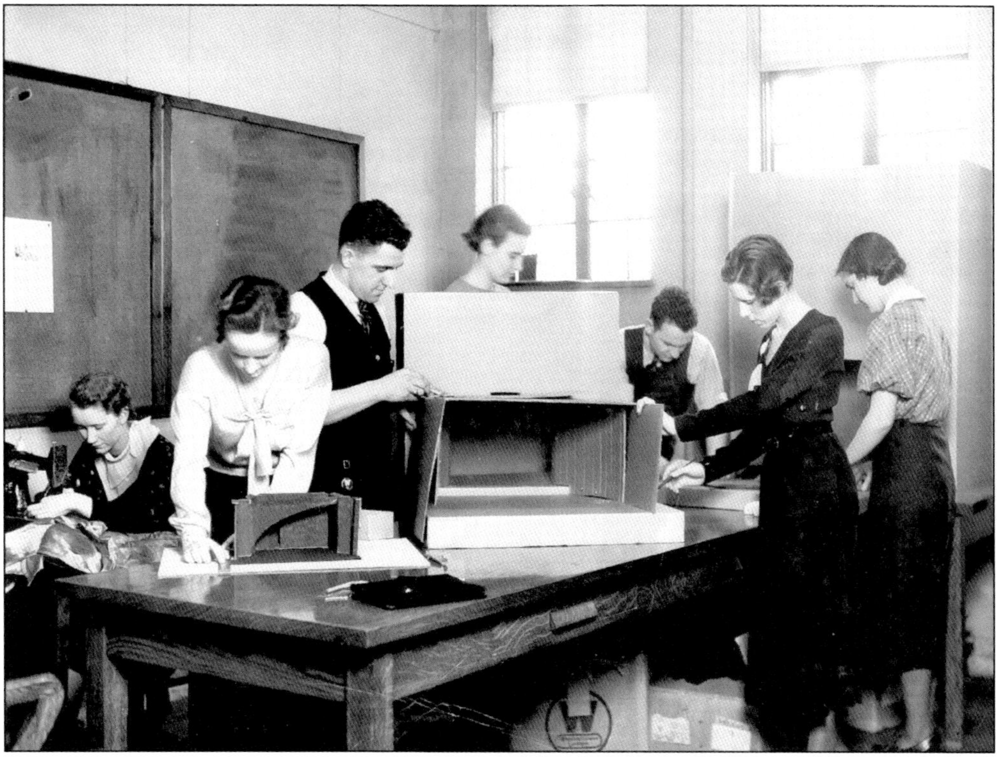

Many behind-the-scenes stagecrafts, from set design to make up, transformed extensive drama and musical productions in the Little Theater (above in the 1930s) and Beeghly Theater (below in the 1980s).

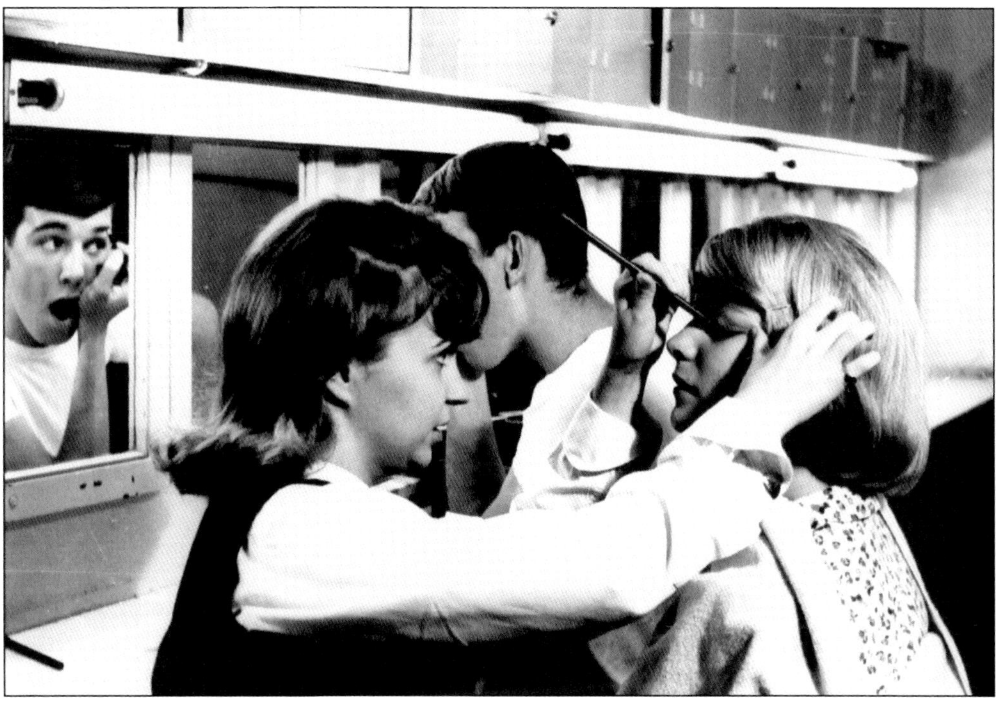

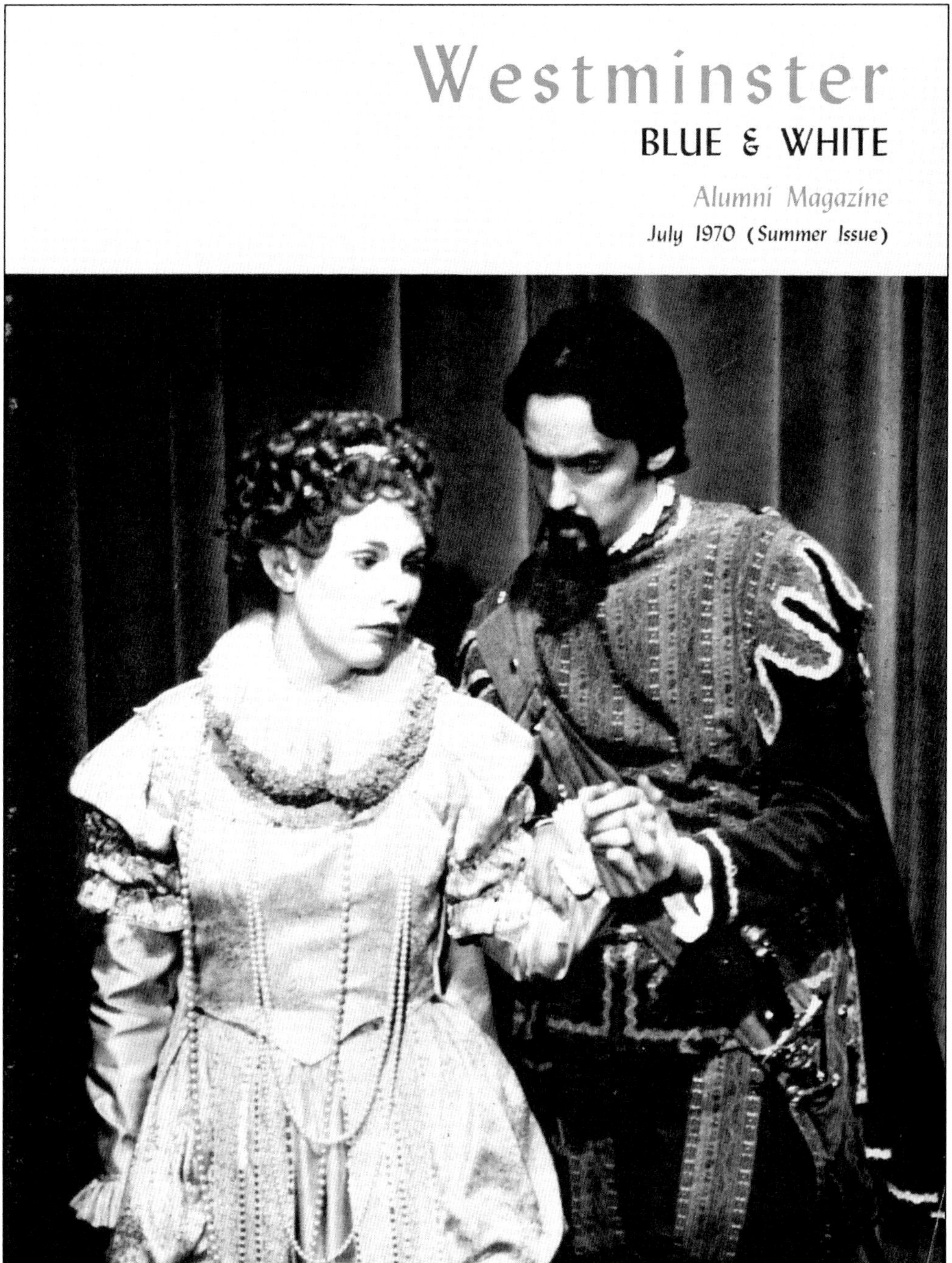

Main stage plays drew theater lovers to the college. The 1970 production of *Mary Stuart*, which starred Deborah Holt and David Reinhardsen, served as front-page news in the *Blue and White*, Westminster's publication for alumni and friends. The quarterly magazine debuted in the mid-1930s and eventually changed to *Westminster College Magazine* in 1982.

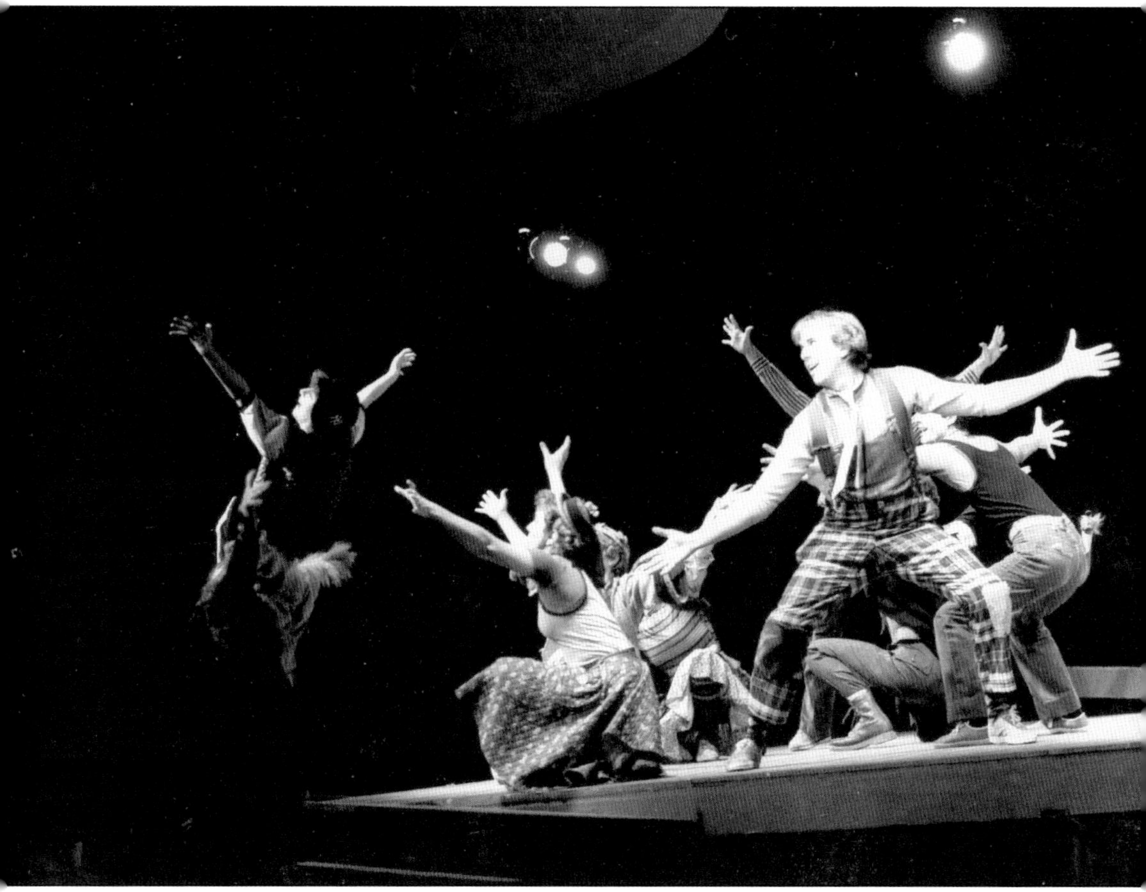

Godspell: A Musical Based on the Gospel According to St. Matthew headlined a 1980s season in Beeghly Theater. The show, an off-Broadway and Broadway sensation, relied upon clowning, pantomime, and acrobatics.

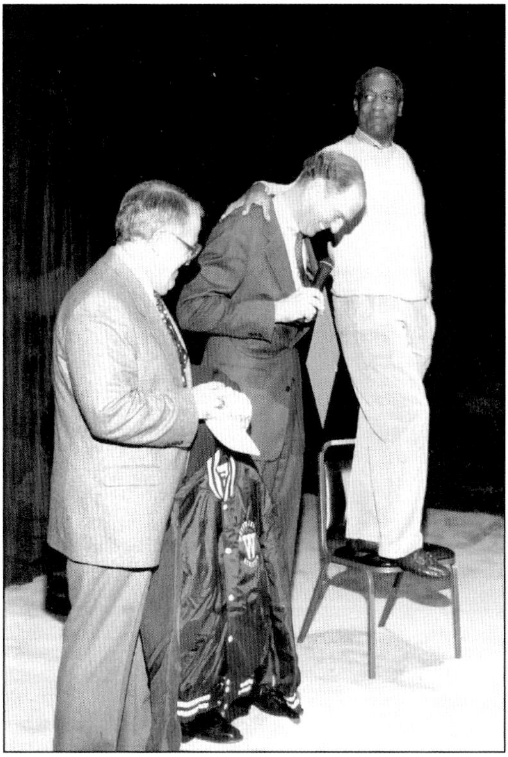

Since the late 1960s, the Celebrity Series has offered a broad range of entertainment from soloists to dancers and symphonies to comedians. The shows draw standing-room-only crowds and make Westminster a cultural hub. Dr. Joe Fusco and Pres. Tom Williamson welcome comedian Dr. Bill Cosby to the Orr Auditorium stage.

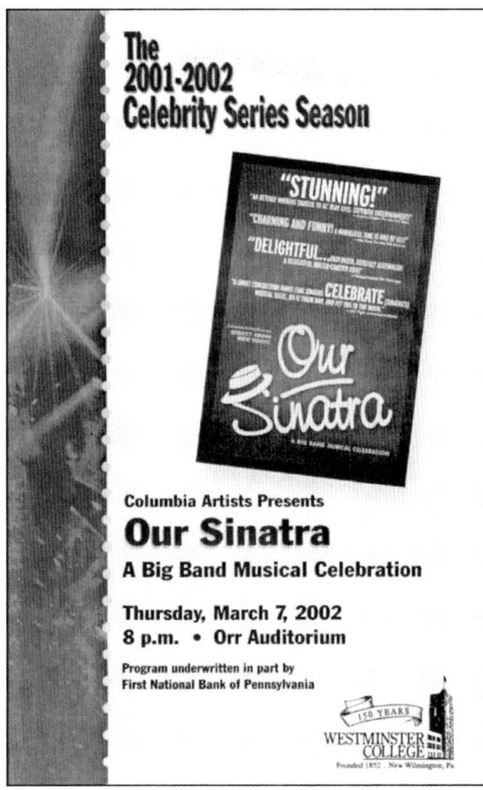

Other celebrities who have performed or lectured on campus include Margaret Bourke-White, Ogden Nash, Peter Nero, Maya Angelou, Leah Rabin, Marcel Marceau, and many more.

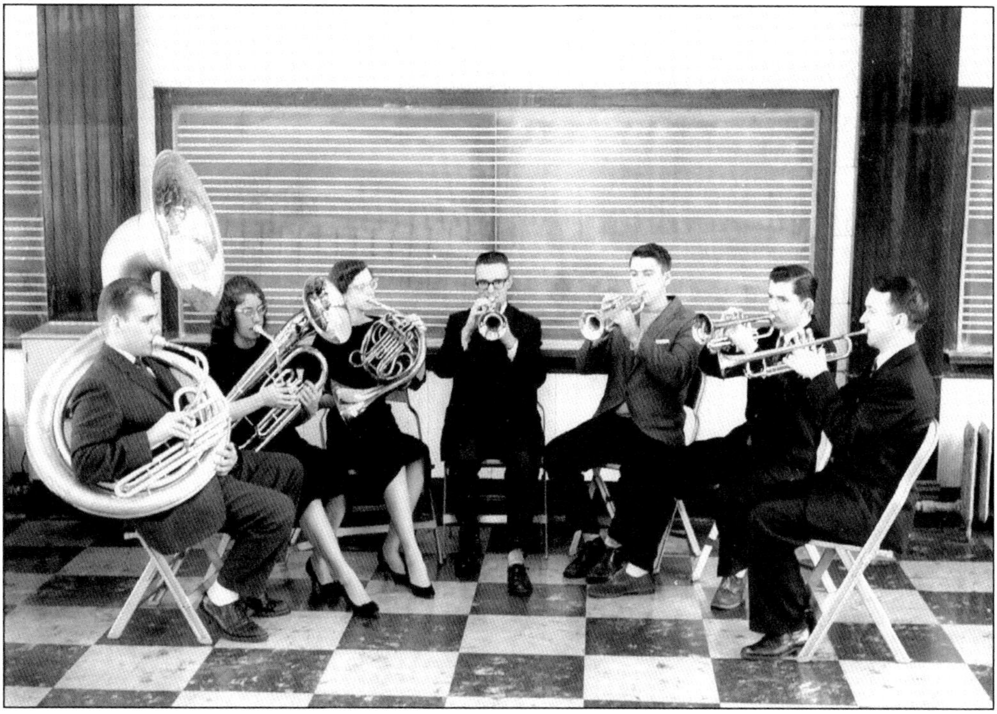

The jazz band, in the mid-20th century, provided entertainment for many campus activities.

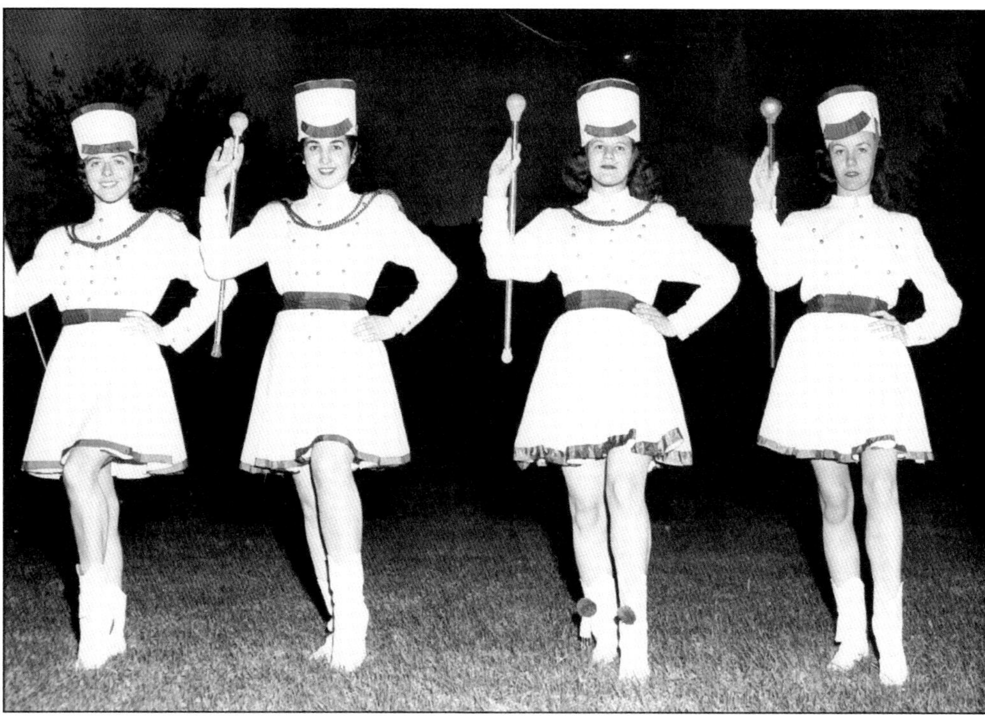

Leading the marching band during parades and half-time performance were the majorettes of the 1950s.

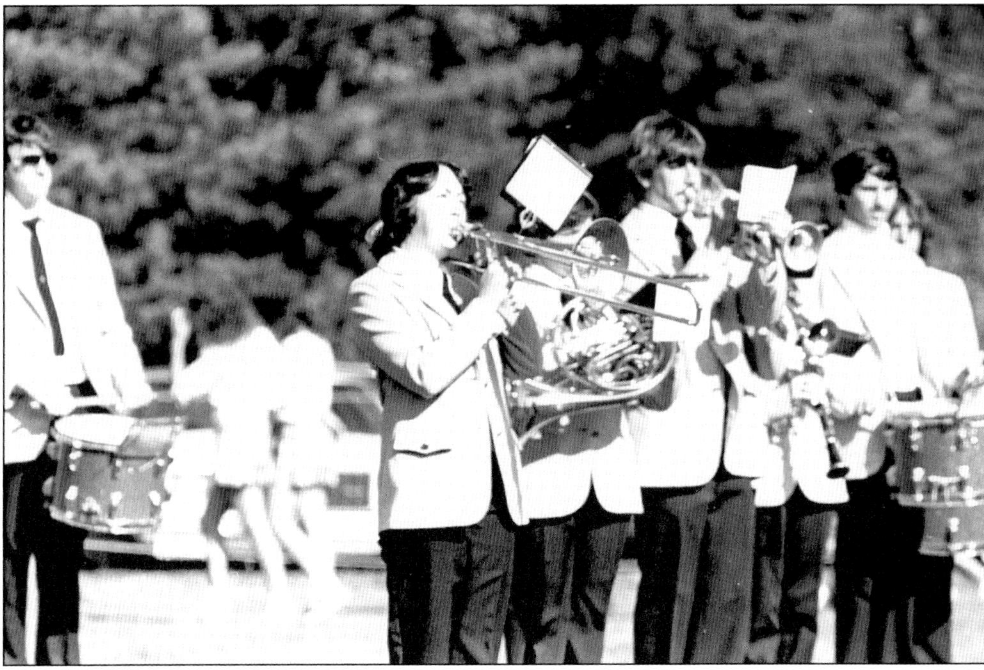

The Titan Marching Band has performed regularly at football games for decades. In 1981, their uniforms consisted of powder blue blazers (above). More traditional attire was worn for the homecoming parade in 1988.

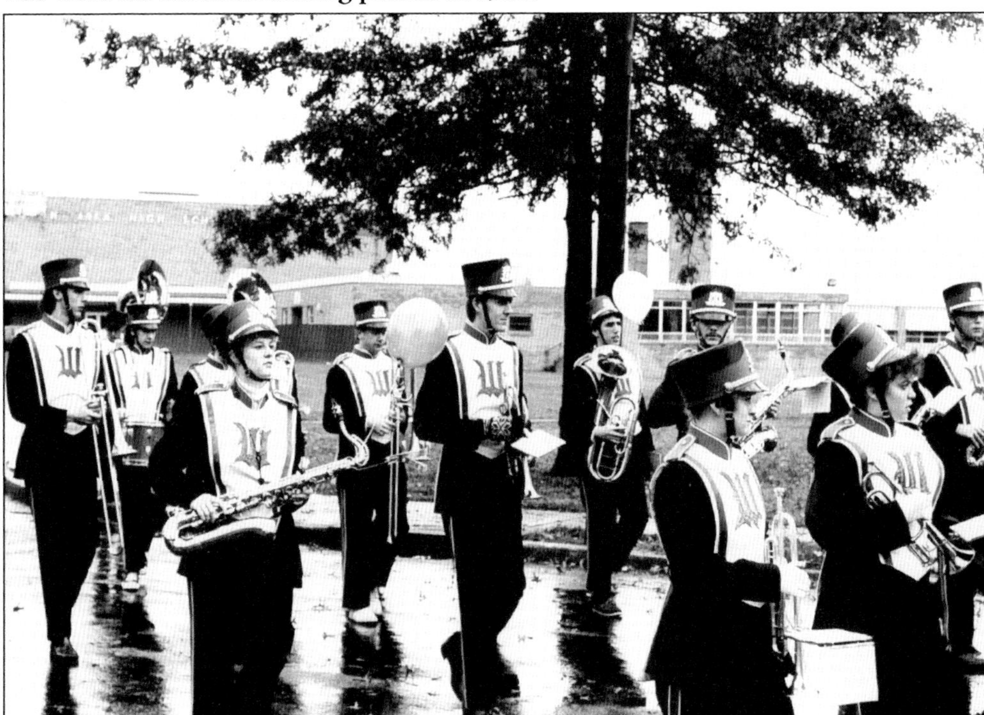

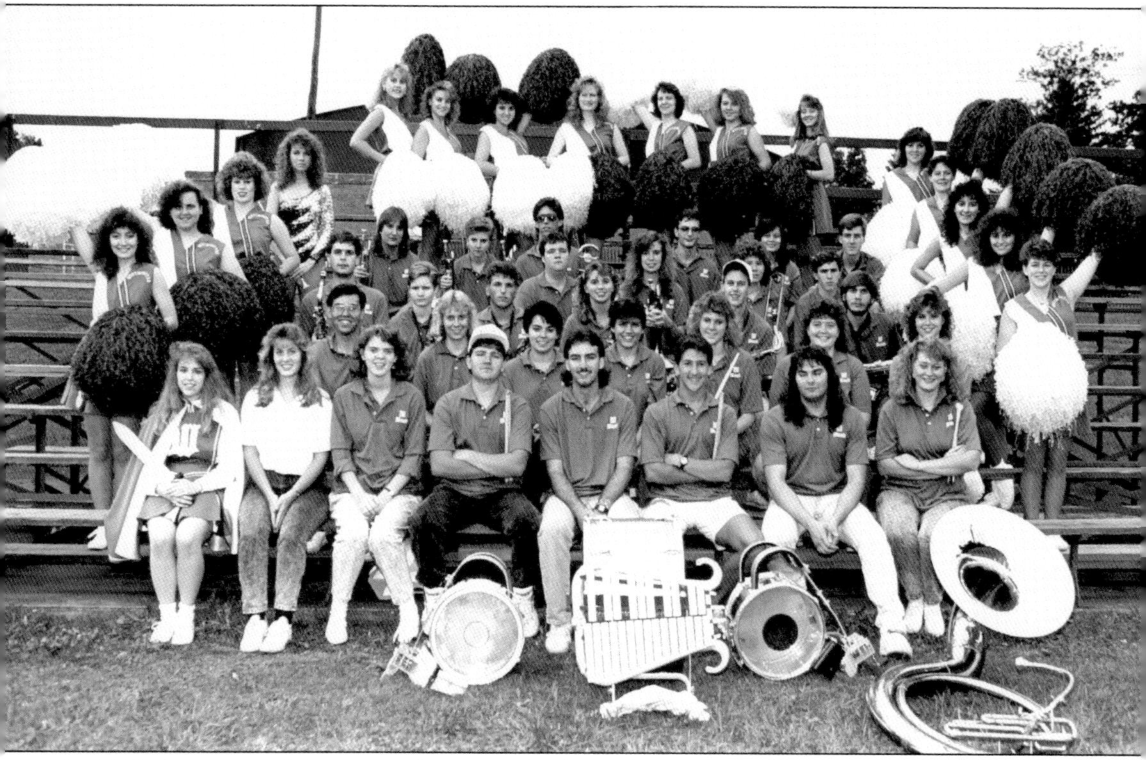

By 1989, the spirited Titan Marching Band adopted a relaxed style and was spontaneous in its performances at Burry Stadium.

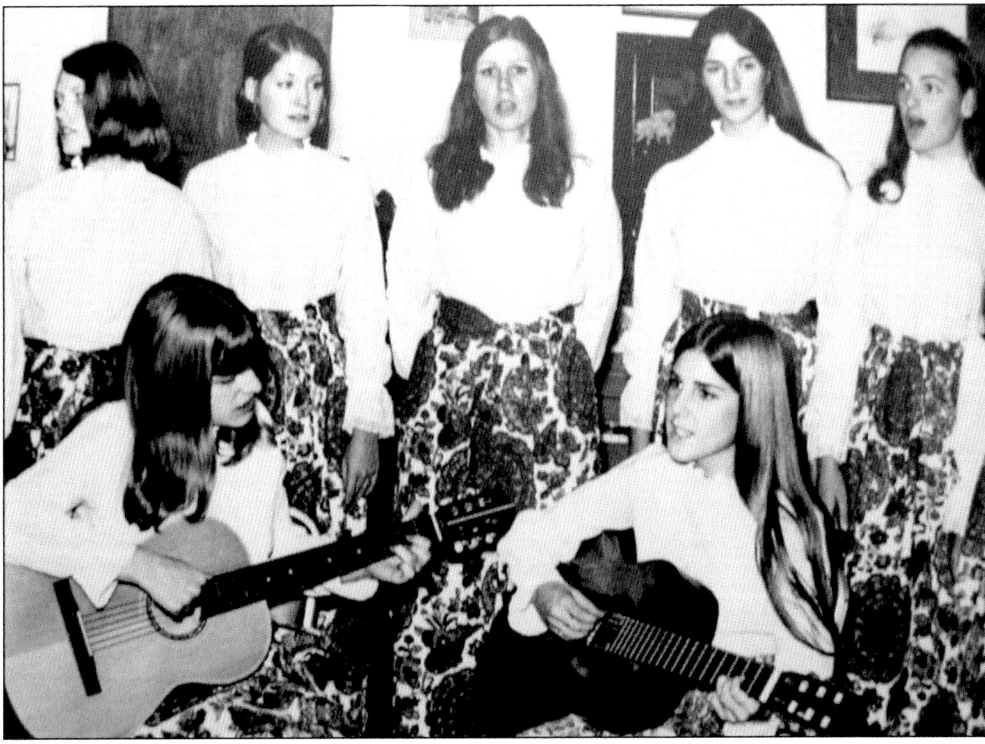

Girl singing groups were popular everywhere in the late 1960s and early 1970s. Westminster was no exception. The New WilmingTens were much in demand for performances at social and community events in the region.

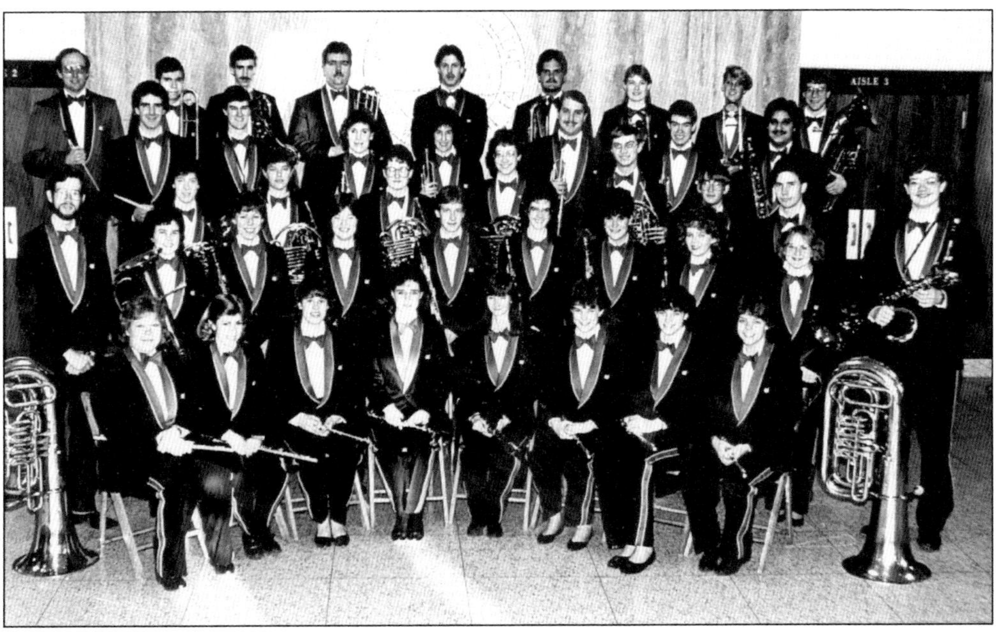

The Westminster Symphonic Band, led by Dr. Grover Pitman in 1985, showcased the talents of collegiate musicians, many of them majoring in sacred music or music education.

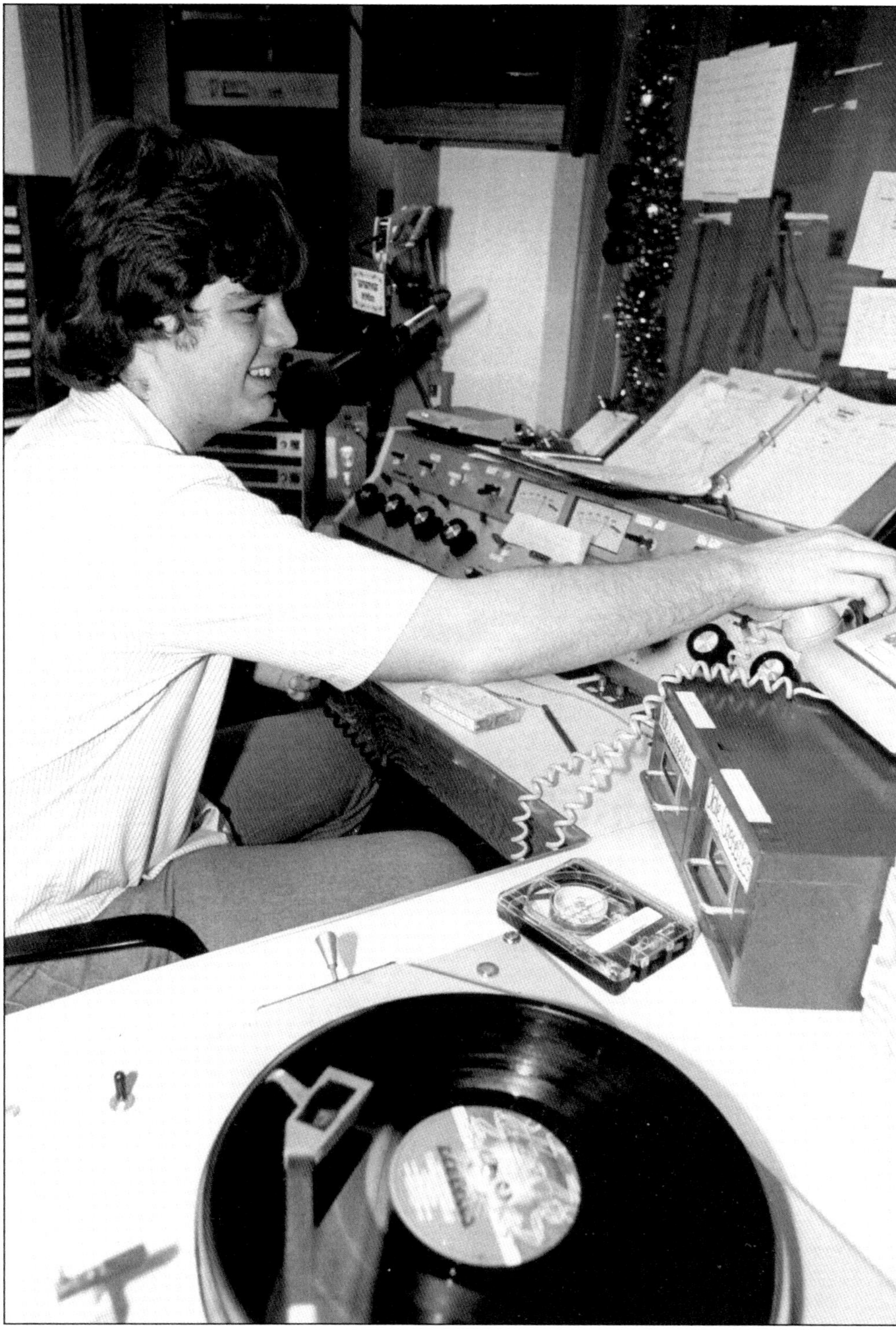

WKPS, at 88.9 FM, began daily broadcasts in 1968. It was the college's first licensed station. The station's call letters signify the student broadcasters who helped to launch it: Tom Wensel, Jeff Kellam, Mark Klinger, Rick Packer, and Richard Stevens.

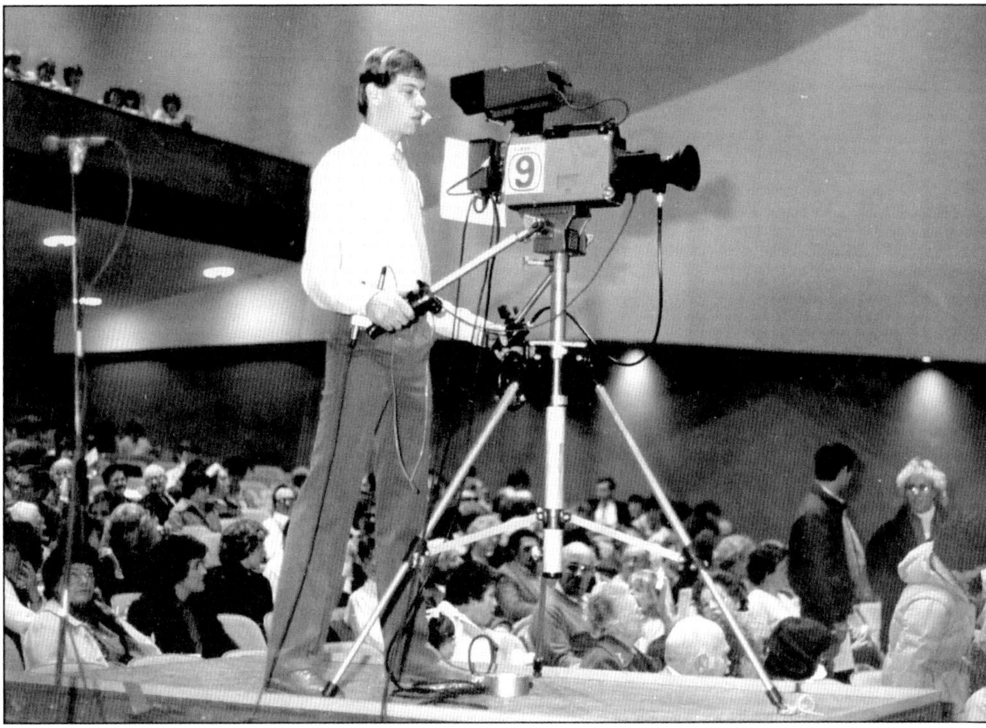

The first live telecast by WWNW-TV, the Westminster cable station, featured a concert by the college orchestra. The show emanated from the stage of Orr Auditorium.

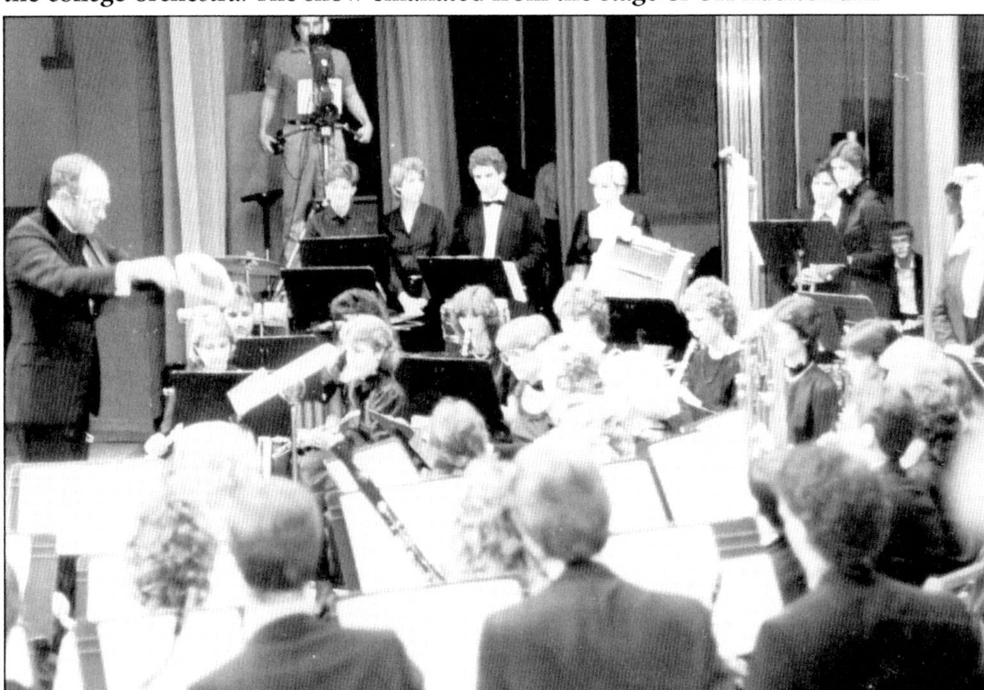

Five

Special Places, Special Memories

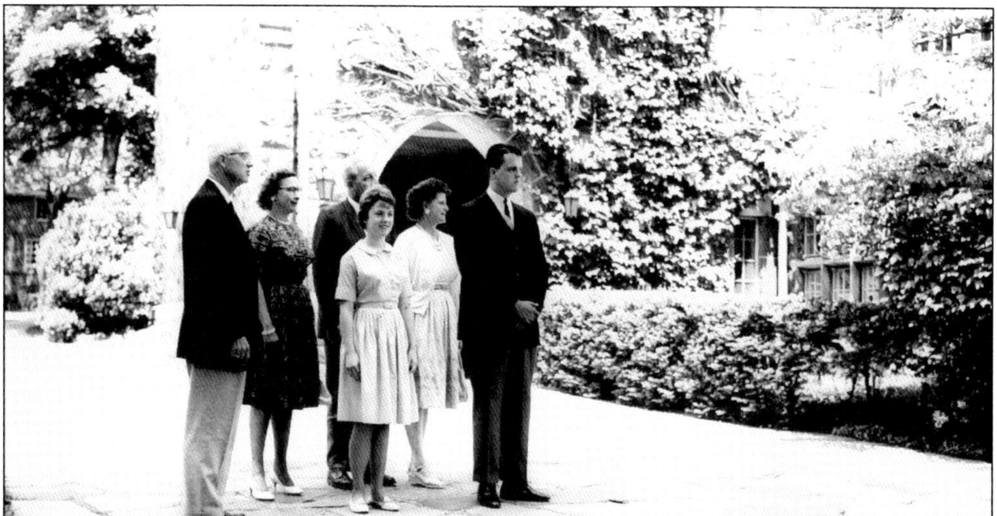

It is impossible to visit the Westminster College campus without being struck by its natural beauty, the dramatic Collegiate Gothic architecture, and the warmth of its people. As Pres. Tom Williamson commented in the foreword, "There is a line from an old Beatles song that goes 'There are places I remember, all my life.' Westminster has many such places. It is, after all, that sense of place that beckons us to keep coming back to this beautiful campus again and again to experience a certain tranquility that we can not quite describe." That "sense of place" begins for most with their first campus visit, usually with parents and usually in the junior or senior year of high school. And, although clothing styles have evolved and the interview now is less formal, today's prospective students are greeted with the same warmth as those pictured here in the 1950s. For most undergraduates, Westminster holds many special places and special memories.

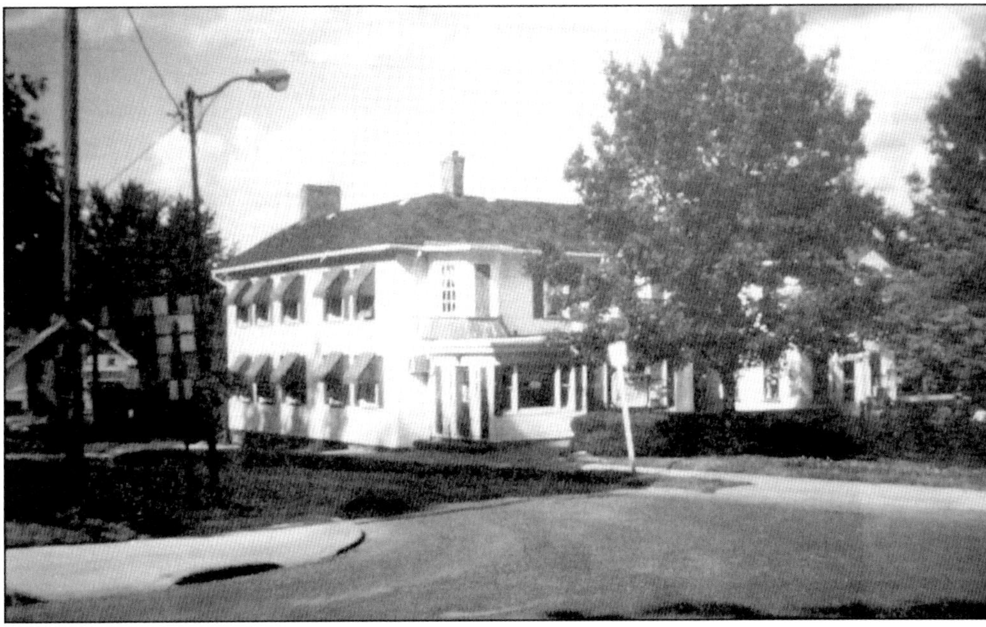

The ultimate dining experience for students and parents was The Tavern, which opened in 1935. For decades the establishment was presided over by a welcoming Cora Durrast. Situated in the center of New Wilmington and aside the borough's main stoplight, The Tavern was renowned for sticky buns, ham loaf, fruit shrubs, and chicken pie. In 1947, it was listed in Duncan Hines's popular guide, *Adventures in Good Eating*. (Photograph by Dewey Dewitt.)

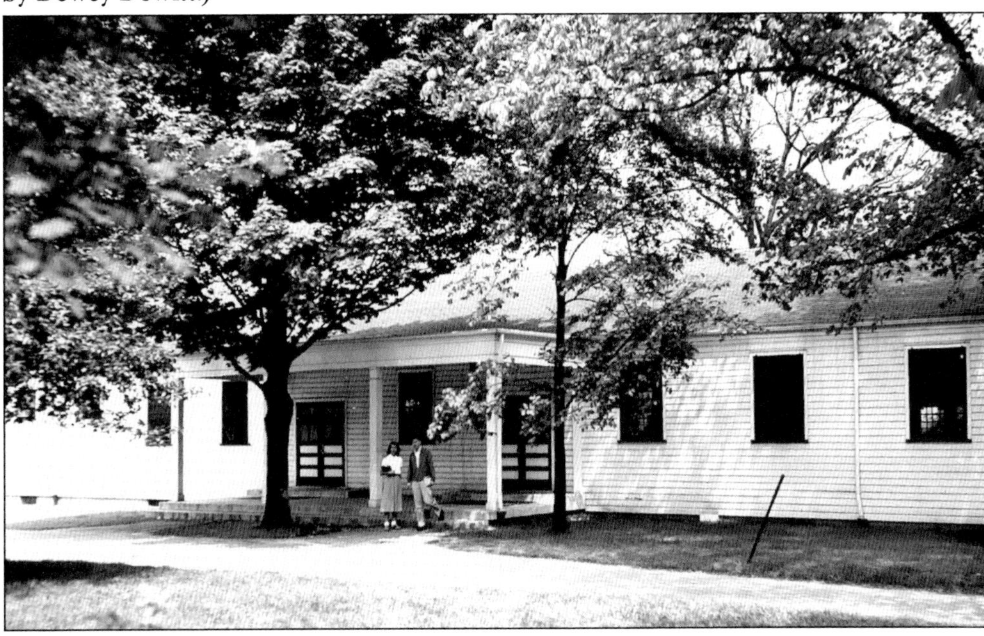

The original student recreation hall was dubbed the Titan Union Building and later just the TUB. It was actually an army surplus building. A modern Walton-Mayne Student Union Building opened in 1958. The original union building remains in use by the college's physical plant department.

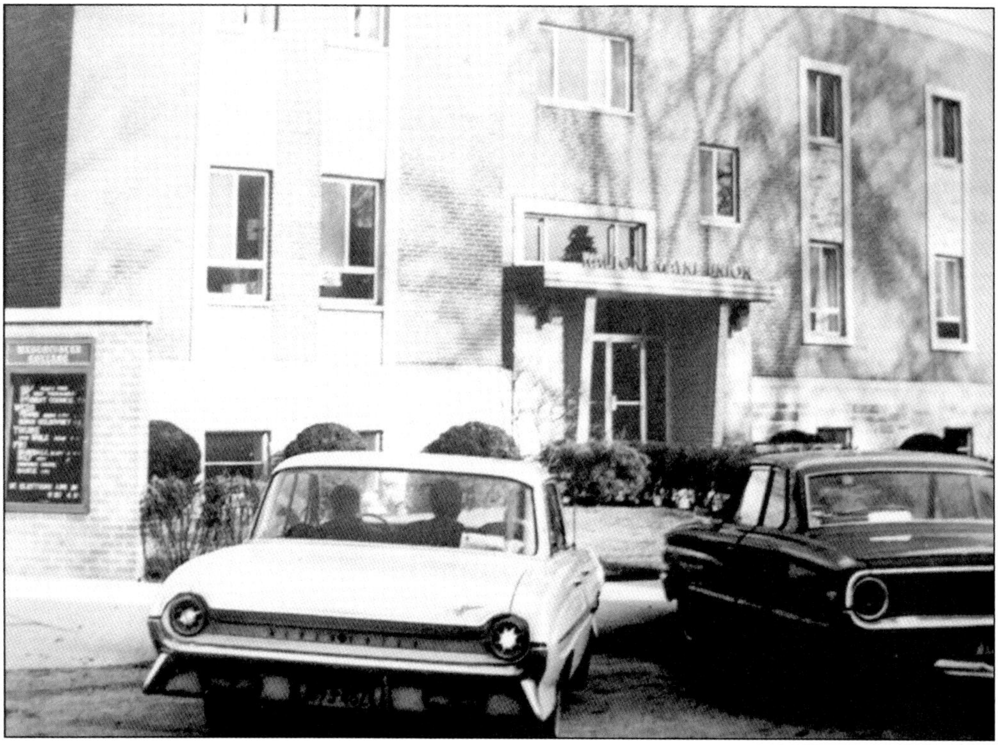

For about 45 years, the Walton-Mayne Student Union Building, generally dubbed the TUB, was home to all forms of student entertainment, from weekend dances and concerts to daily rounds of bridge and 500 rummy.

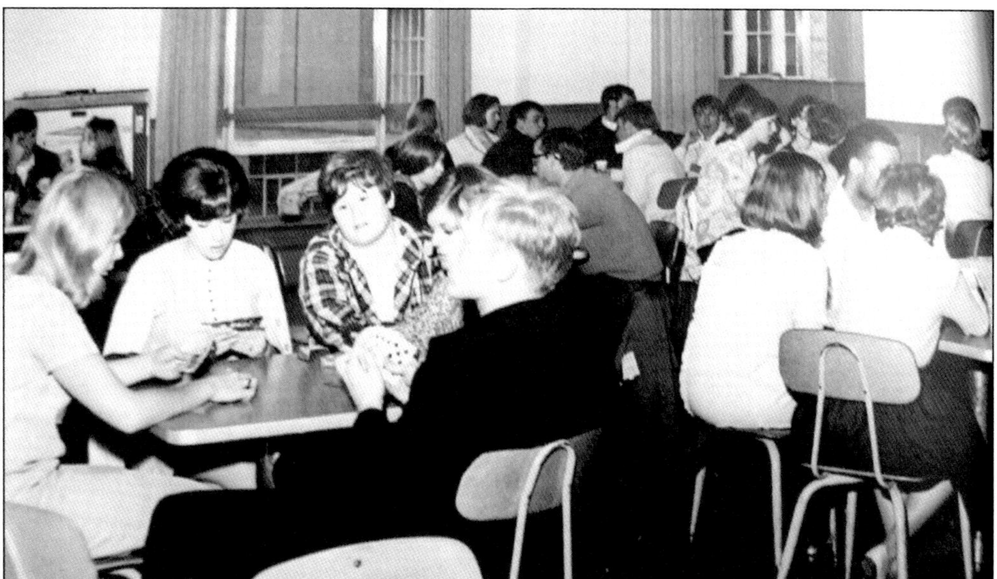

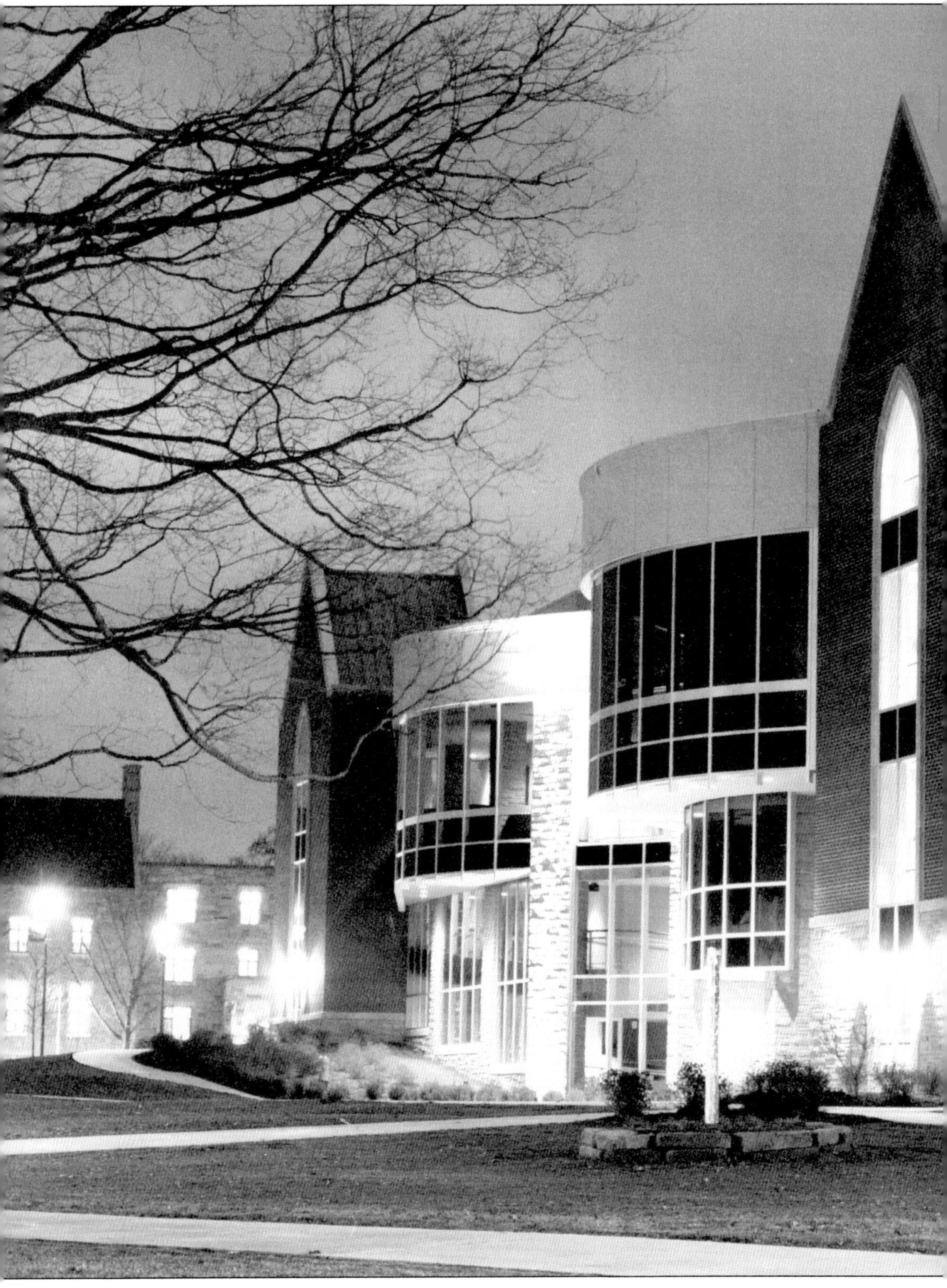

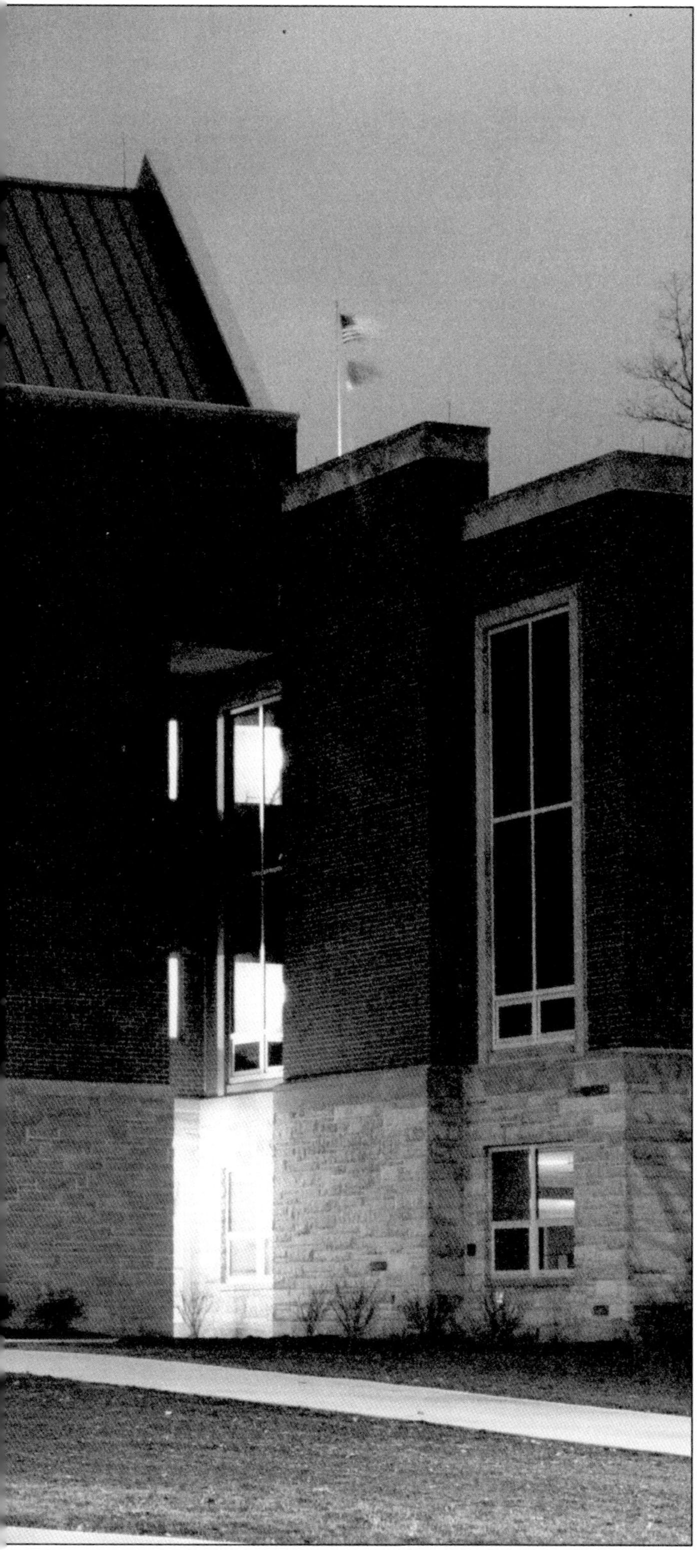

Inventive architecture joined together the Walton-Mayne Student Union with the Thompson Clark Freeman Science Halls to form an expanded structure. Opened in 2003, the McKelvey Campus Center is the hub of student activities. It incorporates banquet rooms, conference centers, offices, lecture halls, and dining facilities. Not long after opening, students petitioned to have the dining area rechristened the TUB, such was their affection for the name.

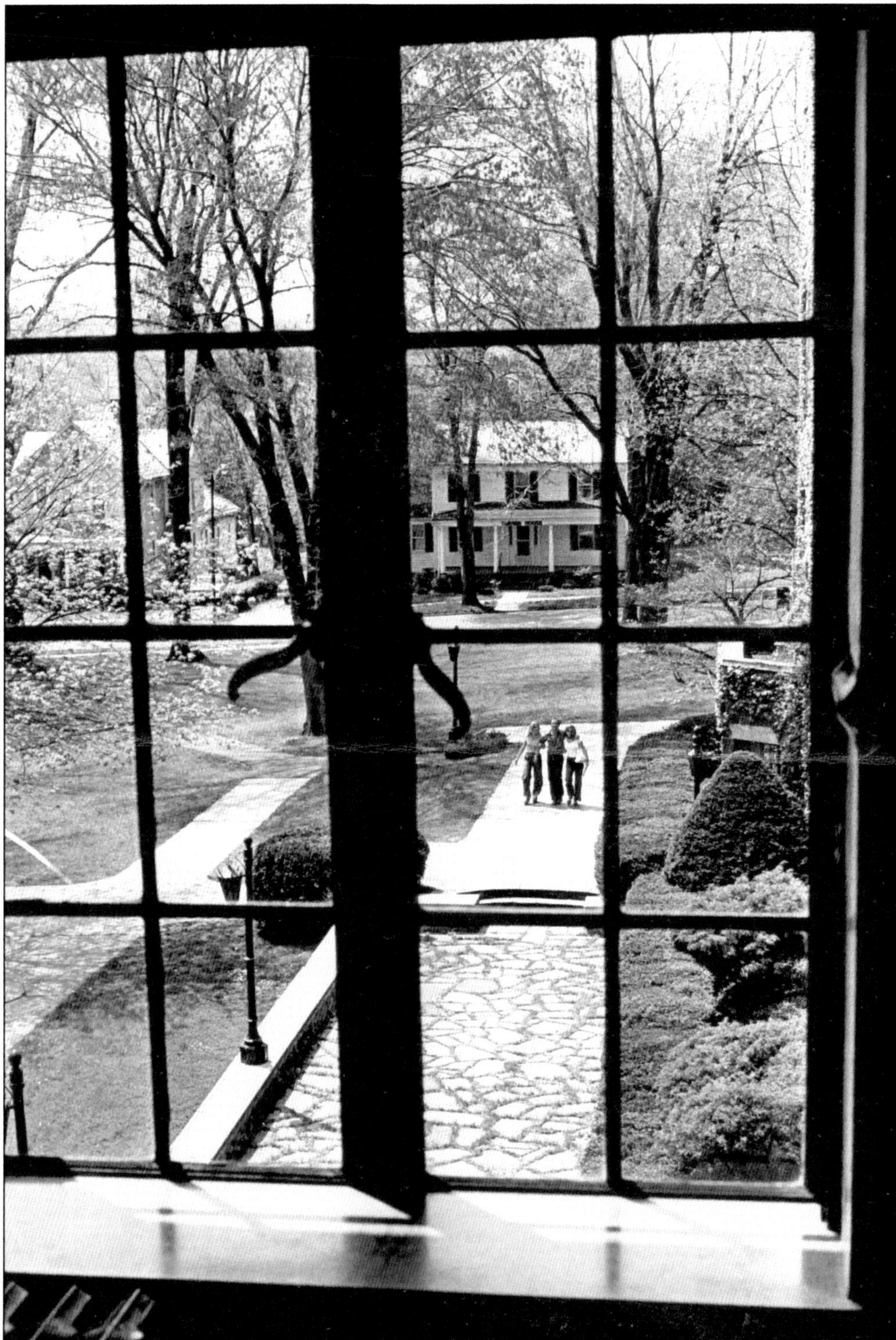

The gracious patio and walkway attached to Old Main Memorial is known as Senior Terrace. Custom limits access to only graduating seniors and alumni.

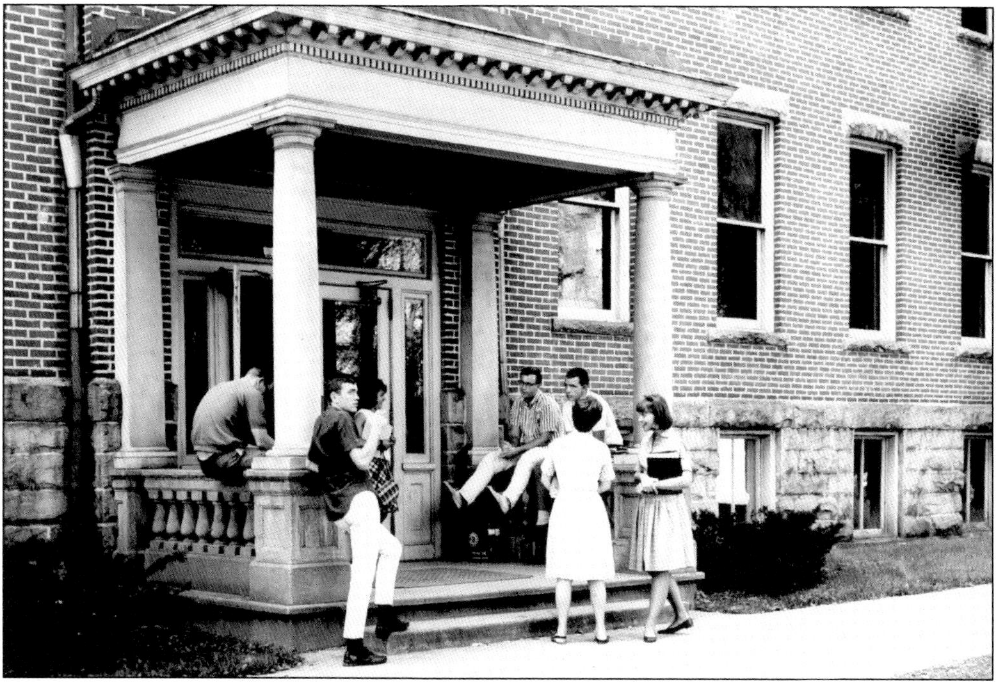

During the late 1950s, Westminster's many restrictions enforced a decorum, which included dresses for women and shirts and ties (and sometimes jackets) for men. More casual clothing was frowned upon.

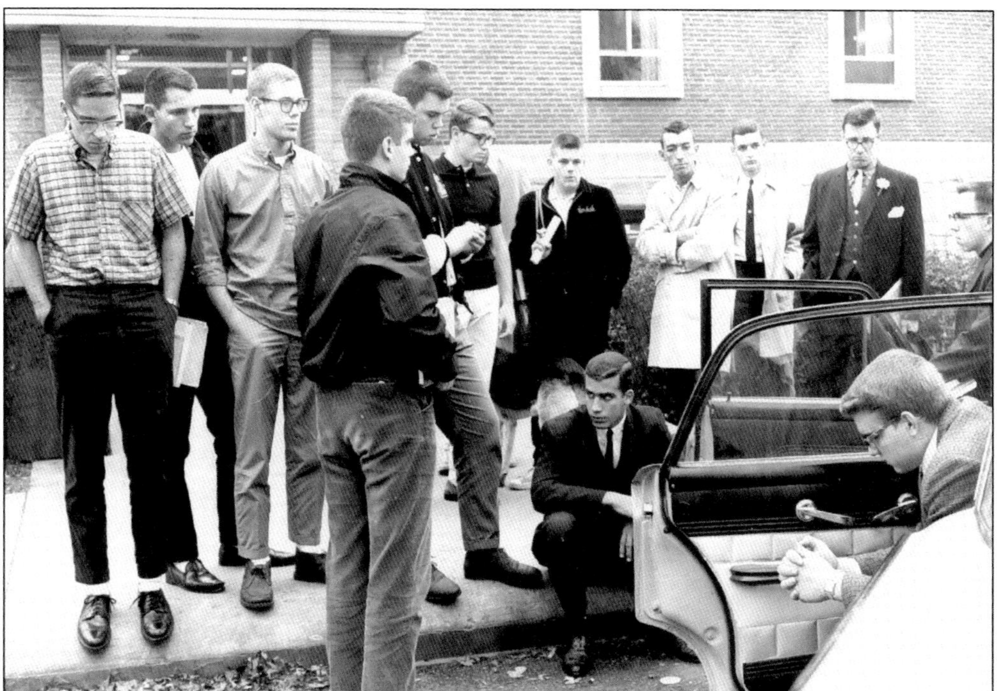

Many Westminster students heard about of the assassination of President John F. Kennedy via radios in their dorms or cars on November 22, 1963.

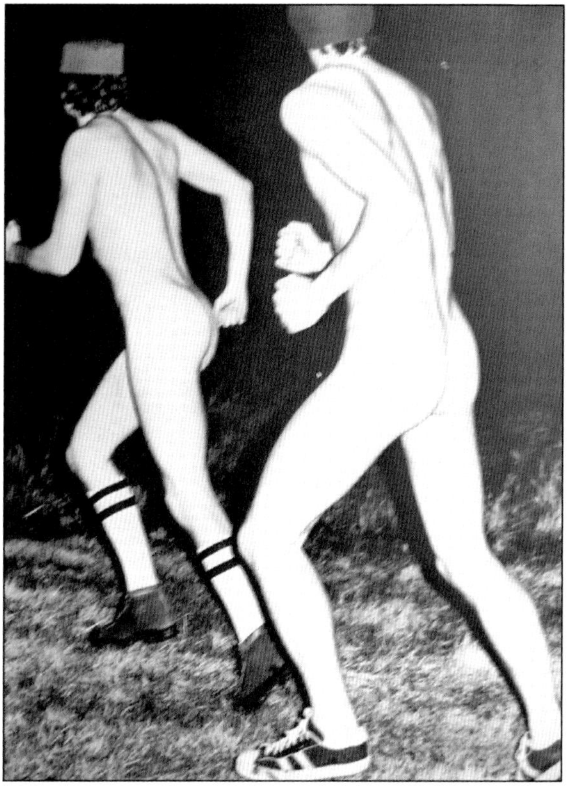

In the early 1970s, streaking caused a minor sensation at the Oscar ceremonies and on Westminster's campus.

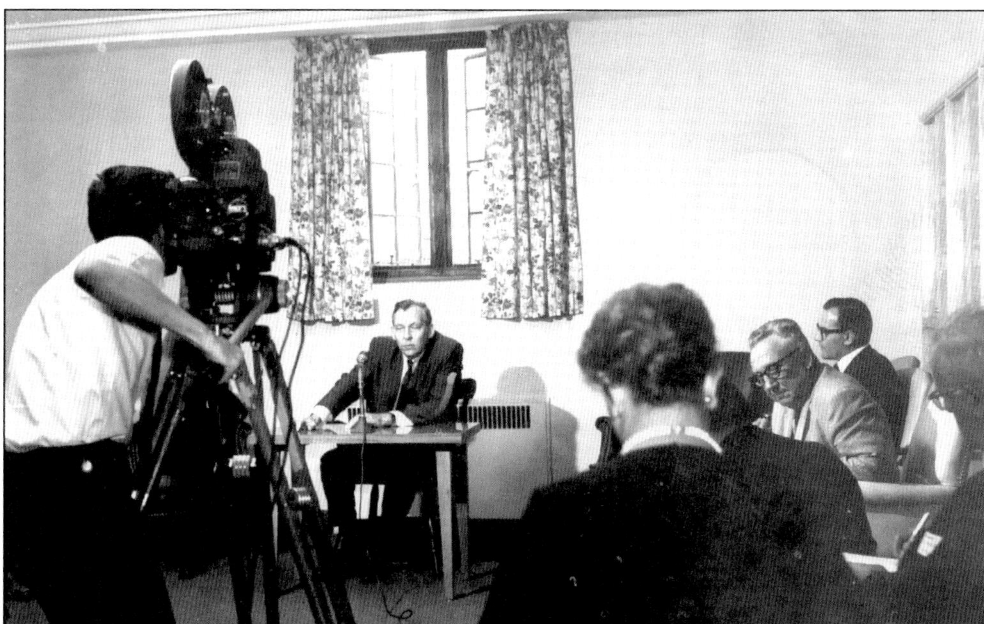

During 1973, campus unrest—at Westminster and elsewhere—involved student protests. In New Wilmington, the actions centered on a number of issues, ranging from accusations of racism to the desire for less restrictive dormitory policies. Pres. Earland I. Carlson held a news conference to discuss the state of campus affairs.

Special Section

See Page 7

The Westminster Holcad

FIRST PUBLISHED IN 1884

Student Association

See Page 8

ol. 85 No. 10 Westminster College New Wilmington, Pennsylvania 1970

WE ARE NUMBER ONE

Task Force Submits SA Constitution

by Dave Downton

At its meeting last Friday, the Task Force finished working out the details in the constitution for the proposed Student Association and voted unanimously to adopt the documents which they had prepared in their first formal vote of the school year. They also set the following dates for briefing students, faculty, and administration and for a student referendum: Oct. 5–representatives from the task force will be in the fraternity houses at 7:30 and all other campus housing at 11 p.m. to discuss the proposed constitution and Association; Oct. 8-the majority of the task force will meet in the TUB lounge to talk with any interested persons; Oct. 9-there will be a student referendum to adopt the documents printed in the paper below; and Oct. 14–representatives of the Task Force will meet with all members of the faculty and administration in an informal briefing and discussion session.

The constitution printed below consists of the following parts: The preamble to the constitution is a philosophical statement of the overall role of the student at Westminster.

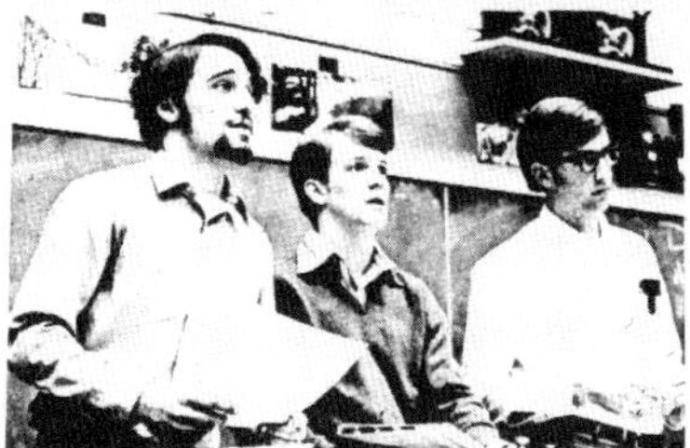

THE PROBLEMS OF LEADERSHIP—seem to be reflected in the faces of S.A. officers Cooper, Scott, and Metzler as the trio attempts to steer the current open dorm question over a rocky road.

Incident Provokes Reaction Sit-in, Injunction Spark WC

by Chip Thistlethwaite

Events in the wake of the recent 'Burry Incident' that broke Tuesday, May 11 have followed in rapid fashion.

B.S.U. and Share held meetings to decide courses of action. In his meeting with Share, and B.S.U., Dr. Harold Burry flatly denied having made any such racist statement. Later, a letter from President Earland Carlson distributed to students claimed that the statement had been made; that it was in reference to a skit seen on a network television program.

The seemingly conflicting stories provoked a sit-in by 35 Westminster students, many of them members of Share, at 1:25 p.m., Friday, May 14. They sat on chairs, desks and on the floor in Old Main, but allowed administration officials to come and go as they pleased.

The sit-in was for the purpose of obtaining an explanation from Dr. Carlson of how the investigation of the incident had been made. The demonstrators were asked to leave at 6:15 by Phillip A. Lewis, dean of the College, or face a possible court injunction.

Claudia Miller, Ed Freeborn, Steven Hikes, Paul Beltz and Paul Henderson, plus the legal term '30 John Does' were listed as 'conspirators'.

Bierbach Unanimous MVP New Win Streak Set At 15

by John Campbell

Westminster College concluded its 1970 football season with an undefeated season, a national championship, and a foundation for more of the same next year.

The 1970 Titans became the fifth undefeated squad in the history of Westminster, all under the guidance of Coach Harold Burry. The teams of 1953, 1956, and 1964 all had identical 8-0 marks while the 1955 edition finished with a record of 6-0-1. In 19 years of coaching at Westminster, Dr. Burry has compiled the remarkable record of 119 victories, 30 defeats, and four ties, a winning percentage of 778. Before the 1970 season Dr. Burry ranked sixth among all NCAA College Division coaches.

Titan wins this past season came, in order, over Marietta 26-6, Susquehanna 38-0, Lycoming 28-0, Waynesburg 51-0, Heidelburg 40-20, John Carroll 20-6, Carnegie-M Mellon 27-7, and Geneva 13-0. The Titans led in the ratings of Division II of the NAIA since the Lycoming victory.

This was the inaugural year of the NAIA Division II football program. Division II was created in order to give the 148 true small colleges across the nation deserved recognition.

With the regular season ended, and the Titans 8-0, Westminster accepted a bid to play nearby Edinboro State in the semi-finals of the national championship. After some talk of a journey to Three Rivers Stadium in Pittsburgh, the game was played at Taggert Stadium in New Castle before some 6500 fans. The Blue and White looked impressive in jumping to a 13-0 halftime lead and coasting to a 20-7 victory.

In the championship game last Saturday Westminster met Anderson College of Indiana, again in Taggert. About 5000 fans showed up to see the contest.

The third quarter displayed the defense that made the Titans unbeatable all year as a fumble and a goal-line interception stopped two Blue and White drives. The fine passing of Mark Manley and receiving of Kirk Carpenter coupled for two touchdowns and four extra points in the waning four minutes of the game, but one last symbolic interception by Don Grimm ended the contest and the Titan quest for the national title.

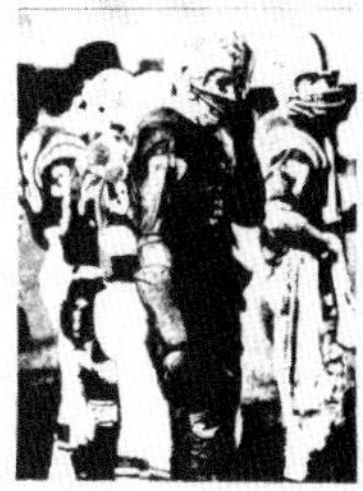

S A Rewrites S G Constitution

by Dave Downton

The Task Force met again in three three-to-four-hour sessions on Sept. 16, 18 & 22 in their effort to complete the constitution and related documents for the proposed Student Association. At Tuesday's meeting and continuing at tonight's meeting they expect to complete the details in the proposed constitution.

January Approaches; A Westminster First

by Glennah Ruiz-Valera

As the first January Term at Westminster approaches, students and faculty are showing great anticipation and excitement, which makes us wonder just what the campus will be like during January. This is the first time anything like this has happened in Westminster, so undoubtedly there will have to be adjustments as different contingencies appear. Nevertheless, we are going to try and give you a preview of what WC will be like next month.

Although registration for January has already been completed, there is still a drop-add period coming.

A green drop-add card can be picked up at the registrar's office next week.

Students actually dropping a course to add another (remember, only phys. ed. can be taken simultaneously with another course during January) must get the signature of both the instructor whose course he is dropping and the instructor whose course he is adding. January Term enrollment is not handled through the regular channels, and this is the only way in which instructors can know the final enrollment in their courses.

The signatures and course cards must be picked up at the various instructors' offices. For visiting instructors, cards can be picked up at the respective department offices.

A memo with the schedule of room assignments for January will be sent before the end of this term.

Many of us have been wondering just how many people will be gone during January. According to Dr. Rogers' data, about 350 students will be off campus. Seventy-seven students are enrolled in Independent Study, which will be taken by many away from Westminster. A group of 50 students are participating in the Philadelphia exchange program, while at least 68 others are enrolled in courses to be taken at 18 different 4-1-4 colleges. Ninety-three students are participating in Westminster's own travel seminars. This year they are to visit Mexico, the Middle East, Germany and Austria.

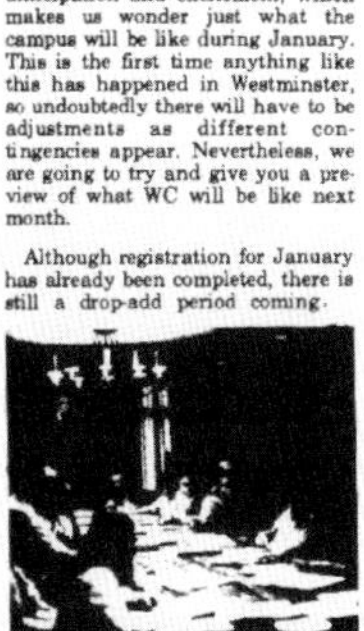

MORE DEBATE—Task Force views the problem of establishing a Student Association.

Carlson Unveils Plans

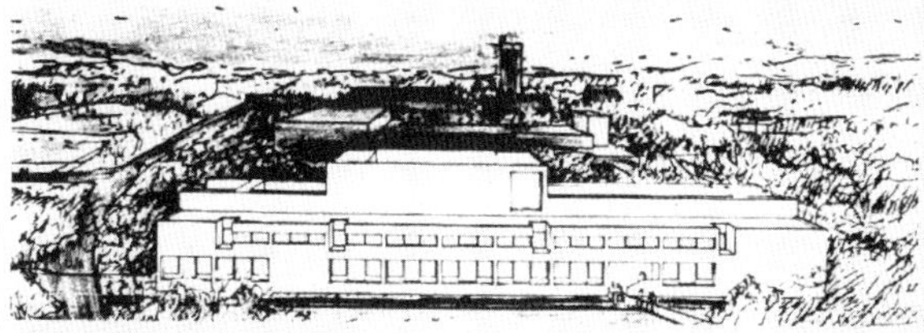

HOYT SCIENCE RESOURCES CENTER—The new science building will be named for Alex Crawford Hoyt, trustee emeritus of Westminster College, and chairman of the Board of the First National Bank of Lawrence County. The Hoyt Science Center will cost an estimated $2,750,000. If sufficient funds are on hand, construction bids will be let

Westminster's student body was abuzz with all types of activities in 1970. The Titans won a national football championship, collegians protested, the student government was dissolved, "J-Term" began, and so much more in only one week.

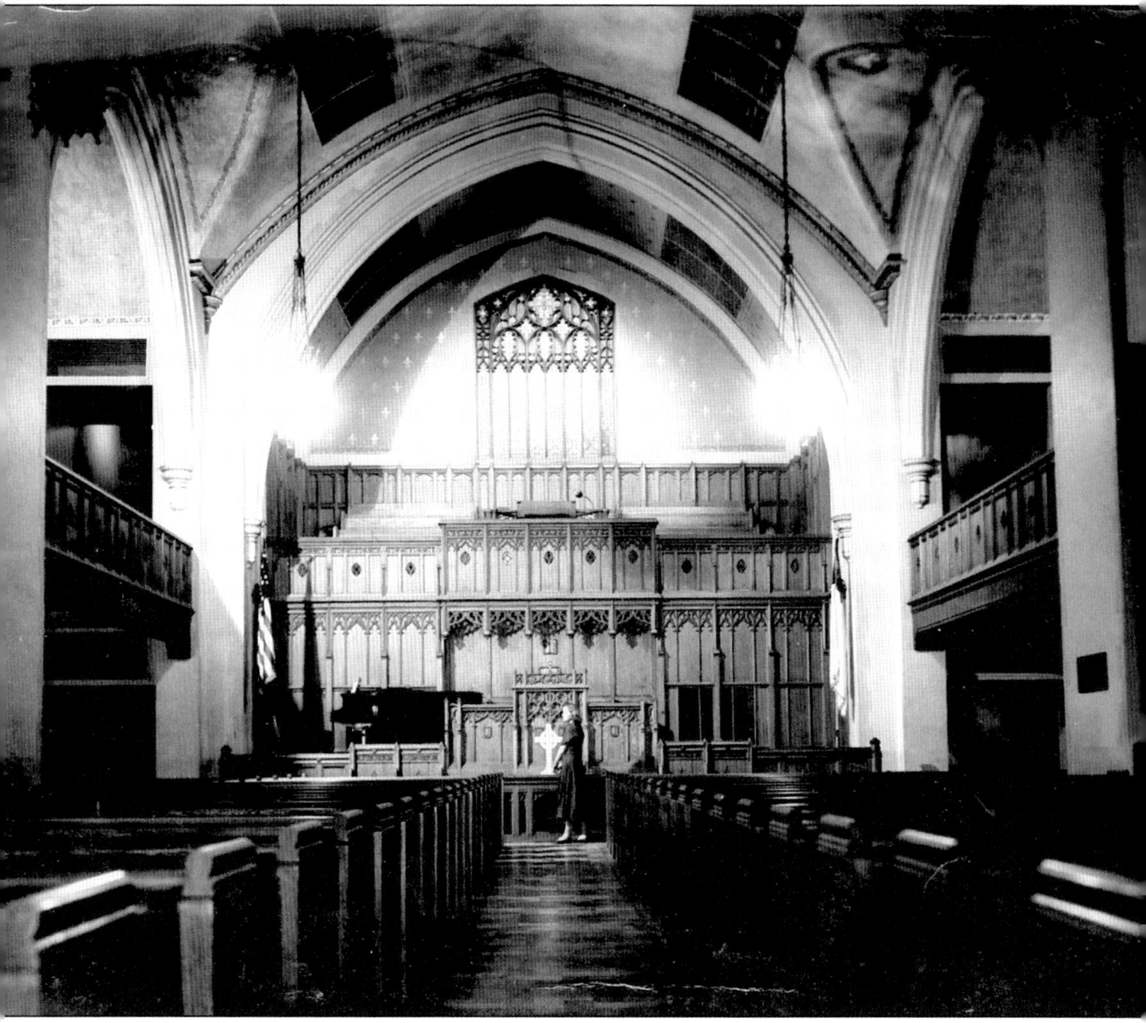

Wallace Memorial Chapel continues to be the site of many worship services, memorials, plays, weddings, inaugurations, vespers, and moments of private prayer. It is named for the sixth president, Dr. W. Charles Wallace. This photograph captures the original chapel decor.

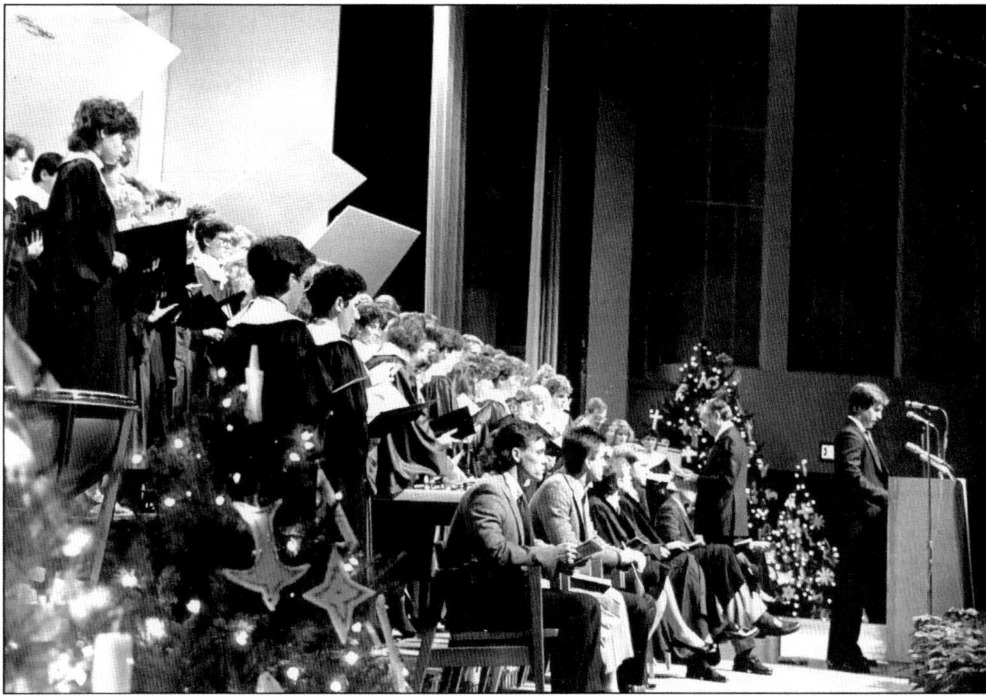

Christmas Vespers have been called Westminster's Christmas Eve. For decades, the service has drawn students and the community together in song and prayer.

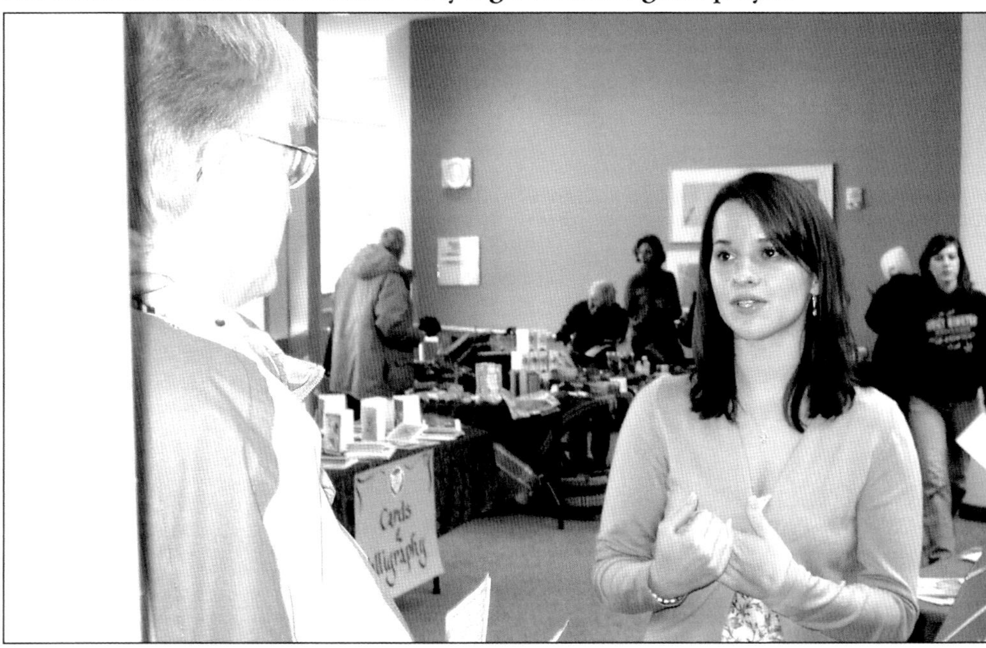

The Young Presbyterian Scholars (YPS) program began in 2004 as a means of attracting high-achieving students. Presbyterian ministers nationwide may nominate youth from their congregations. On campus, YPS students often join in service projects, such as an alternative gift market (above) to raise funds for global humanitarian causes. Californian Jessica Widemann was an early YPS participant.

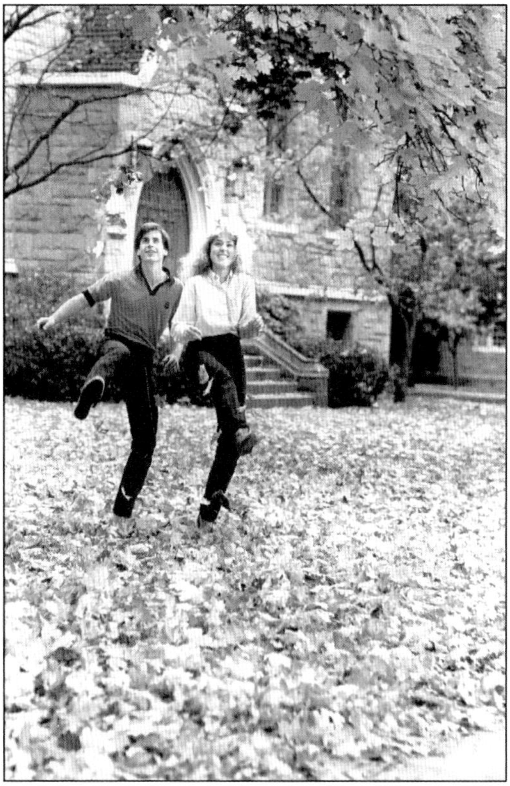

Nowhere is more radiant in the fall than New Wilmington.

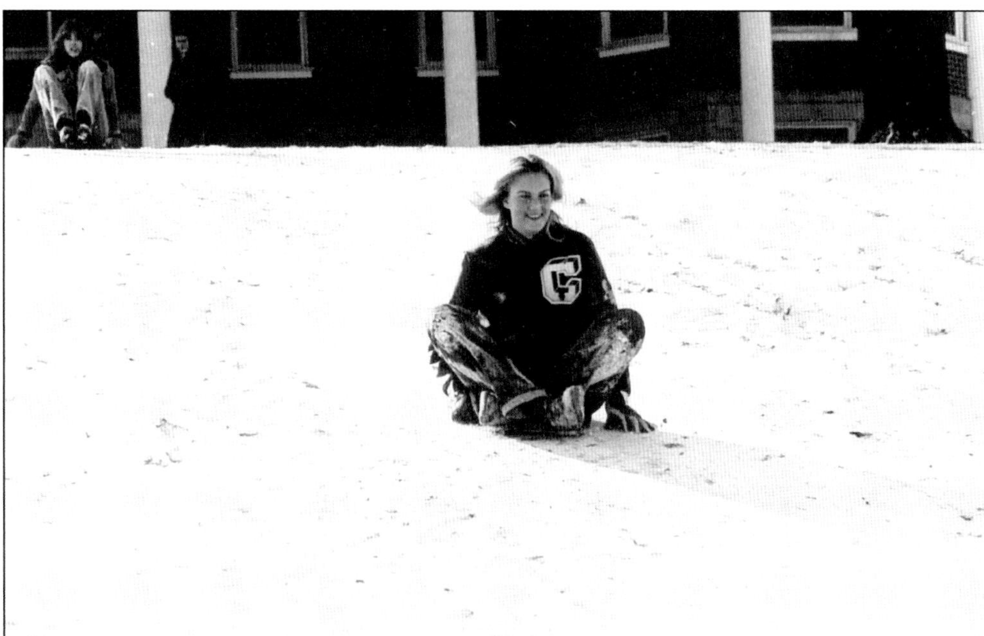

Northwestern Pennsylvania shares its beauty with the students of Westminster. Frosty days are remembered for sledding (usually on trays swiped or "borrowed" from the dining halls).

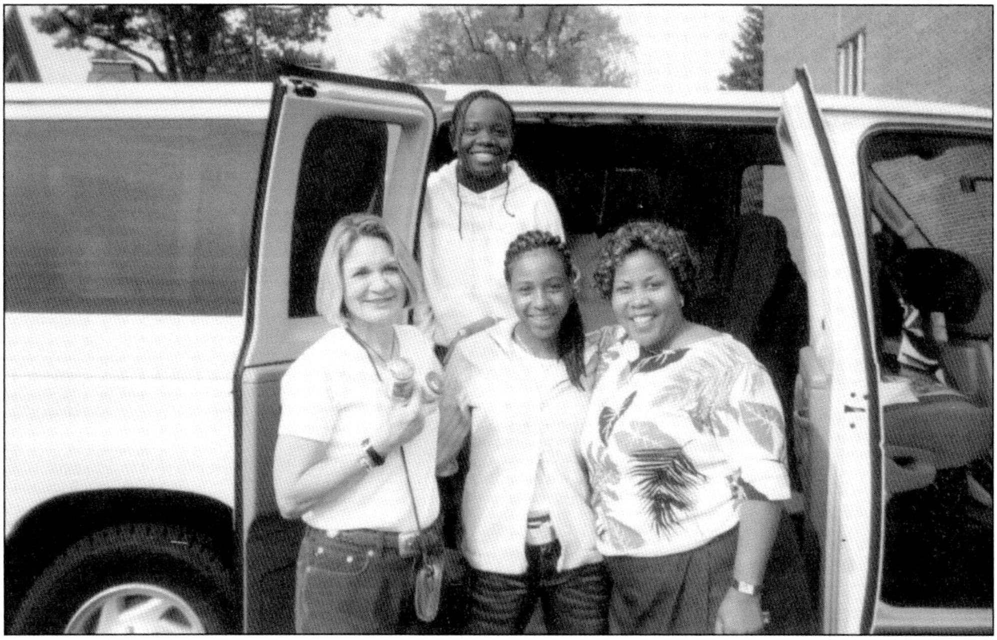

The Black Student Union and the office of diversity services has supported students through special events and programming. Among the activities have been field trips hosted by Dr. Elizabeth Ford (left), former advisor; and Rev. Jeanette Hubbard (right), director of diversity; with students Angela Duckett (front center) and Olawunmi Lawani.

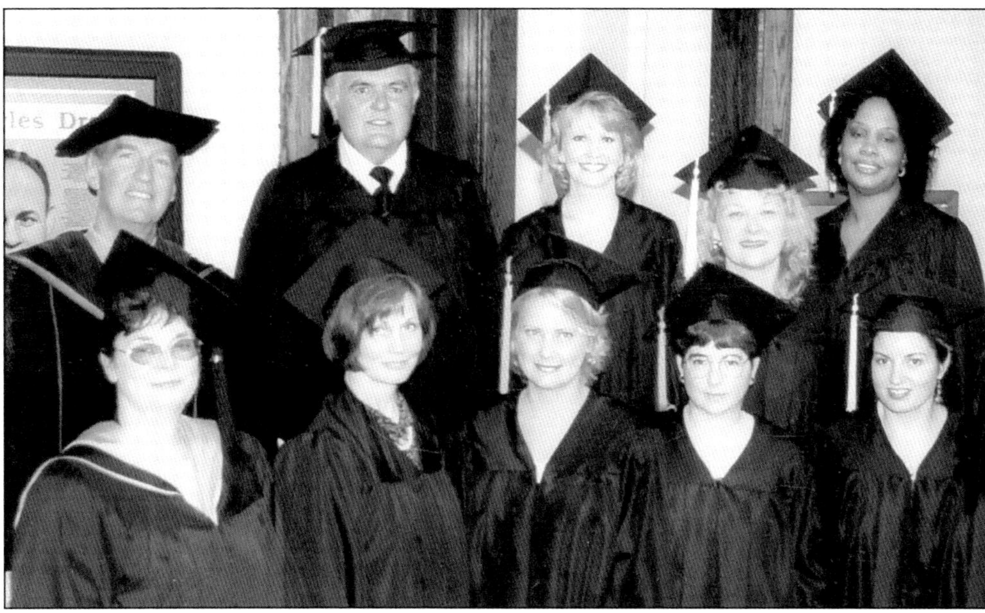

The Lifelong Learning Program, launched in 1975, appeals to non-traditional students who wish to earn their bachelor degrees by taking advantage of a flexible schedule. This program also offers post-baccalaureate students the opportunity for certification in elementary and secondary education, or a second degree in any of the over 40 majors. Degrees are awarded during spring commencement ceremonies. Qualified high schoolers also may enroll in Westminster courses.

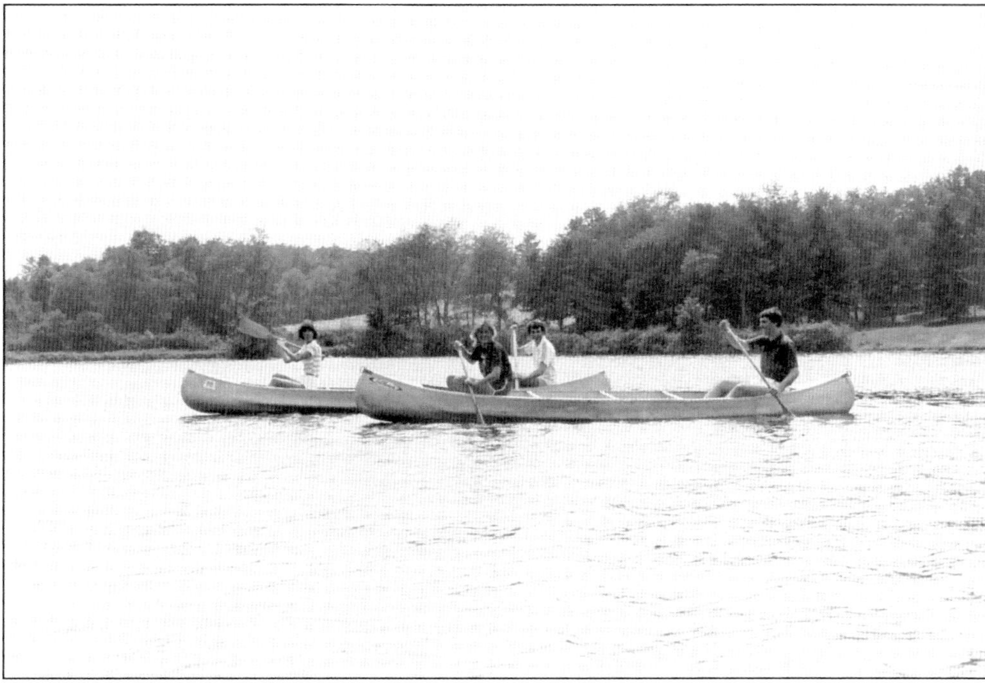

The crown jewel of Westminster's campus is Brittain Lake. Originally, in 1951, it was dug to encompass five acres. In 1956, Pres. Will Orr expanded the lake to its present 15 acres. Students and the community enjoy canoeing and fishing on the lake, which is shaped like the state of Alabama. Interestingly, Orr's wife Eloise hailed from Alabama.

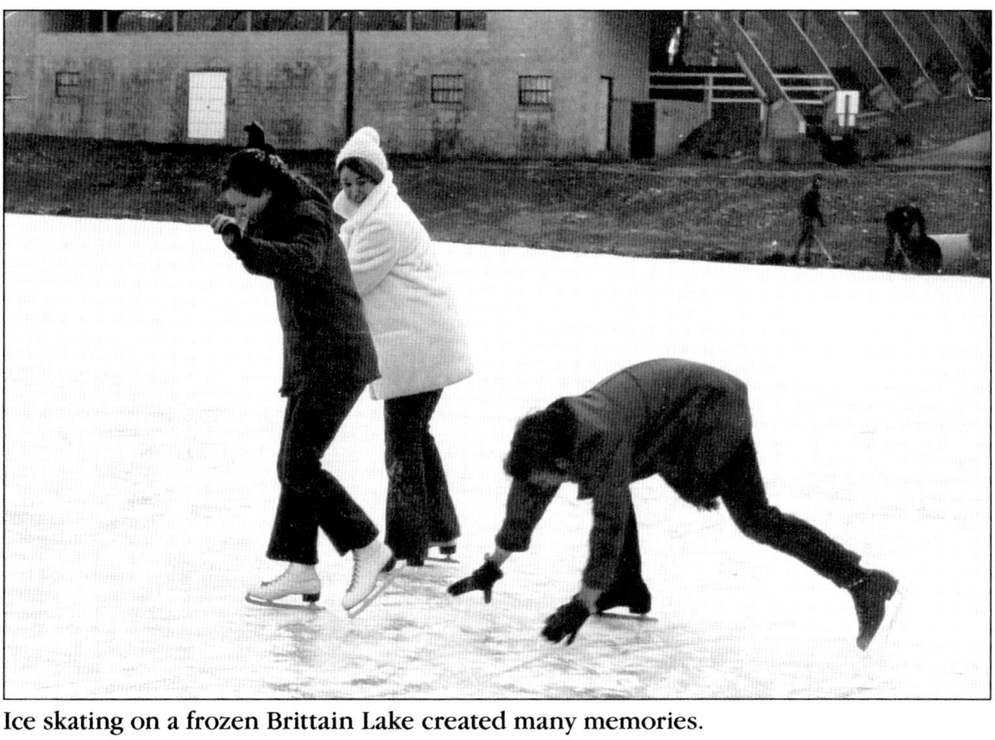

Ice skating on a frozen Brittain Lake created many memories.

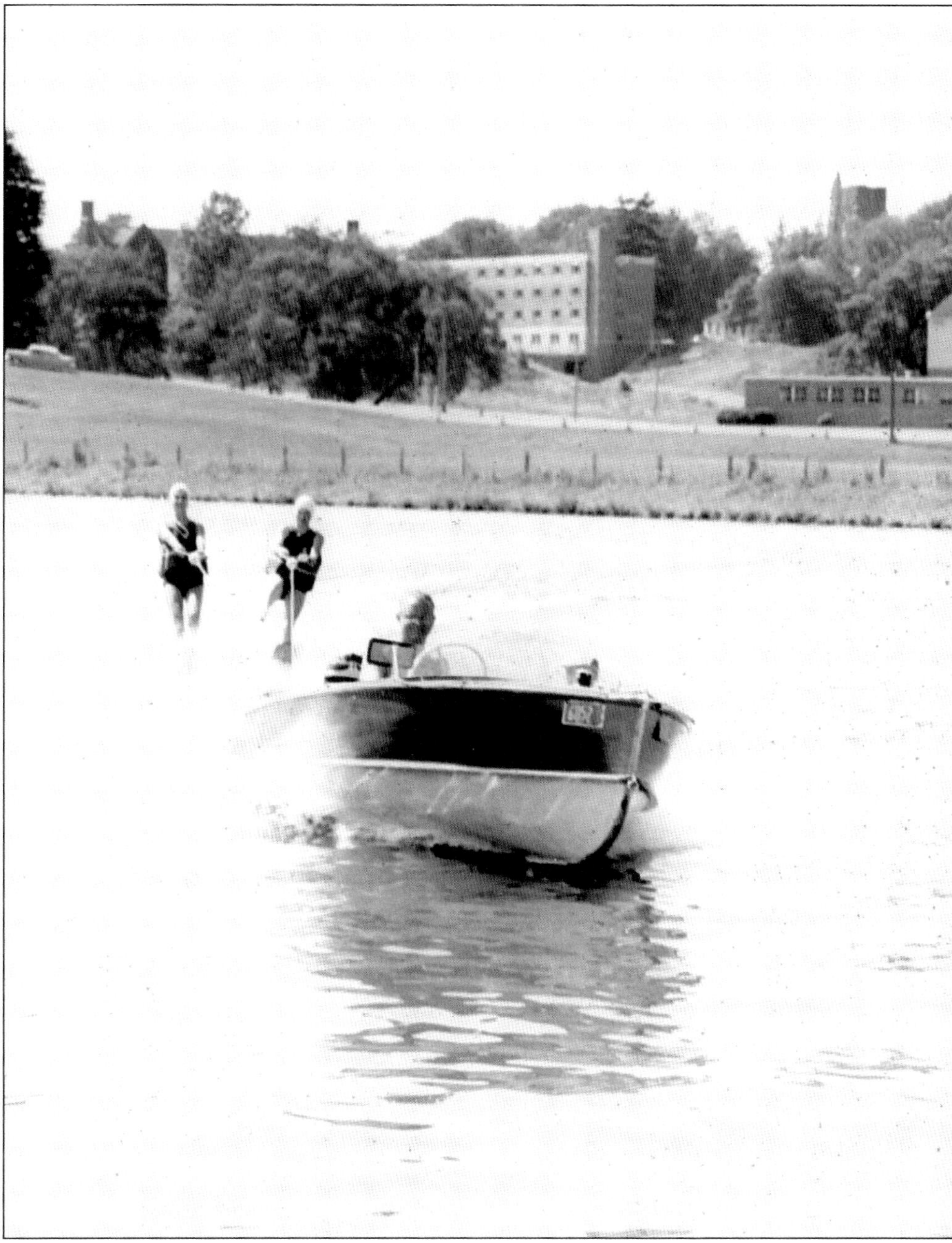

Pres. Will Orr pressed for the construction of Brittain Lake and loved to powerboat and water ski there despite its relatively small size. He towed students, friends, and family, including his daughter Arlis and her friend Biz Ellis.

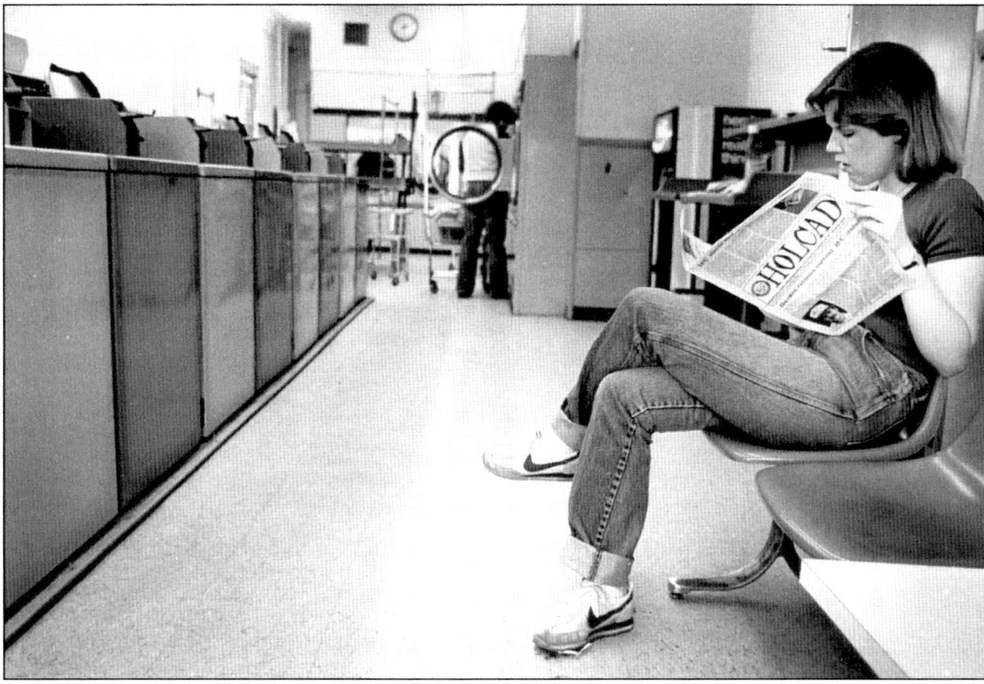

"Downtown New Wilmington" offered few amenities, but the laundromat was a "must see" destination before free washers and dryers were added to the dorms.

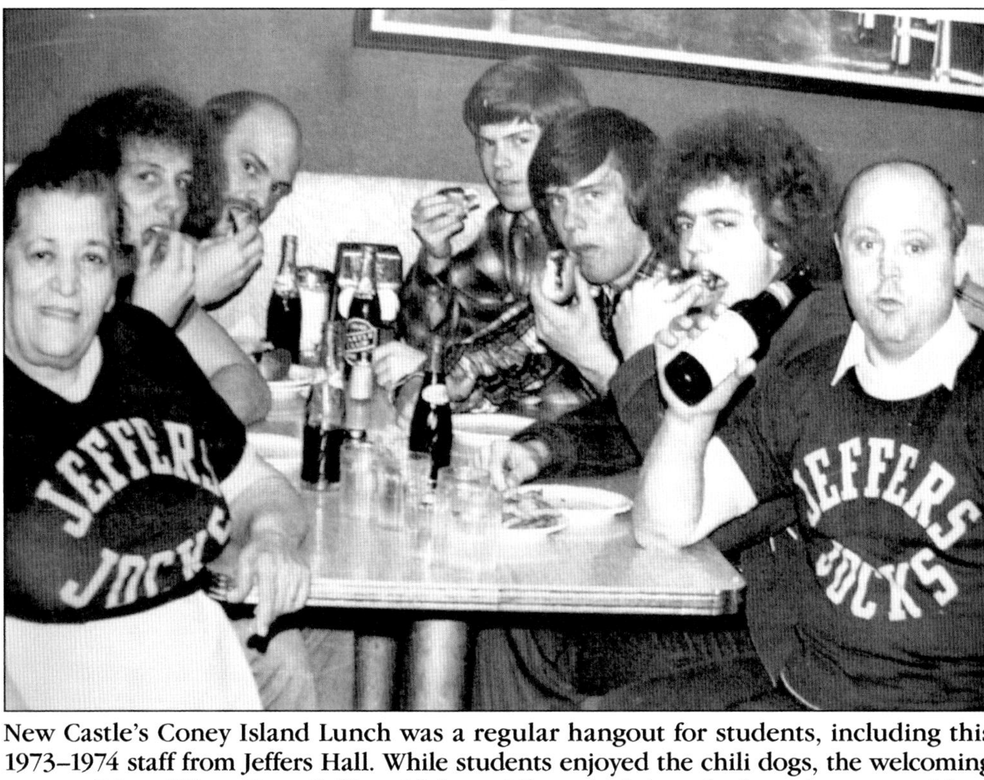

New Castle's Coney Island Lunch was a regular hangout for students, including this 1973–1974 staff from Jeffers Hall. While students enjoyed the chili dogs, the welcoming personalities of Mary Trott (left) and Johnny Mitsos (right) made the visits memorable.

Westminster students never forget the "clomp clomp, clomp clomp" of Amish horses and buggies. The Old Order Amish settled in Lawrence County not long before the college was founded. Amish neighbors parked their buggies in the lot between the Golden Dawn and Gilliand's Market in the 1970s and continue to do so today.

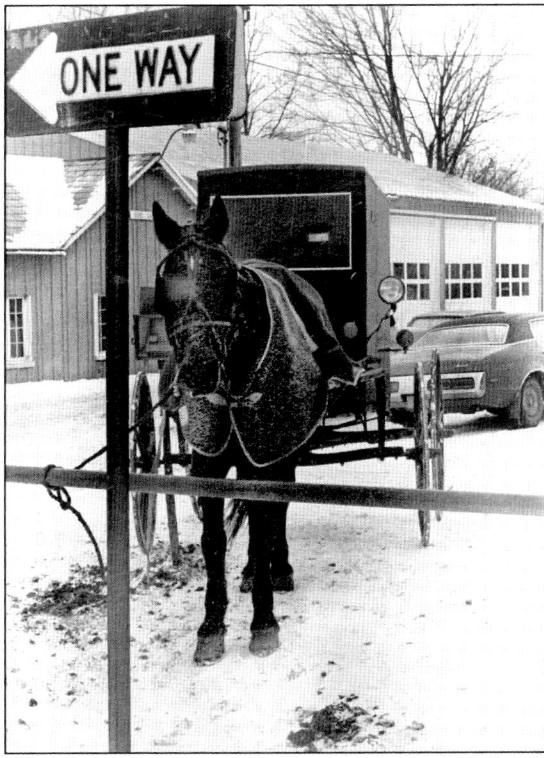

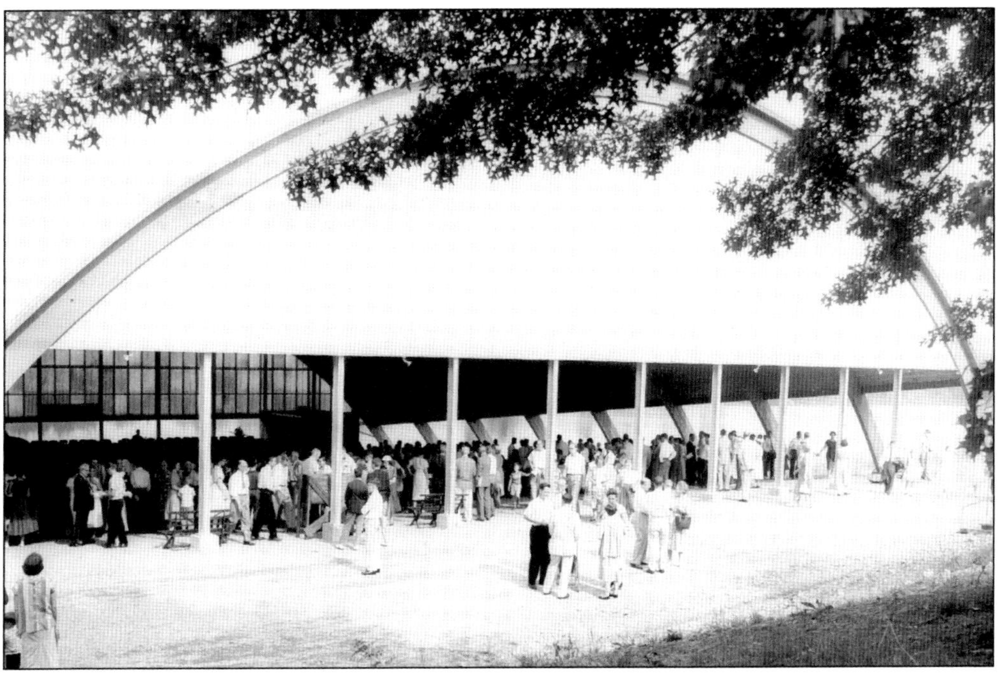

The New Wilmington Missionary Conference has been held nearly continuously since 1906. It utilizes campus facilities and constructed the open-air Anderson Amphitheater in 1958 as a central meeting place. The college utilizes the facility during the rest of the year.

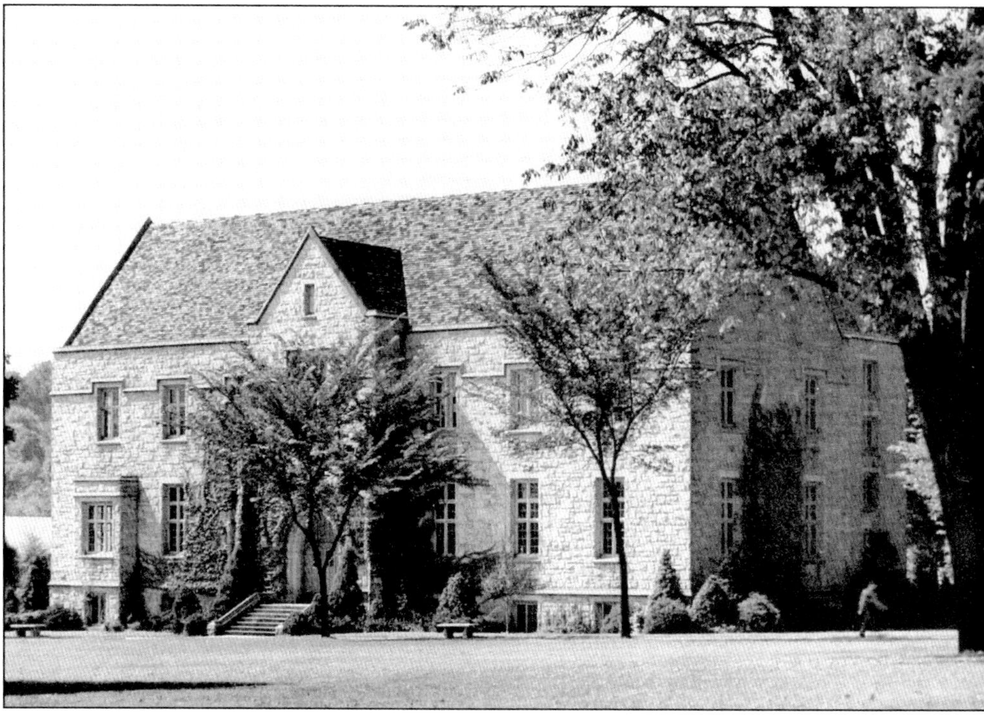

McGill Memorial Library was named for Presbyterian missionary Ralph Gibson McGill. McGill, who served in Egypt, drowned in the Mediterranean in 1926 trying to rescue young children. Opened in 1937, the library was intended to be a place for quiet study. However, the Ferguson Room (below) defied that description and was known to many generations of students as "the Zoo."

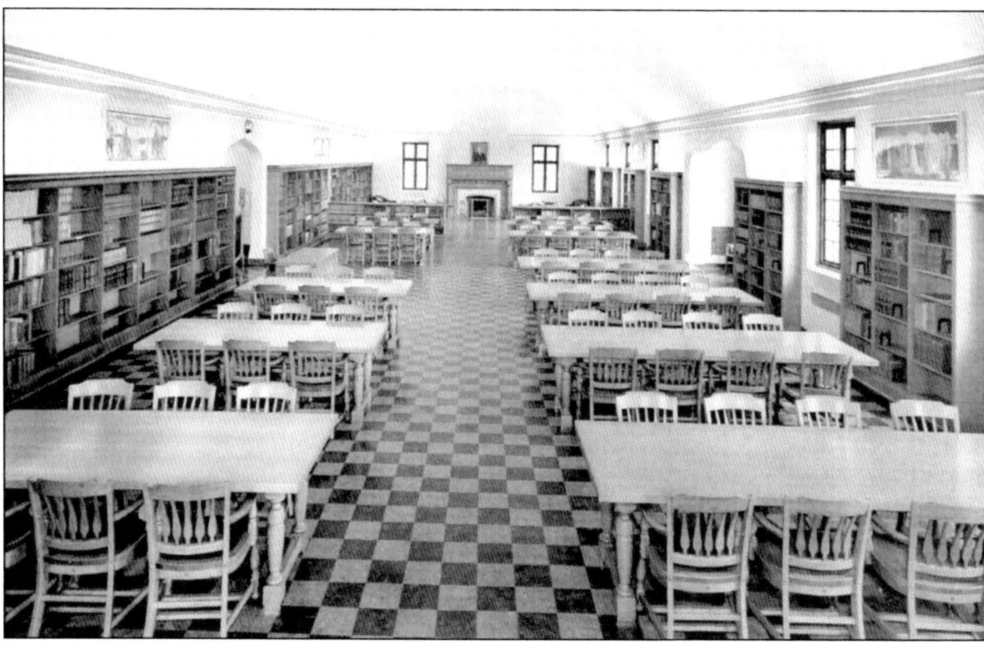

Susan Grandy Graff, class of 1985, raised awareness and the funds to restore Westminster's mummy, Pesed. Pesed was presented to the college by Presbyterian missionary and alumnus Rev. John Giffen. She arrived on campus in 1885 and for the following century took up residence in many places, from Thompson Science Hall to outside the children's center in McGill Memorial Library. Fraternities also were known to kidnap her for short trips to parties and other festivities. Inside the mummy case lid are found initials and dates from "special events" attended by Pesed.

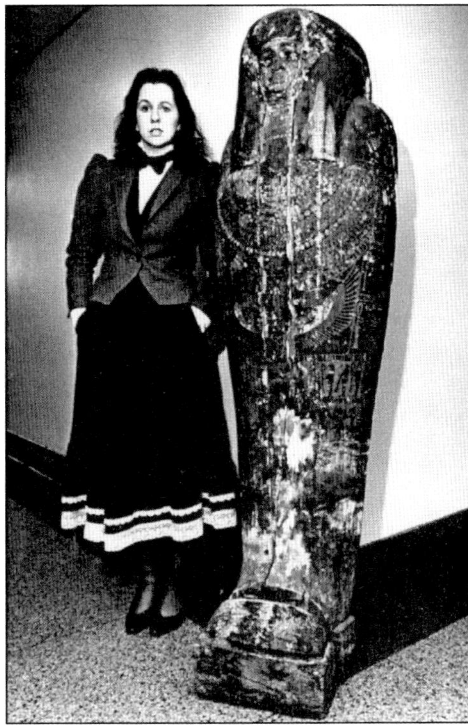

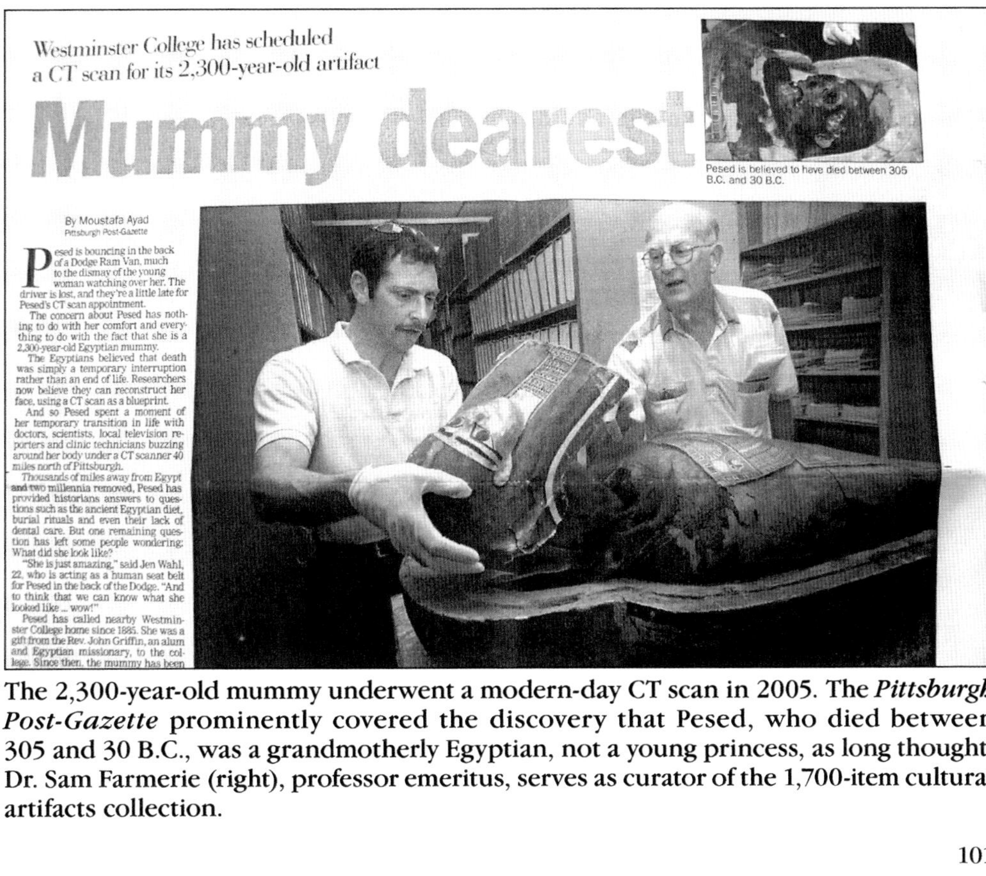

Westminster College has scheduled a CT scan for its 2,300-year-old artifact

Mummy dearest

Pesed is believed to have died between 305 B.C. and 30 B.C.

By Moustafa Ayad
Pittsburgh Post-Gazette

Pesed is bouncing in the back of a Dodge Ram Van, much to the dismay of the young woman watching over her. The driver is lost, and they're a little late for Pesed's CT scan appointment.

The concern about Pesed has nothing to do with her comfort and everything to do with the fact that she is a 2,300-year-old Egyptian mummy.

The Egyptians believed that death was simply a temporary interruption rather than an end of life. Researchers now believe they can reconstruct her face, using a CT scan as a blueprint.

And so Pesed spent a moment of her temporary transition in life with doctors, scientists, local television reporters and clinic technicians buzzing around her body under a CT scanner 40 miles north of Pittsburgh.

Thousands of miles away from Egypt and two millennia removed, Pesed has provided historians answers to questions such as the ancient Egyptian diet, burial rituals and even their lack of dental care. But one remaining question has left some people wondering: What did she look like?

"She is just amazing," said Jen Wahl, 22, who is acting as a human seat belt for Pesed in the back of the Dodge. "And to think that we can know what she looked like ... wow!"

Pesed has called nearby Westminster College home since 1885. She was a gift from the Rev. John Griffin, an alum and Egyptian missionary, to the college. Since then, the mummy has been

The 2,300-year-old mummy underwent a modern-day CT scan in 2005. The *Pittsburgh Post-Gazette* prominently covered the discovery that Pesed, who died between 305 and 30 B.C., was a grandmotherly Egyptian, not a young princess, as long thought. Dr. Sam Farmerie (right), professor emeritus, serves as curator of the 1,700-item cultural artifacts collection.

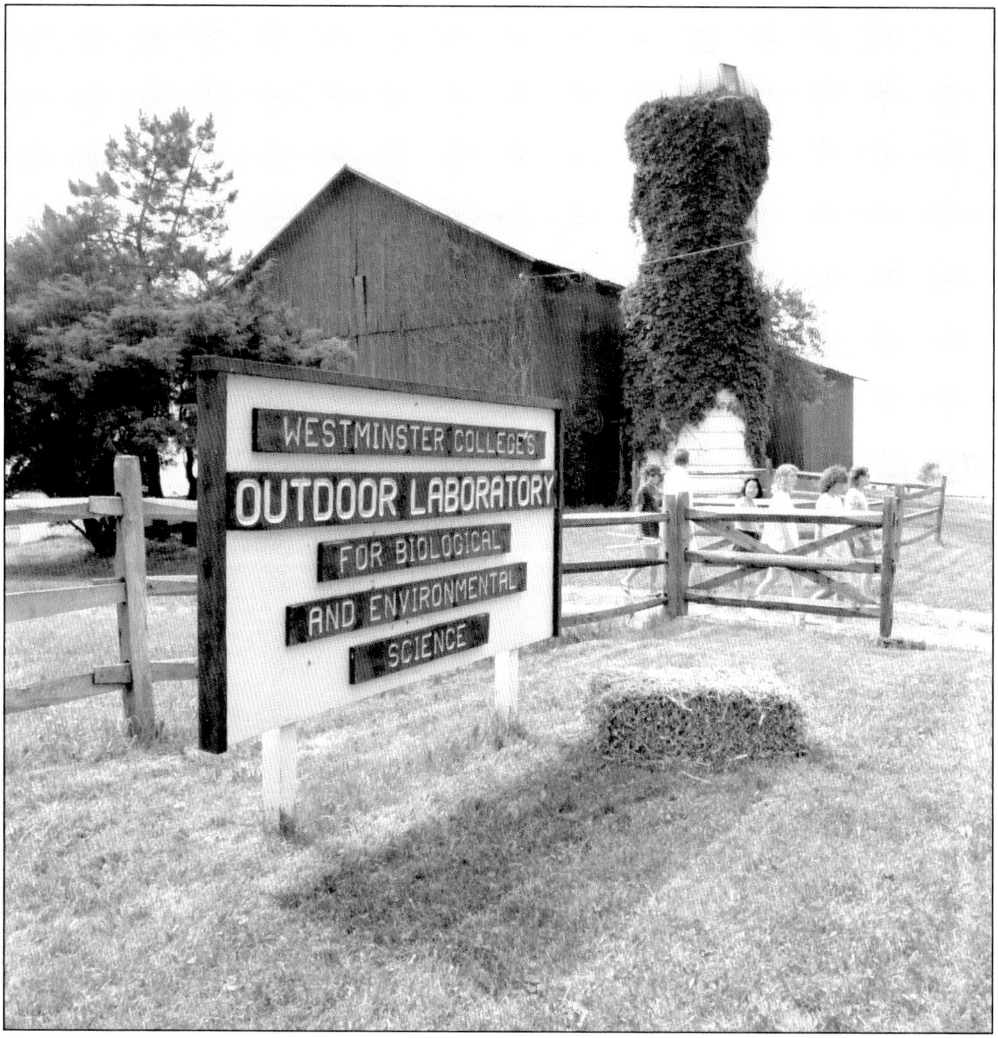

The Outdoor Laboratory is a 50-plus acre facility east of campus. Although Westminster has owned the property starting in 1964, it created the environmental lab in 1980. Today it includes a retrofitted 1877 bank barn filled with labs, research, and equipment space. Other features include the Lucille Frey Nature Trail, the Offutt Microforest with 1,000 trees, a weather station, and the Sandra Edminston Memorial Labyrinth. The facilities are used by environmental classes, art students, and by community and school groups. In addition, the college equestrian team horses are stabled nearby.

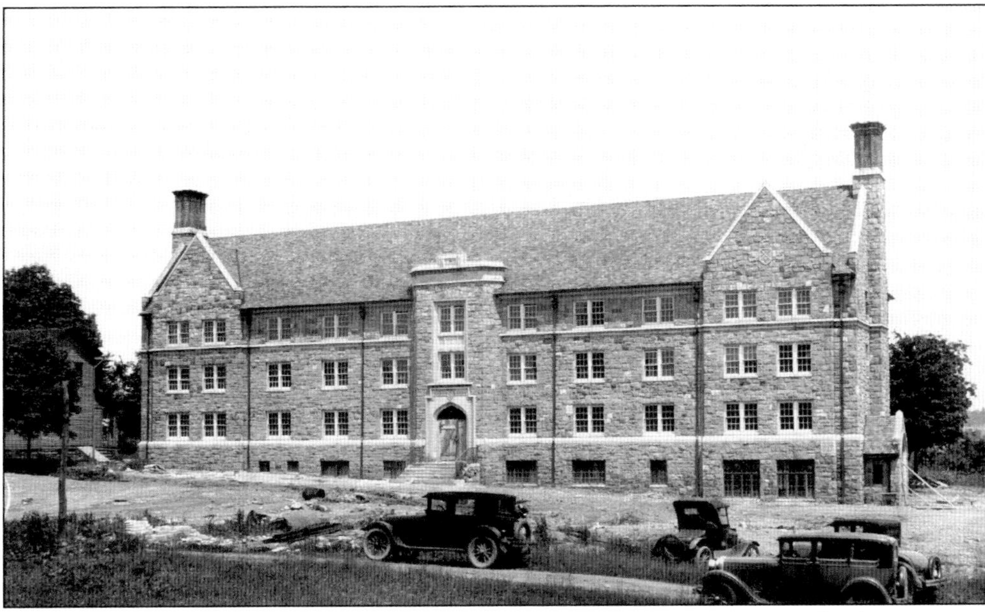

Browne Hall, named for former president Robert Audley Browne, was built in 1928 as part of the main quadrangle. The citizens of New Castle raised the $185,000 for the building and its furnishings. It was originally a men's dormitory and later was converted to a women's dormitory.

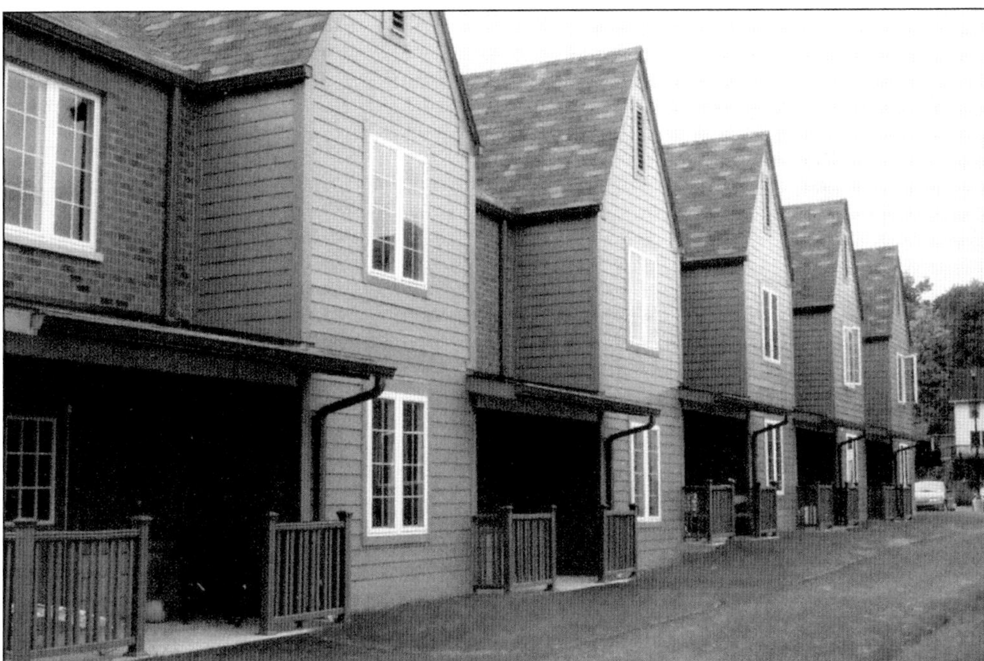

Townhouse living is an option for today's students. Berlin Village, opened in 2006, is a complex of 15 units overlooking Brittain Lake. Each features four bedrooms, two baths, a living room, a kitchen, and laundry facilities.

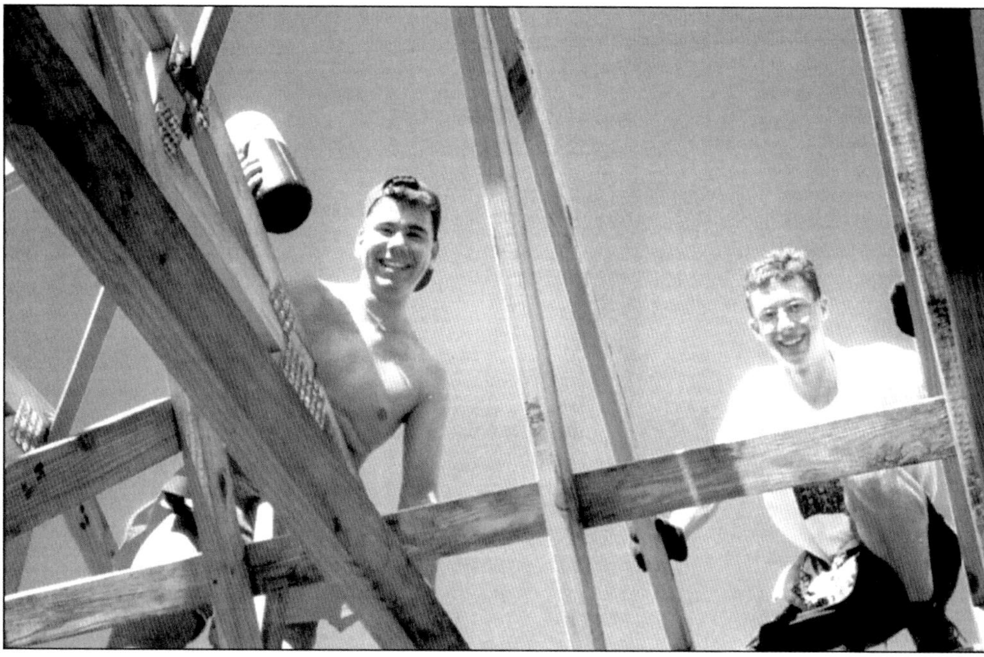

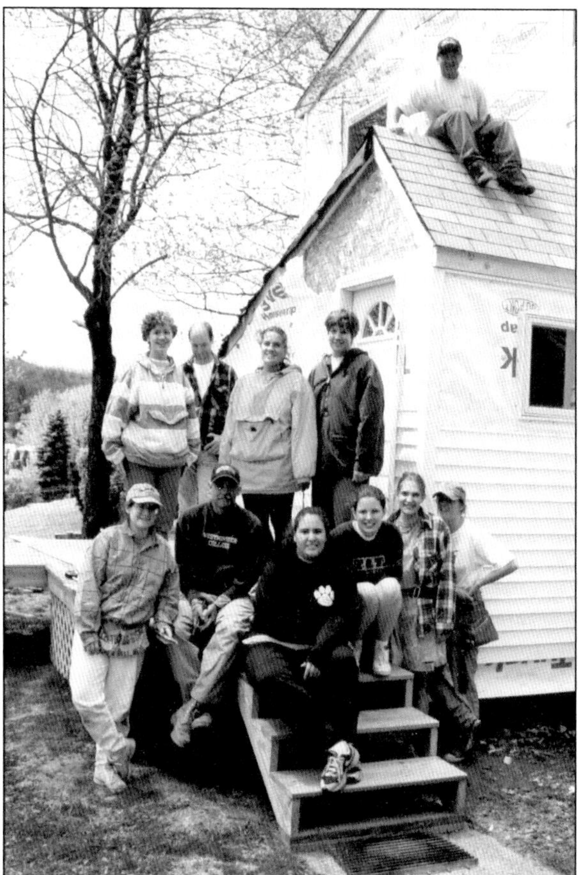

The connection with Habitat for Humanity was begun in 1984 by students Luke Stollings and Tim Cahn (above) when they bicycled across the United States to raise money. A chapter was formed in 1988. Currently it is the largest activity on campus.

Six

ON THE FIELD AND ON THE COURT

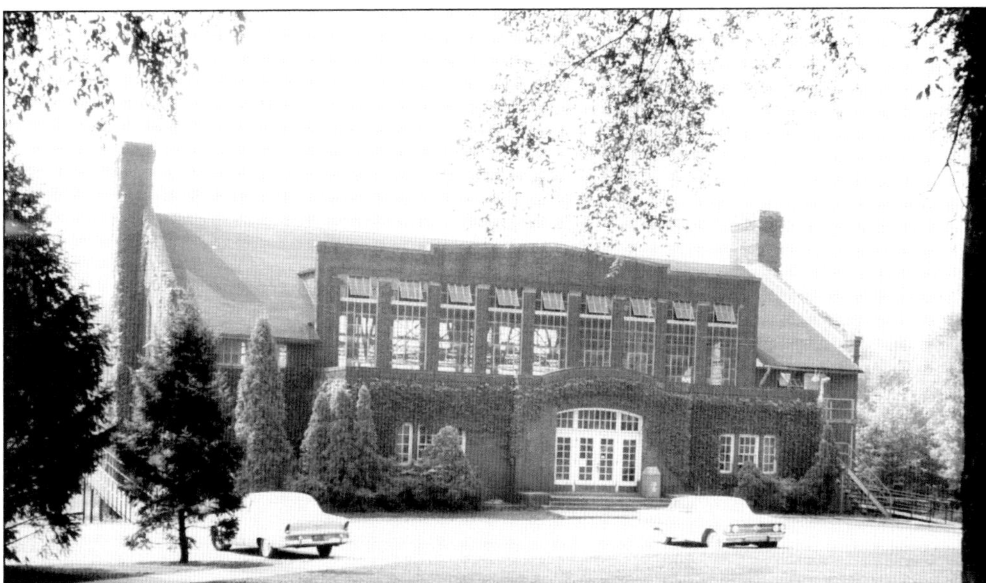

Westminster's first gymnasium was constructed in 1878 and was, according to the college's official history, "a crude, cross-shaped structure. [It was] a project of the Class of 1880" which raised the necessary $900 for construction. "Three wings had sawdust floors and weatherboard walls, but one wing was equipped with ladders, trapezes, bars and other equipment." It stood for 43 years until a new, more solid structure was built in 1921. The second gymnasium (above), complete with a balcony track, became known as "Old 77" in honor of the final string of 77 winning varsity basketball games that took place there. Today, Old 77 houses the Marjorie A. Walker Recreation Center, among other facilities.

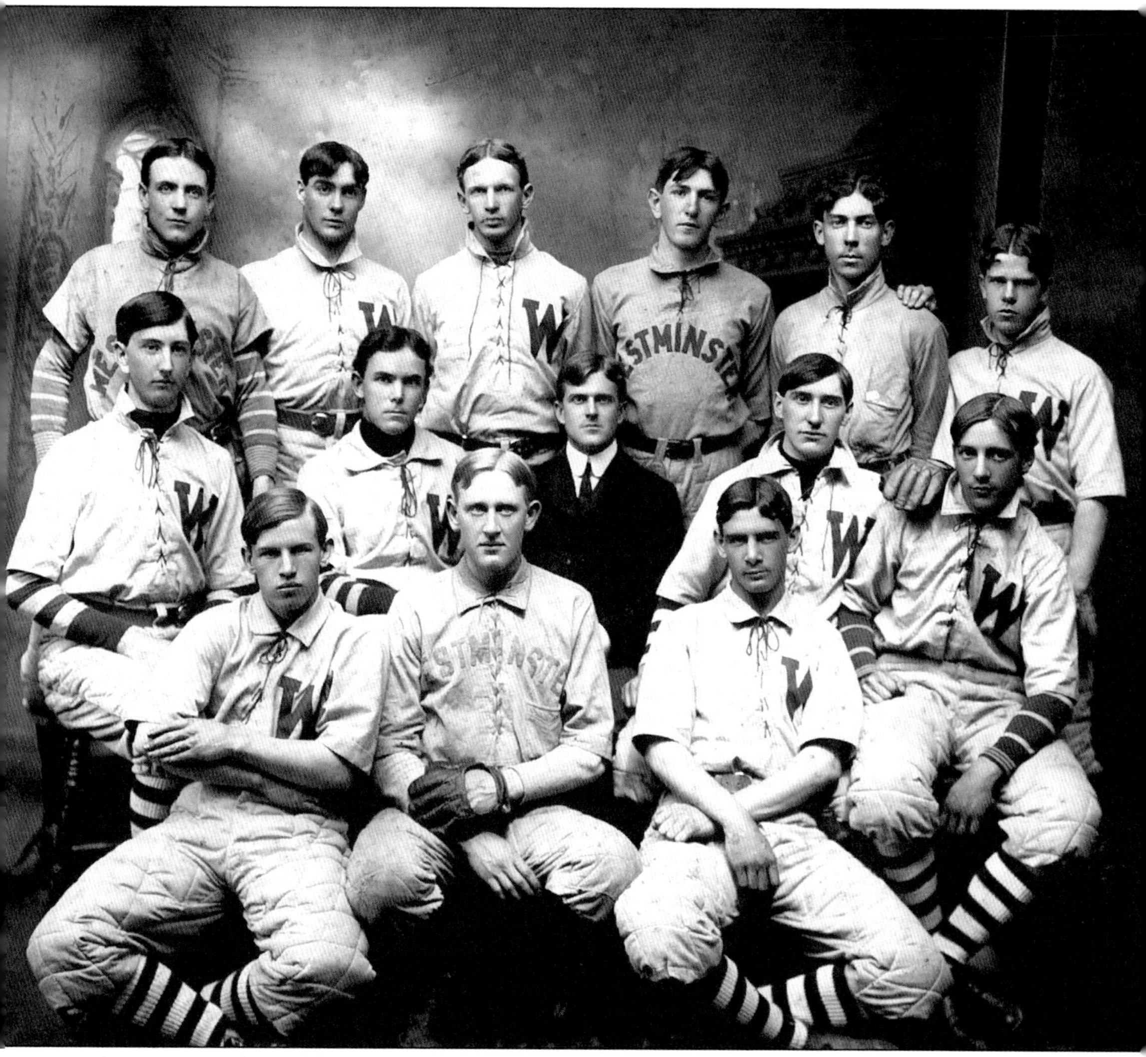

A co-curricular athletic program started at Westminster around 1884 in keeping with the belief that, as one observer noted, "healthy bodies go with healthy minds. Early Westminster advocates of this classical ideal generally took their exercises outdoors." This perhaps explains why the college's first organized sport was baseball. Westminster's team began in 1896 with a full 20-game season and, that same year, won the conference championship. The 1905 team (above and the cover background) sported maroon and grey uniforms. The immediate success of the baseball team prompted the introduction of other sports. During the 1895–1896 academic year a fledgling track and field team took off. Just several years later, in 1902, Westminster won the mile relay at the National Intercollegiate Track and Field Meet.

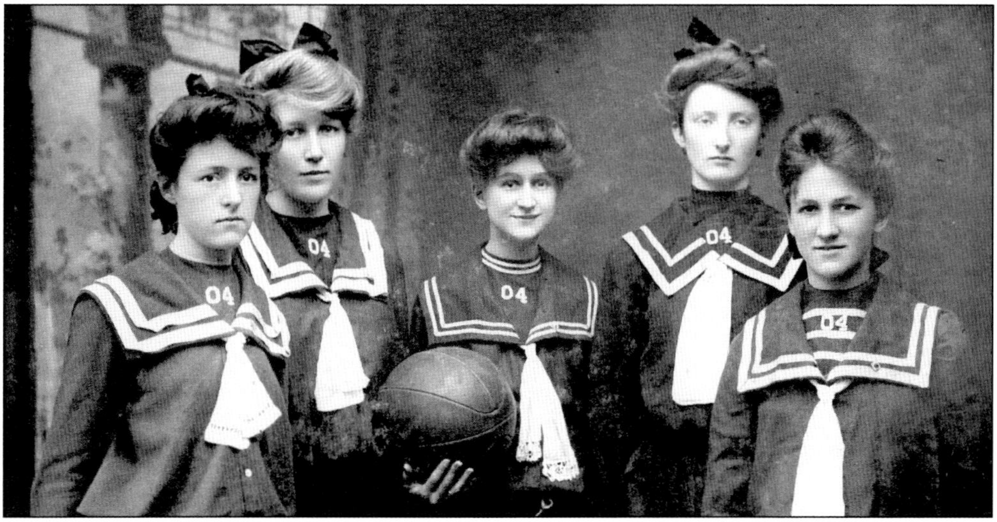

Westminster's coeds quickly embraced athletics, although early contests were limited to intramural competition. The 1904 women's basketball team was decked out in sailor collars. Intercollegiate basketball games for women began in 1910.

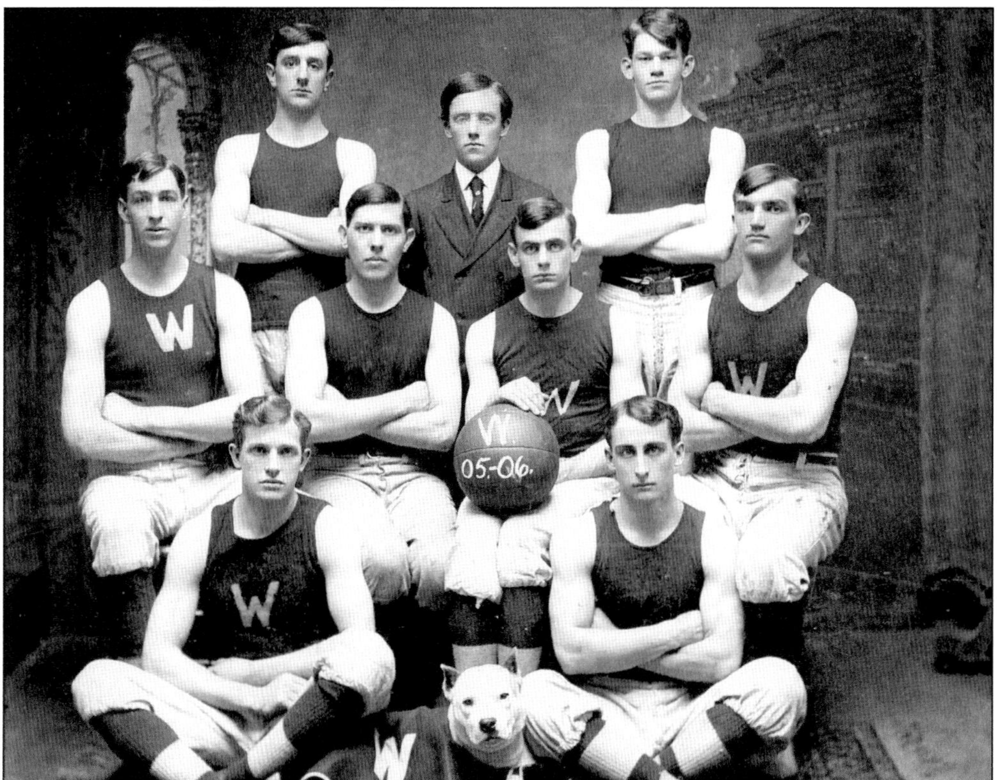

Men's basketball caught on quickly at Westminster and its earliest team was assembled in 1897, just five years after the very first game was played at the YMCA in Springfield, Massachusetts. Westminster's 1905–1906 team (above) took the western Pennsylvania championship. The players even had a canine mascot to cheer them on to victory.

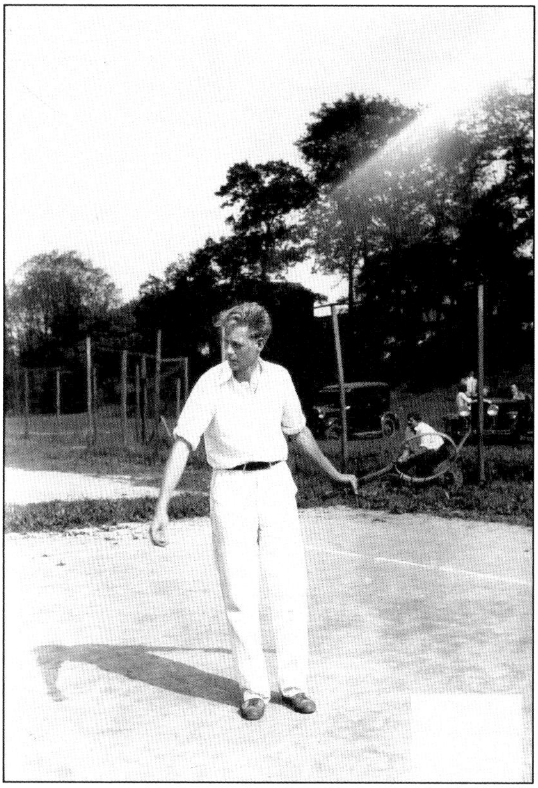

In 1888, a lawn tennis association was formed. During the 1920s and 1930s, spectators (below) watched from their cars in hats and stylish attire. John Witherspoon '31 (left) was a standout on the courts. He went on to become a prominent Pittsburgh physician. The Witherspoon Rooms in the McKelvey Campus Center are named in his memory.

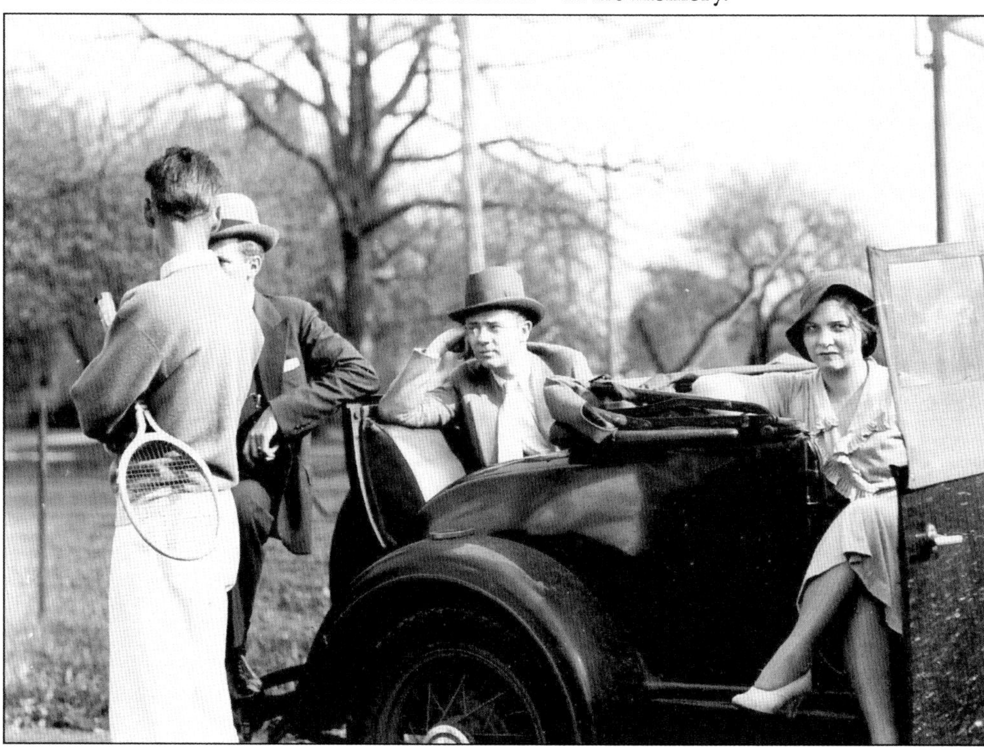

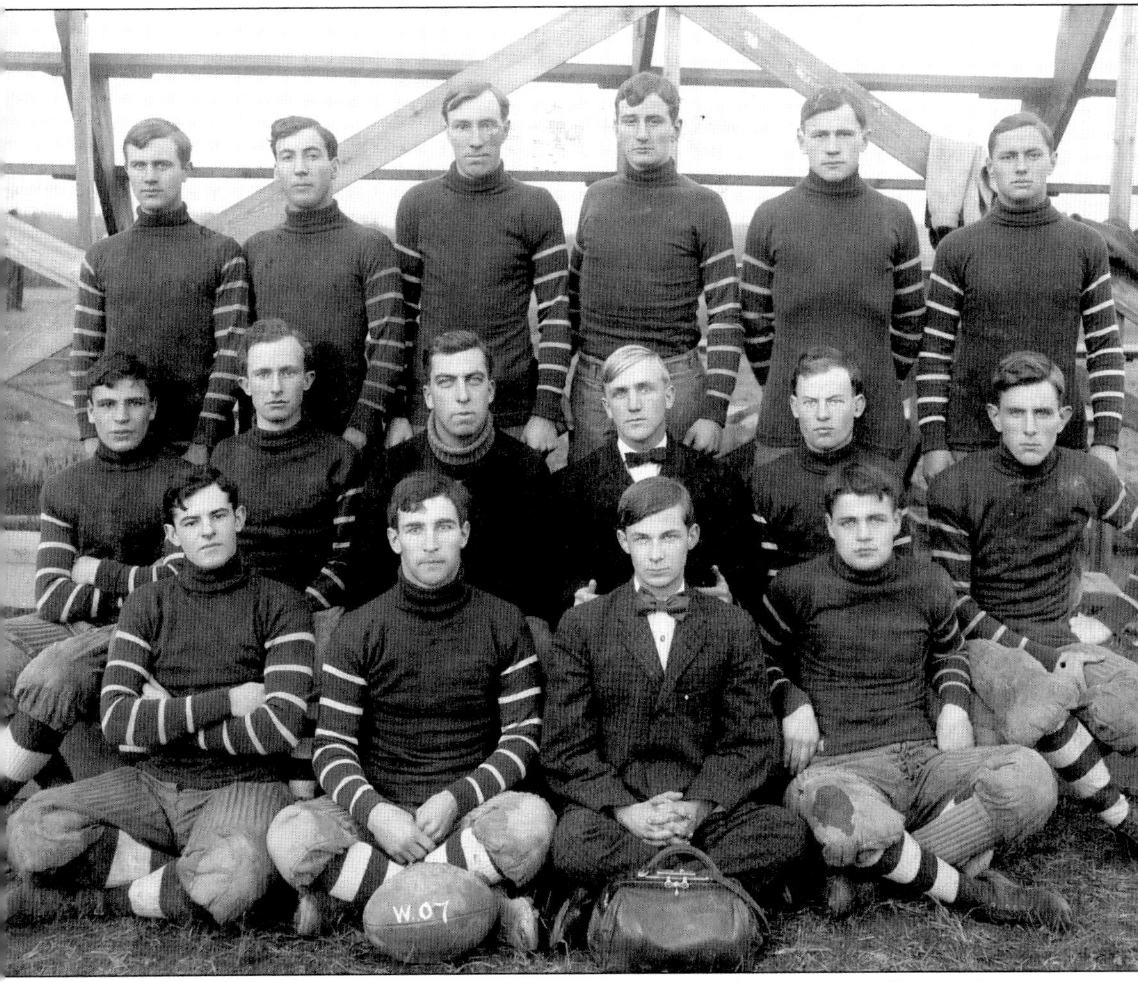

The year 1891 kicked off Westminster's tradition as an intercollegiate football powerhouse. However, all was not perfect during those early years. One college history notes that, in 1892, the *Holcad* "editorialized against [football] as a rough and ungentlemanly sport." By 1907 (above), football was ensconced on the campus. At that time, the uniforms seemed to offer little protection against injury, which may explain the presence of a doctor's bag in the team photograph. As a side note, in 1907, Westminster's tuition rose to $60 per year.

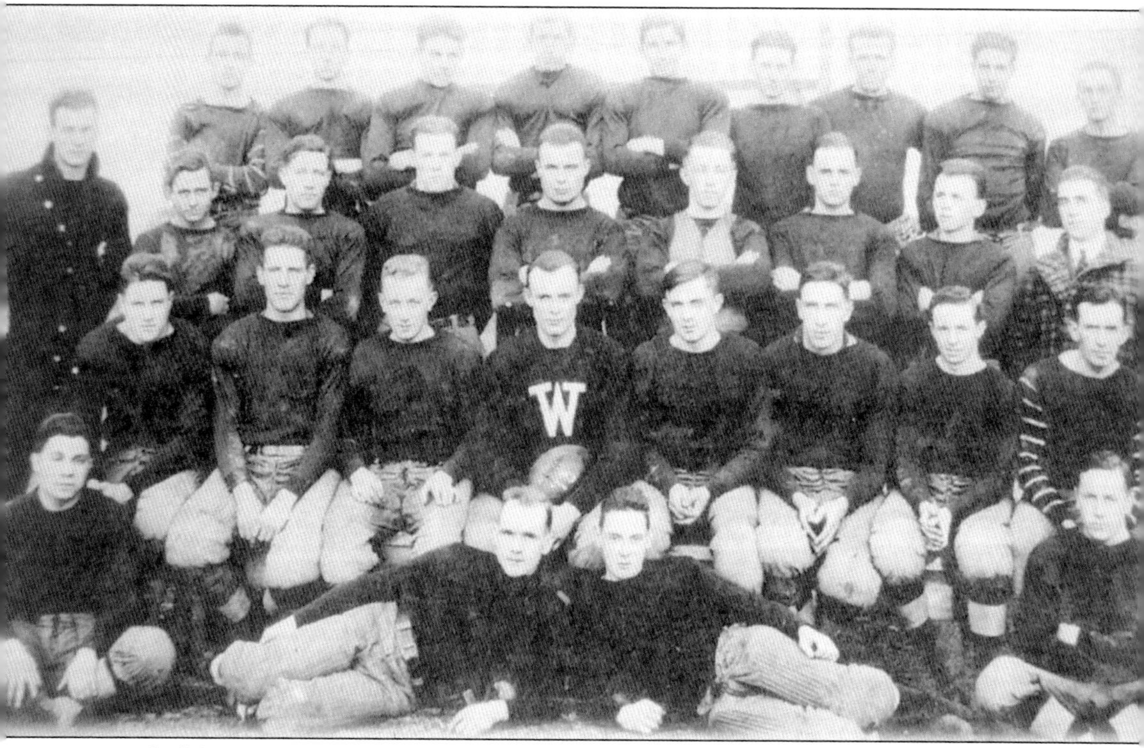

Football has added much to the Westminster experience. Over the years, it has brought a host of inspirational leaders to campus. One was DeOrmand "Tuss" McLaughry, a member of the winning 1913 gridiron team (above) and later a Westminster football coach. In his spare time, McLaughry played professionally for the Massillon (Ohio) Tigers with teammate Knute Rockne. After leaving his alma mater, McLaughry coached at Amherst, Brown, and Dartmouth and was regarded widely for sportsmanship and leadership. Since 1964, the American Football Coaches Association has given the Tuss McLaughry Award, its highest honor, to individuals who have distinguished themselves in service to others. The recognition has been presented to six U.S. presidents, seven generals, five astronauts, and such other notables as Rev. Billy Graham and entertainer Bob Hope.

For many people, Harold Burry '35 (at right, center) was synonymous with Titan varsity sports. Burry, who joined the physical education faculty in 1943, was among the first coaches in the nation to recruit African American players to a historically white campus. Much of the credit for the undefeated 1956 football team goes to Burry's determination to mentor two African American players, Harold Davis (52) and Bill White (10). The duo became Little All-Americans and played for four seasons on Titan teams that compiled a 29-1-1 record. Burry, in 1970, led the Titans to the National Association of Intercollegiate Athletics (NAIA) Division II national championship. As a tribute to its inspiring coach and athletic director, Westminster christened Burry Stadium in 1997. Burry, who coached every Titan men's sport during his career, was inducted posthumously into the College Football Hall of Fame. (Right, courtesy of Darwin Huey.)

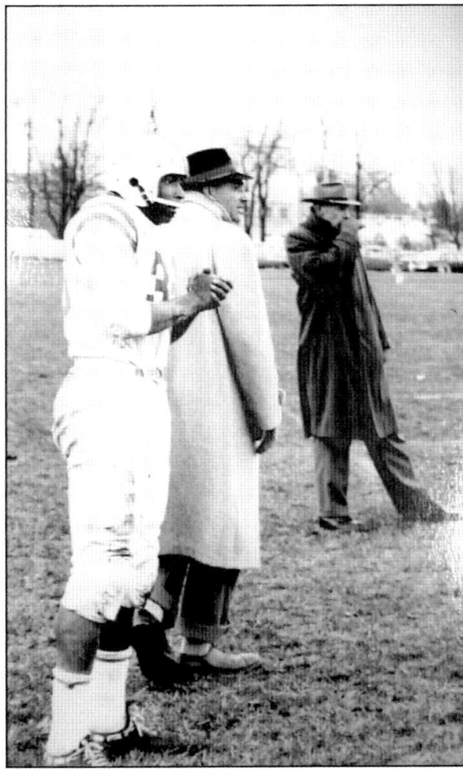

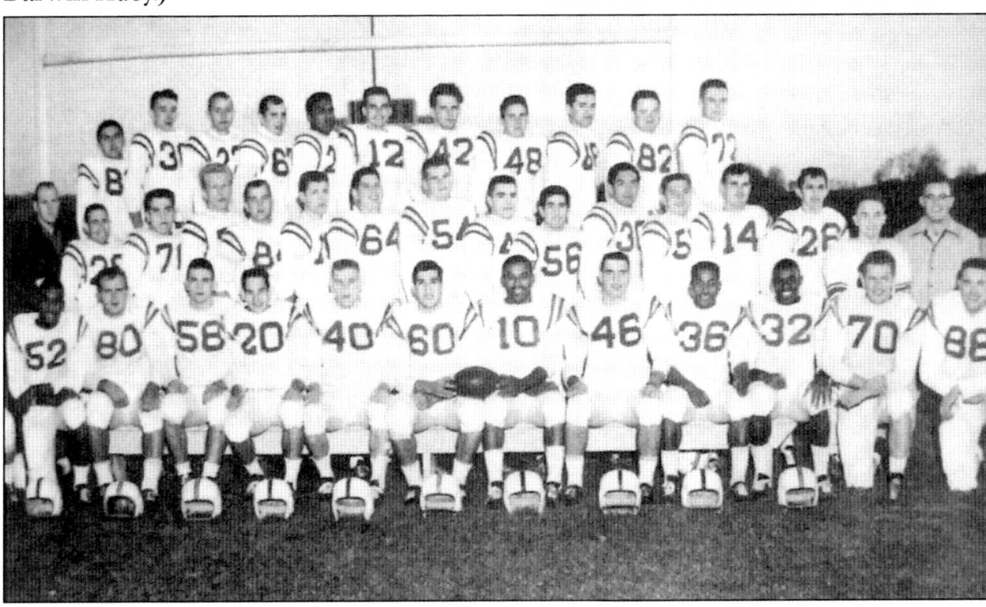

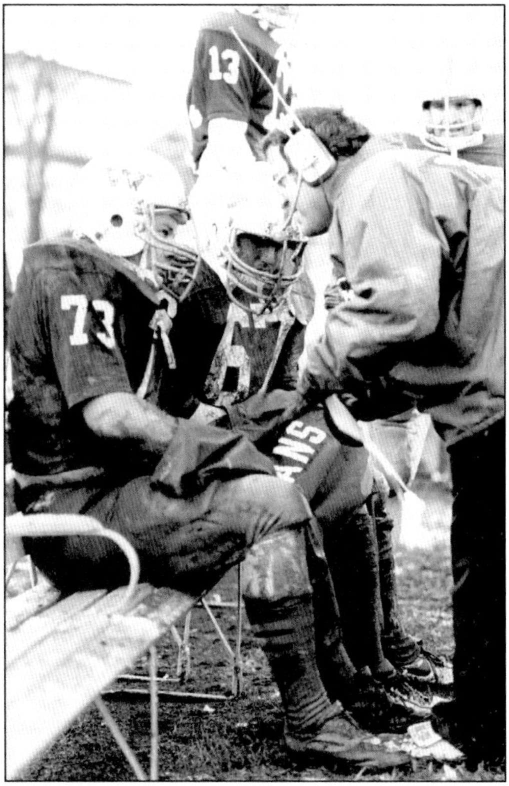

Joseph B. Fusco (left) took over as the Titan's head coach in 1972, staying in the position until 1990 and racking up a series of impressive years, including three perfect seasons and, importantly, four national titles. In 1976, Westminster won the NAIA Division II championship for the second time and repeated the feat in 1977, 1988, and 1989. Tailback Brad Tokar finished his career in 1990 with the school rushing record of 5,269 yards and as a three-time All-American. Coach B. Eugene Nicholson took over in 1991, led the Titans to the national title in 1994 and was named NAIA Coach of the Year. Westminster's football history is captured in *Winning: 100 Years of Westminster College Football* by Dr. William J. McTaggart, professor of English and stadium announcer.

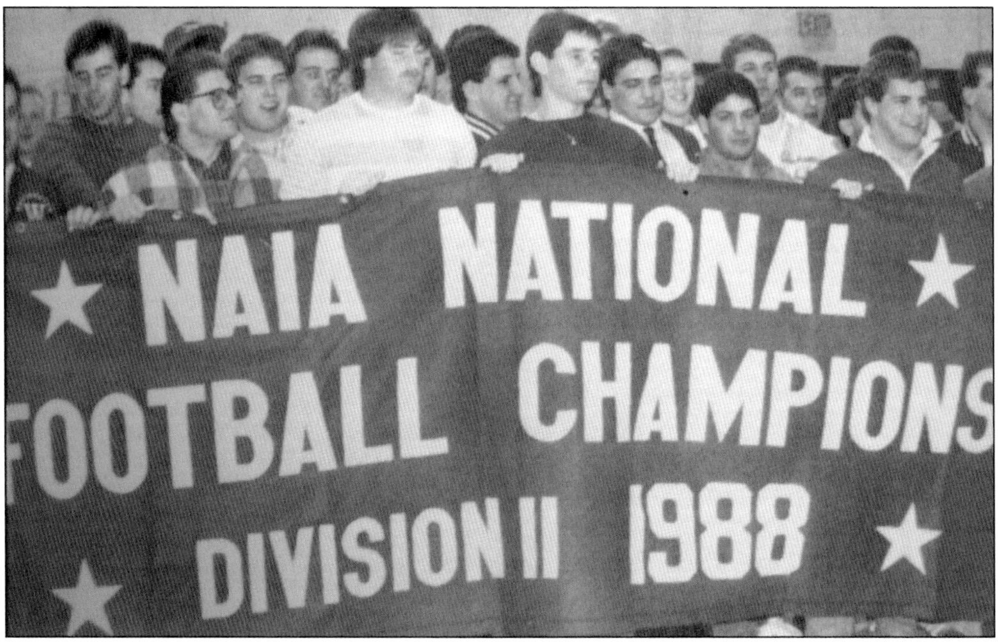

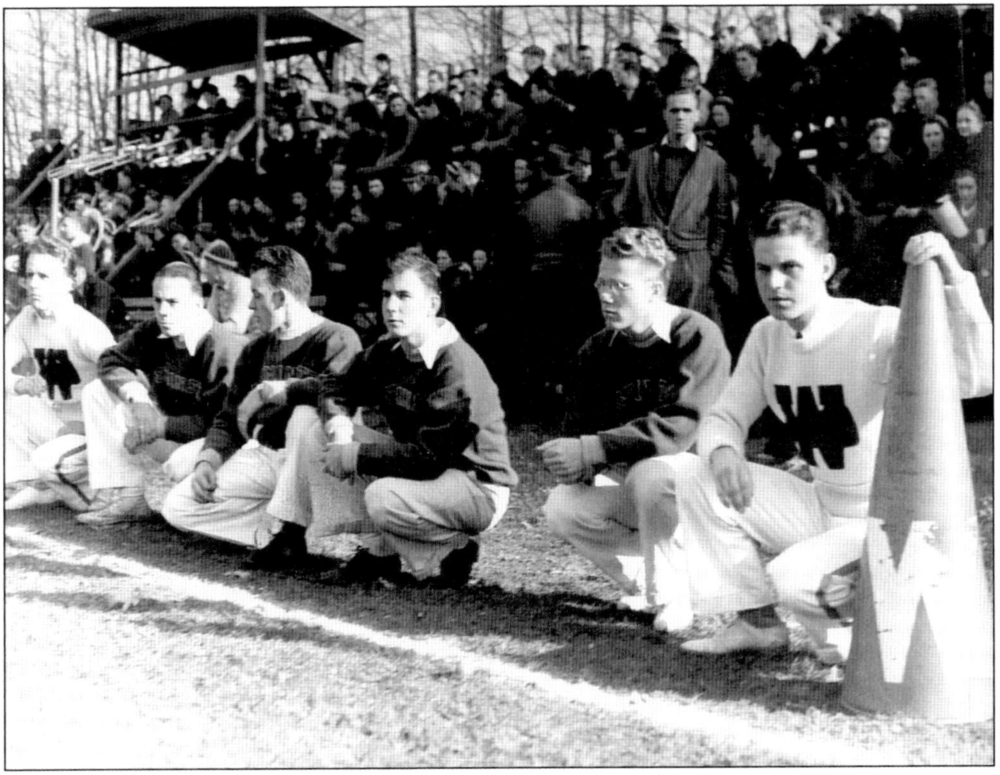

Cheerleading, a concept first adopted at Westminster in 1911, evolved from the selection of a single leader (always a male student) for each game to the formation of an organized squad (above). Over the years, the makeup of the squad has changed from a mix of males and females to all coeds, as in 1966.

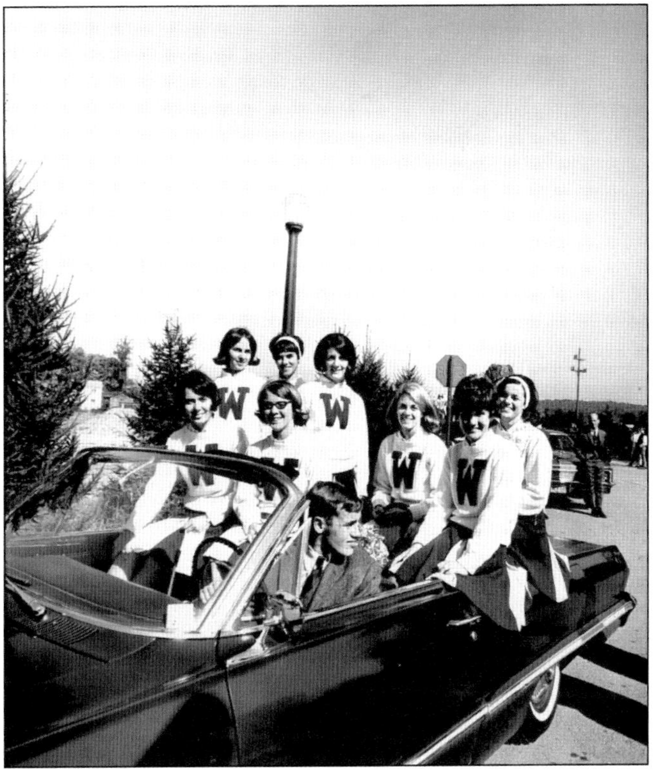

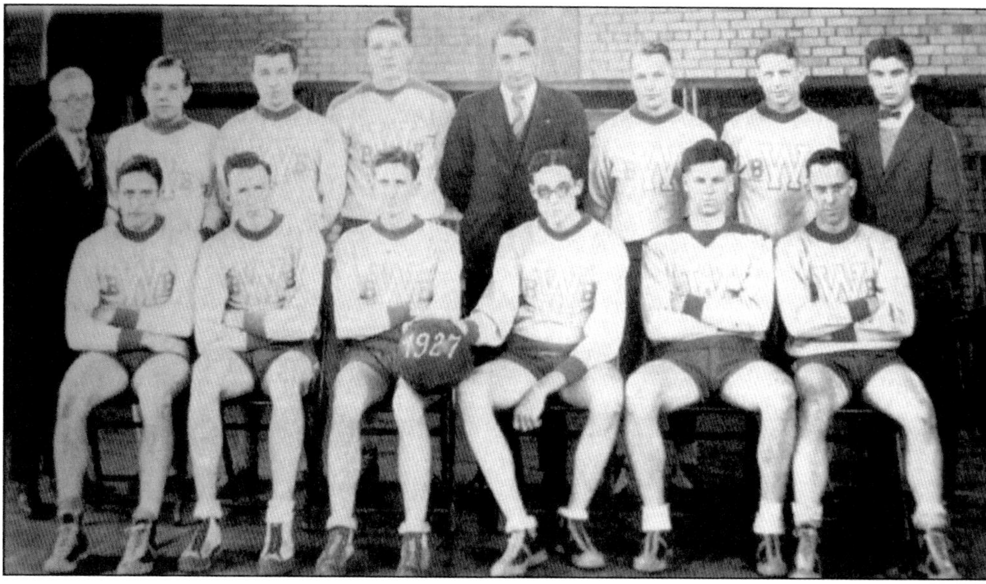

Basketball has been a hallmark of Westminster sports, but during one period (1909 to 1915) the team was limited to intramural activity "on the grounds that [intercollegiate sports] interfered with scholastic work," as the college history states. In the 1920s, the Westminster team was coached by John D. Lawther '19 (second row, fifth from left) who used a then-inventive strategy that relied upon tall players and a zone defense. The concept caused *Holcad* editor Irving L. "Bud" Mansell to dub the 1926–1927 team (above) "The Towering Titans." Lawther's techniques caused a bit of controversy. As an education and psychology professor, he was innovative in the application of sports psychology. Lawther left Westminster in 1934 and moved to Penn State where he drew national attention and penned a number of books on this emerging science. The Towering Titan Organization (TTO) is a group of alumni and friends who provide financial backing to the college's varsity teams. TTO was formed in 1976.

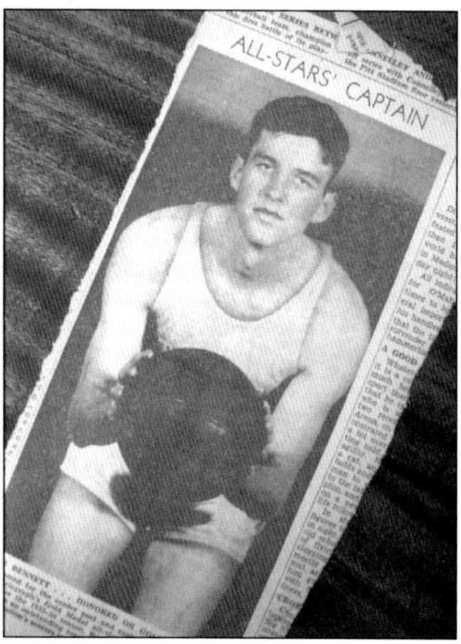

Wes Bennett, a six-foot-four-inch ambidextrous guard, remains one of Westminster's most distinguished athletes. Playing for the 1933–1934 Towering Titans, he was the nation's top scorer and drew the attention of sportswriters from across the country. In 1934, Bennett was College Player of the Year and, during both 1934 and 1935, he was selected an All-American. Bennett played professionally for three years.

Under coach Lawther, the Towering Titans became a part of sports lore when they played the first double-header basketball game ever in Madison Square Garden. The tourney featured four nationally prominent teams: Notre Dame, New York University, St. John's College, and Westminster. The December 29, 1934, competitions were played before 16,128 fans, the largest crowd then to see a basketball game. Westminster beat St. John's 37-33. Wes Bennett (43) was the tournament standout.

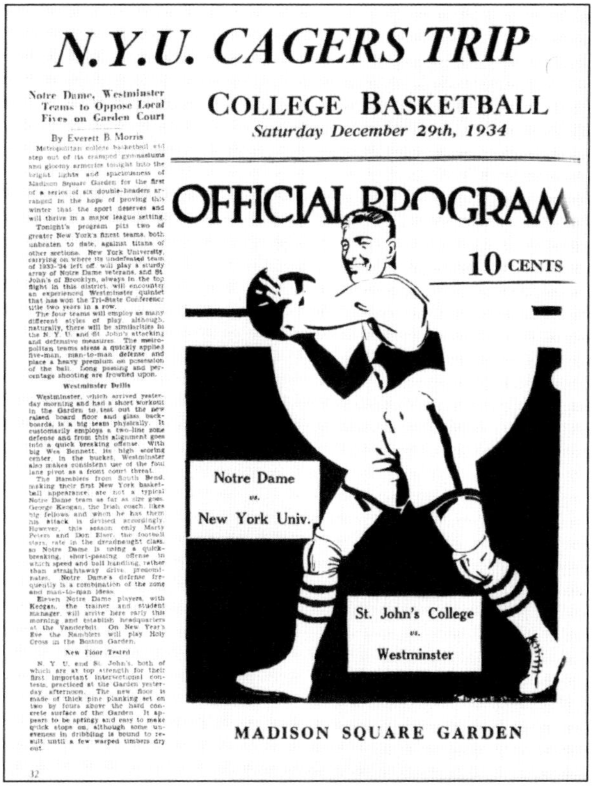

N. Y. U. CAGERS TRIP

Notre Dame, Westminster Teams to Oppose Local Fives on Garden Court

By Everett B. Morris

Metropolitan college basketball will step out of its cramped gymnasiums and gloomy armories tonight into the bright lights and spaciousness of Madison Square Garden for the first of a series of six double-headers arranged in the hope of proving this winter that the sport deserves and will thrive in a major league setting.

Tonight's program pits two of greater New York's finest teams, both unbeaten to date, against titans of other sections. New York University, carrying on where its undefeated team of 1933-'34 left off, will play a sturdy array of Notre Dame veterans, and St. John's of Brooklyn, always in the top flight in this district, will encounter an experienced Westminster quintet that has won the Tri-State Conference title two years in a row.

The four teams will employ as many different styles of play, although, naturally, there will be similarities in the N. Y. U. and St. John's attacking and defensive measures. The metropolitan teams stress a quickly applied five-man, man-to-man defense and place a heavy premium on possession of the ball. Long passing and percentage shooting are frowned upon.

Westminster Drills

Westminster, which arrived yesterday morning and had a short workout in the Garden to test out the new raised board floor and glass backboards, is a big team physically. It customarily employs a two-line zone defense and from this alignment goes into a quick breaking offense. With big Wes Bennett, its high scoring center, in the bucket, Westminster also makes consistent use of the foul lane pivot as a front court threat.

The Ramblers from South Bend, making their first New York basketball appearance, are not a typical Notre Dame team as far as size goes. George Keogan, the Irish coach, likes big fellows and when he has them his attack is devised accordingly. However, this season only Marty Peters and Don Elser, the football stars, rate in the dreadnought class, so Notre Dame is using a quick-breaking, short-passing offense in which speed and ball handling, rather than straightaway drive, predominates. Notre Dame's defense frequently is a combination of the zone and man-to-man ideas.

Eleven Notre Dame players, with Keogan, the trainer and student manager, will arrive here early this morning and establish headquarters at the Vanderbilt. On New Year's Eve the Ramblers will play Holy Cross in the Boston Garden.

New Floor Tested

N. Y. U. and St. John's, both of which are at top strength for their first important intersectional contests, practiced at the Garden yesterday afternoon. The new floor is made of thick pine planking set on two by fours above the hard concrete surface of the Garden. It appears to be springy and easy to make quick stops on, although some unevenness in dribbling is bound to result until a few warped timbers dry out.

32

COLLEGE BASKETBALL

Saturday December 29th, 1934

OFFICIAL PROGRAM

10 CENTS

Notre Dame vs. New York Univ.

St. John's College vs. Westminster

MADISON SQUARE GARDEN

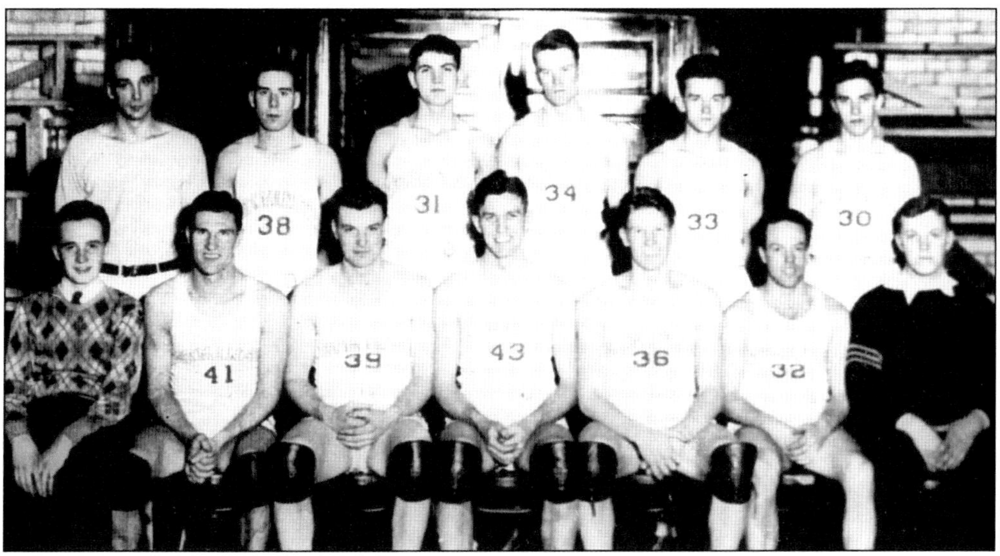

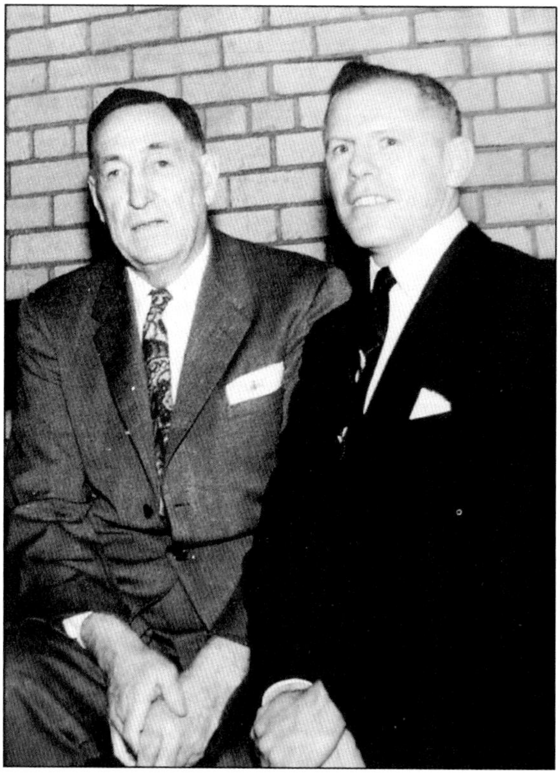

Grover C. Washabaugh (left) arrived in New Wilmington in 1937 to coach football and basketball. His football team, however, suspended play during World War II. Despite a lack of men on campus, the basketball team continued to compete and, in 1946, was the top-scoring team in the country. Washabaugh coached the Titans to 77 consecutive victories. Charles G. "Buzz" Ridl '42 (right) joined the coaching staff in 1956–1957 and propelled the Titans to even greater acclaim. After leaving Westminster, Ridl took up coaching duties at the University of Pittsburgh and became a nationally recognized Division I coach. He subsequently returned to Westminster as athletic director. The Field House gym was named in Ridl's honor in 1996.

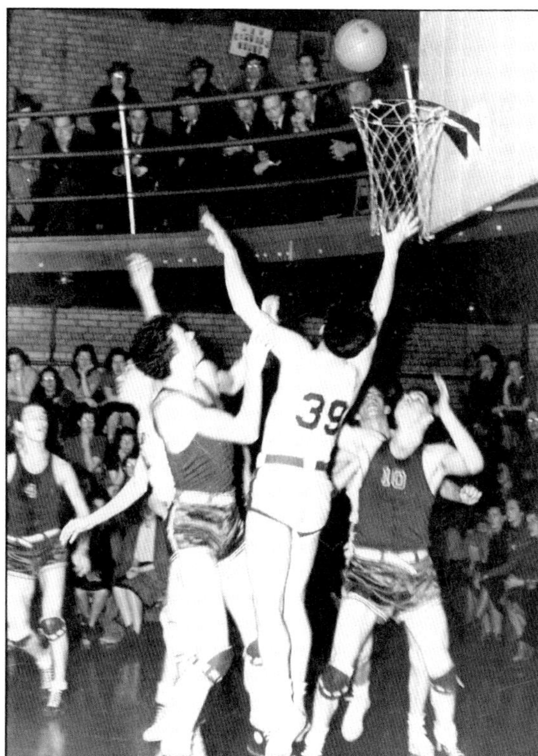

During the 1939–1940 season, spectators in Old 77 enjoyed watching competitions from the bleachers and precariously from the banked balcony track.

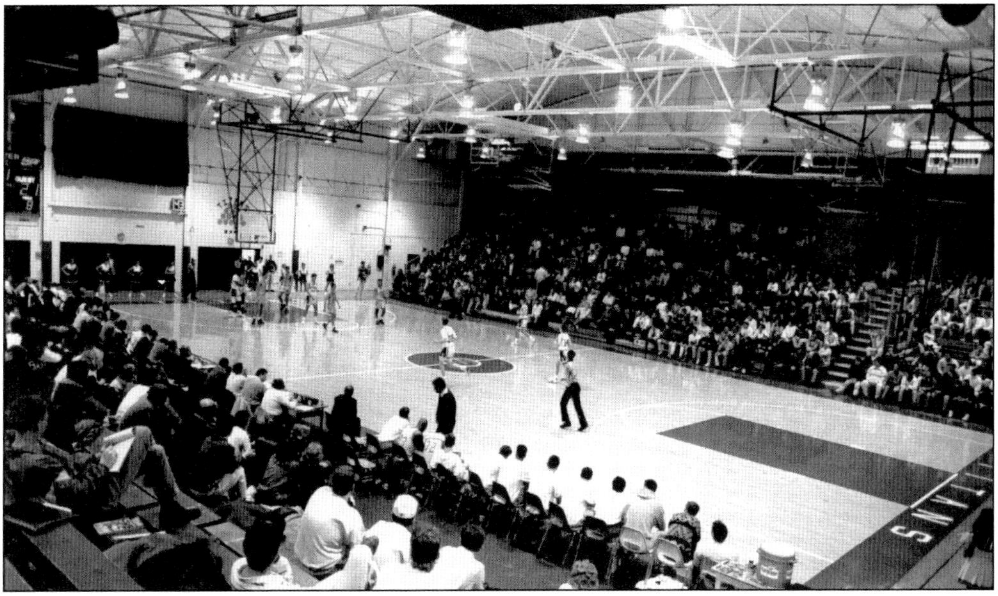

In 1951 Titan basketball moved to the hardwood of Memorial Field House, named for the college's war dead. Jim Riley was a standout in the years 1955–1957 and was the only Titan to be a three-time basketball All-American. A high-water mark for the Titans came during 1959–1960 when the team (below) traveled to Kansas City for the NAIA tournament, following an impressive 24-3 season. The team lost in a dramatic semi-final game.

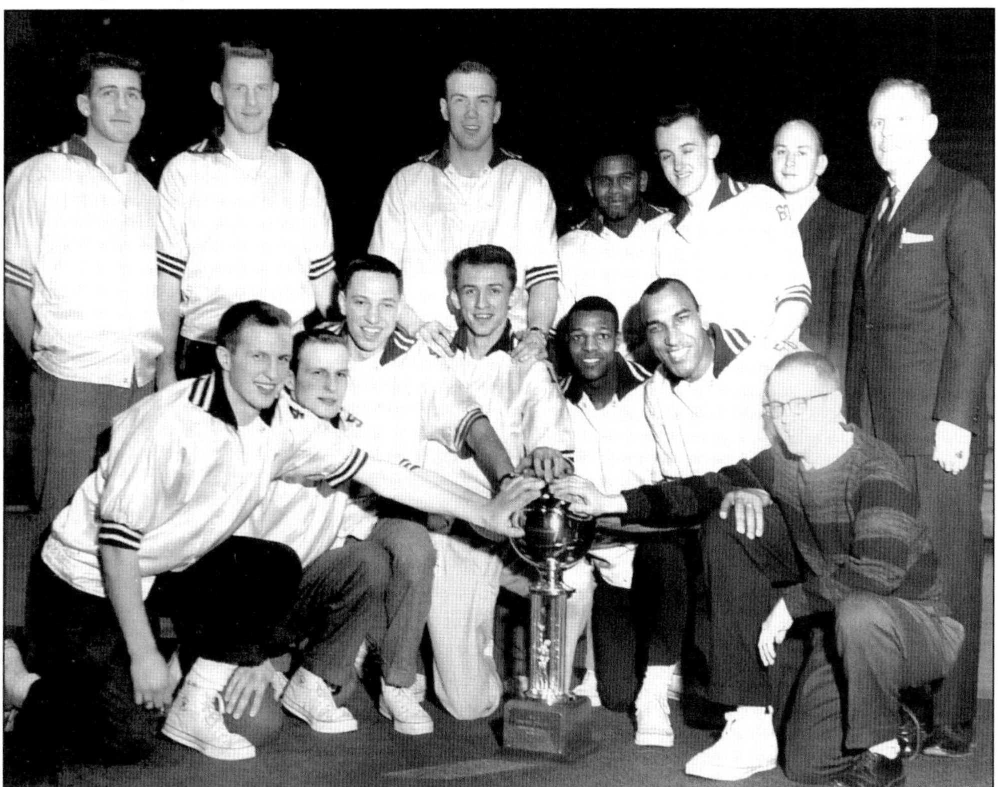

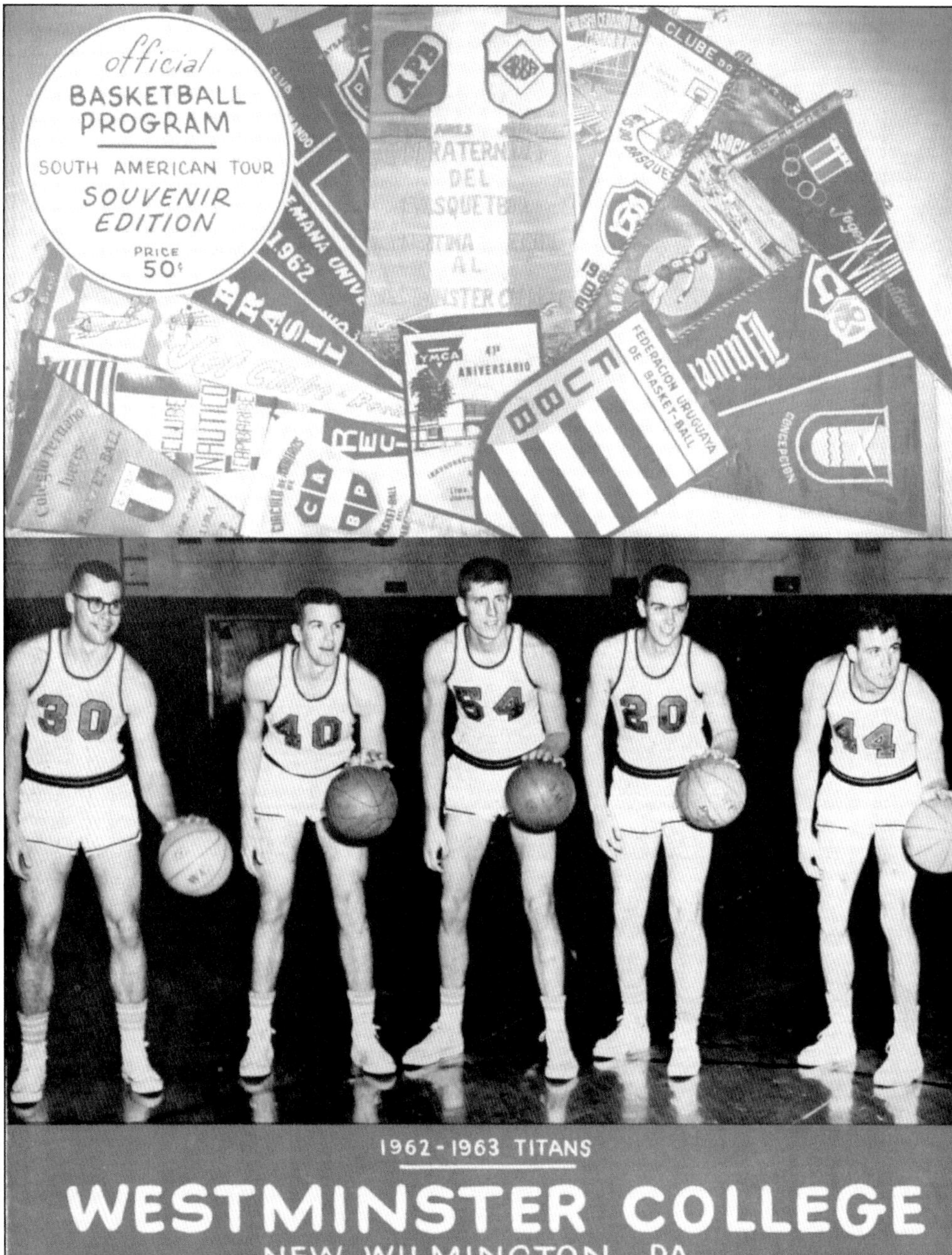

The 1961–1962 Titans, with a strong 26-3 record, were picked by both the Associated Press and United Press International as the United States' No. 1 small college team. Charles "Buzz" Ridl was named NAIA Coach of the Year. Unfortunately, the team lost in the final to Prairie View A&M of Texas. The U.S. State Department and Amateur Athletic Union selected Westminster for a six-week goodwill tour of South America. The Titans were joined by Grambling State University, a historically black college in Louisiana whose team included future professional standout Willis Reed. The tour was featured in a commemorative program (seen here) the following season.

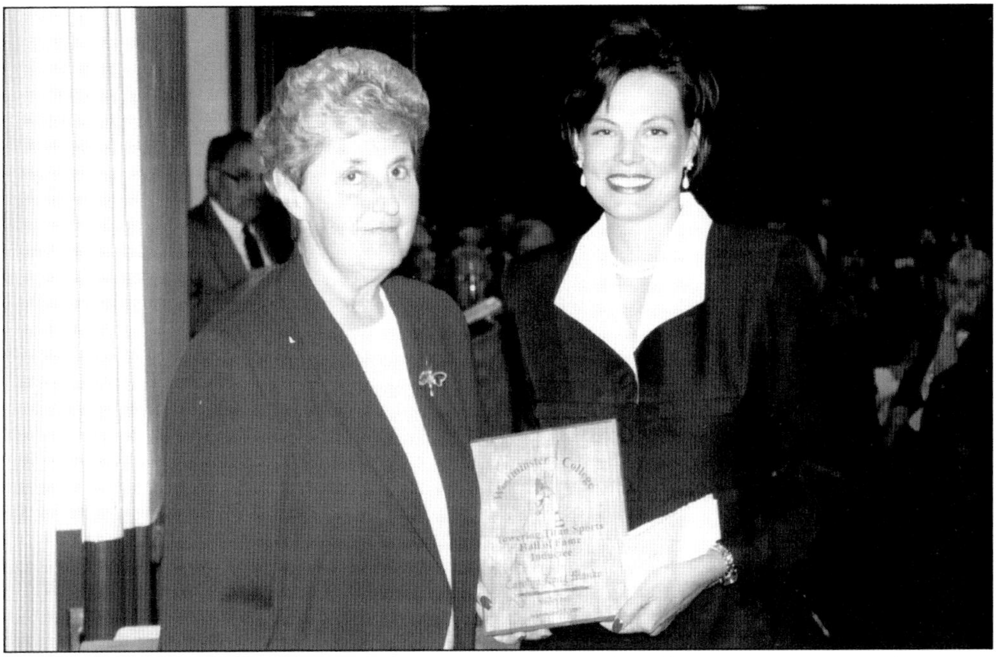

Women's sports blossomed in the 1970s. Title IX, a federal law requiring parity between men's and women's sports, spurred the growth in women's athletics everywhere. Leading the drive on campus were Irene Walters and Marjorie A. Walker, seen above on the left. They coached the Lady Titans in a range of sports from field hockey (in 1982 below) to badminton, tennis to table tennis, and swimming to volleyball and golf. Plus, they and others were responsible for training the cheerleaders and the Titannaires drill team. Many coeds from the late 1960s and early 1970s remember compulsory calisthenics sessions, which the staff usually led to a recorded routine by health maven Bonnie Prudden. Walker championed the induction of many women into the Titan Hall of Fame, including volleyball standout Carolyn Long Manko '92, seen above on the right.

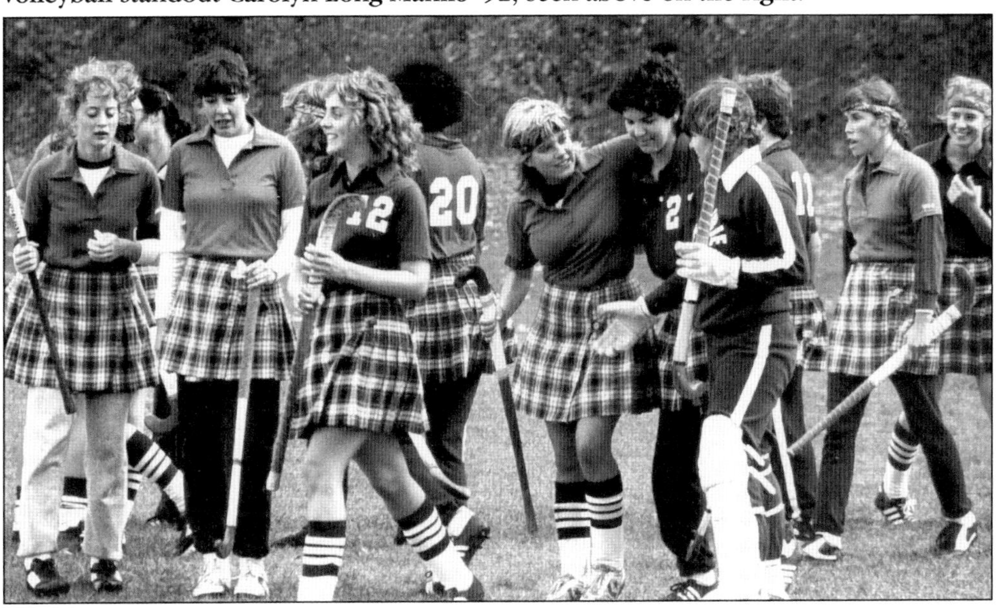

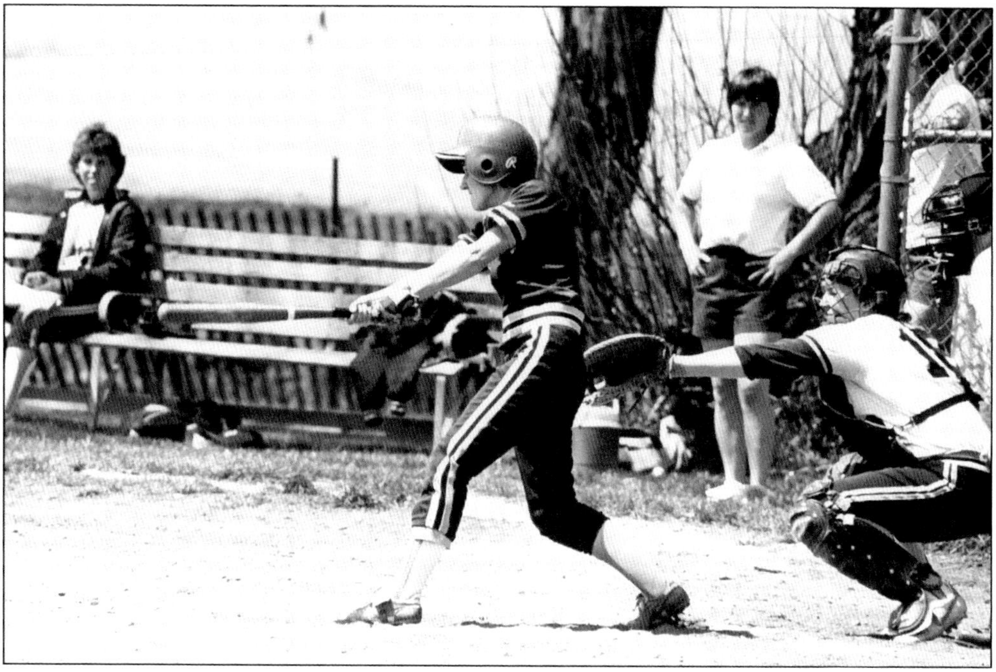

Westminster coeds first played softball in 1886. The sport changed little over the following 100 years, as evidence at a centennial game played by the Lady Titans in 1986. Rev. Dr. Wayne Christy, professor of religion, coached the team which went to two national tournaments.

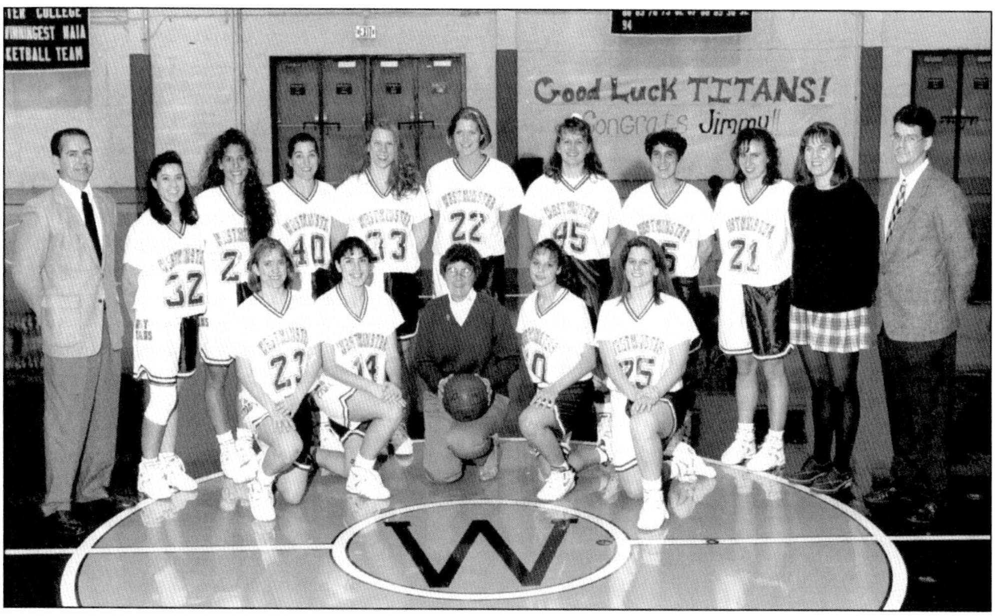

The Lady Titans basketball squad of 1994–1995 was led by S. Kipley Haas (first row, third from left), who was the head coach for 22 years. On the team was Deanna Kaczynski Seruga '97 (first row, fourth from left), who scored 1,148 points during her college career.

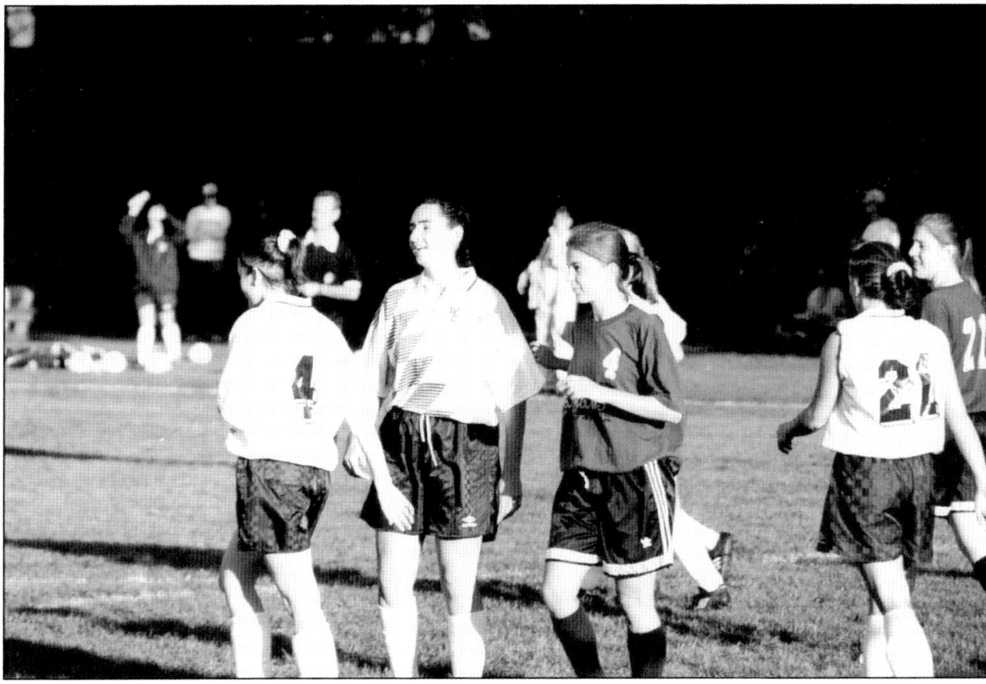

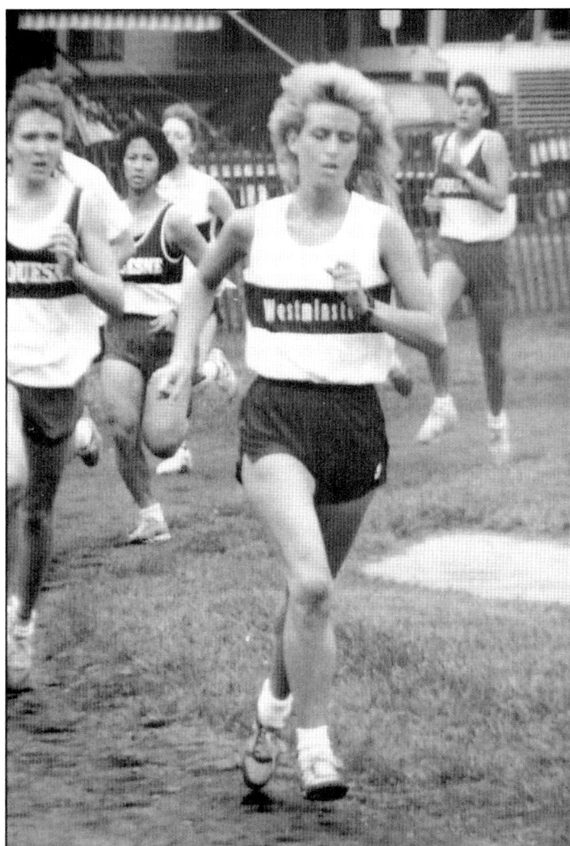

Women's soccer has been enjoyed as an intercollegiate sport since 1997. It was first introduced as a men's sport by coach Harold Burry in the mid-1940s when soccer was yet a novelty in the United States. Played then for several years, soccer returned after a hiatus of several decades. Track and field and cross-country have remained popular with both men and women.

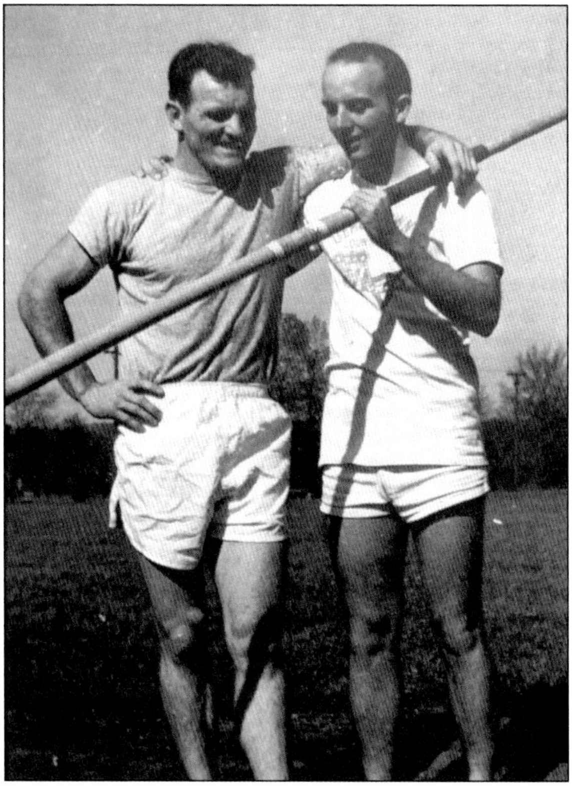

During the 1958 season, student John Shaffer (right) participated in the pole vault. He received instruction from Bob Richards, the two-time Olympic gold medal winner. Richards also competed in the Olympic decathlon and was known as "The Vaulting Vicar" because he was an ordained minister.

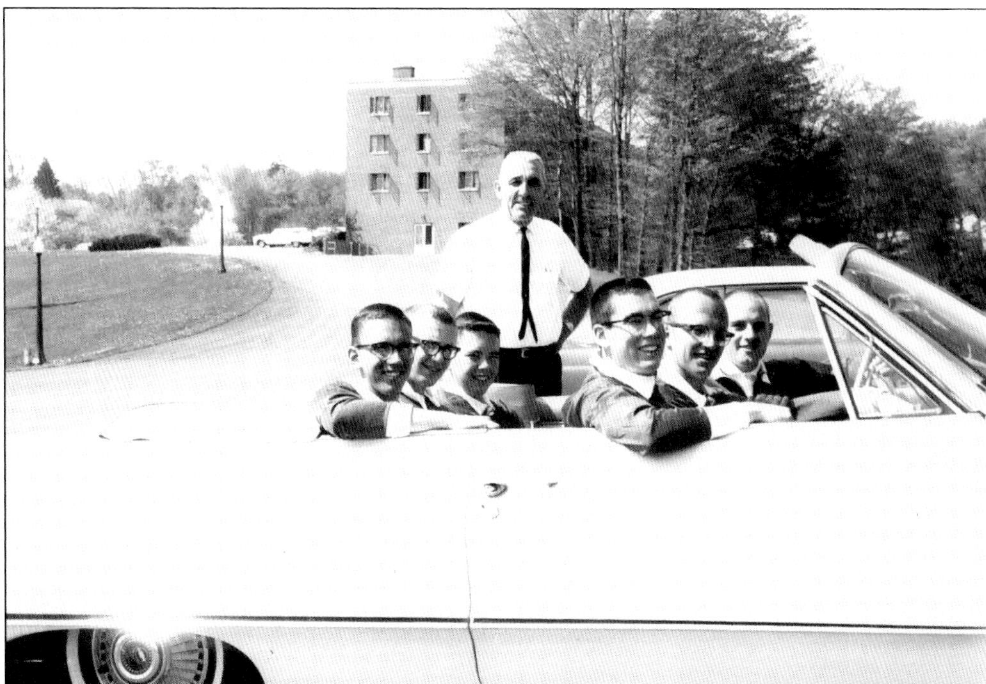

Golf became a varsity sport at Westminster in 1934. Harold Burry, seen here standing in 1963, coached the team for nearly 20 years.

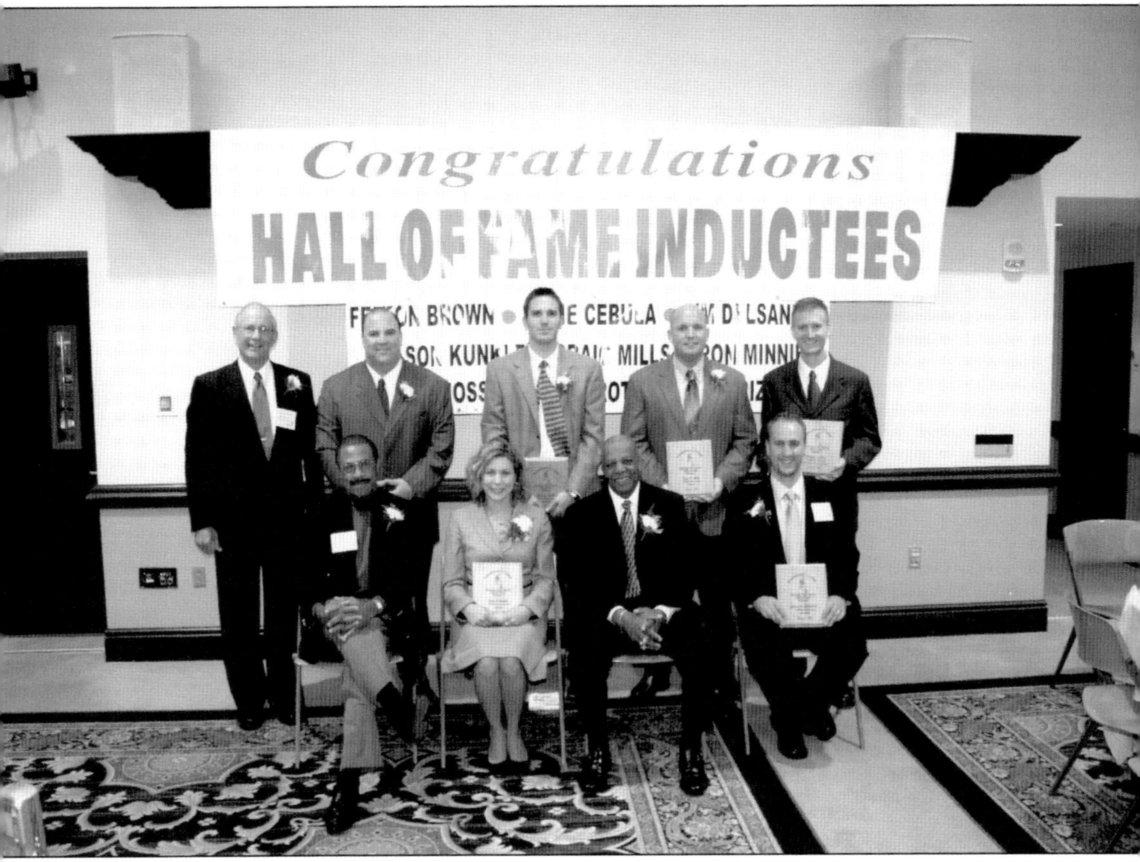

The Titan Hall of Fame has recognized student athletes since its inception in 1963. The Hall of Fame includes standouts from all intercollegiate sports. Honorees are saluted with special half-time ceremonies during a football game. Hall of Fame plaques are displayed prominently in the Washabaugh Lobby at Memorial Field House. The 2006 inductees were, from left to right, (first row) Felton Brown '60, track and field; Janie Cebula '97, volleyball; Ron Minnie '60, track and field and basketball; and All-American Jim Delsandro '97, basketball; (second row) Bill Moss '57, football and track and field; Lou Perrotta '94, football; Jason Kunkle '95, swimming; Craig Mills '96, football; and Tony Pizon '97, track and field and cross-country.

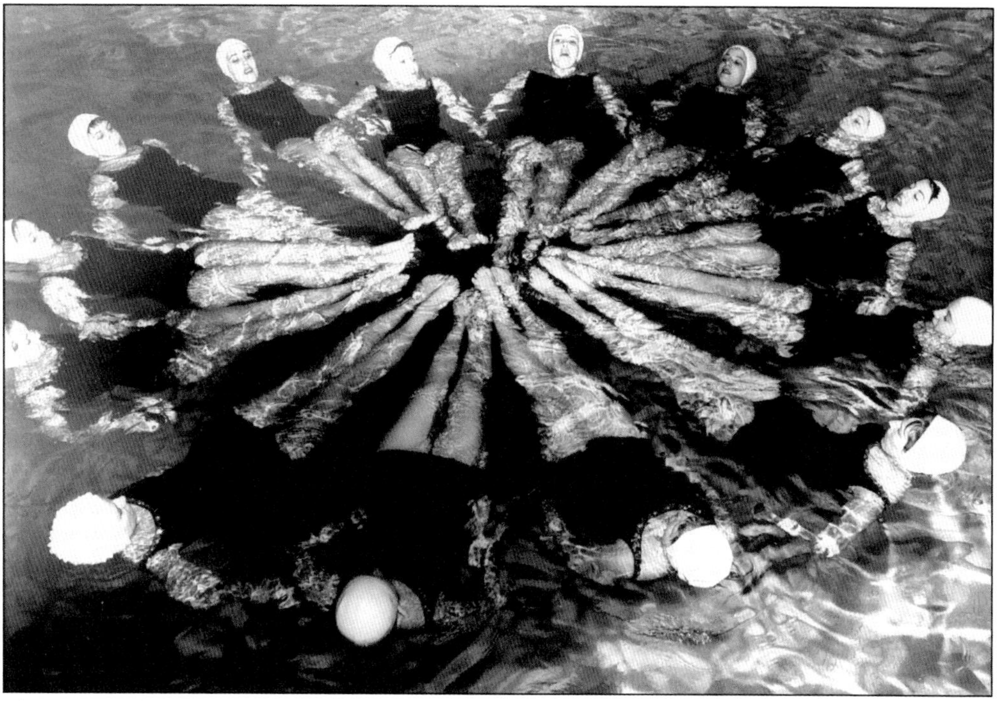

The Mermaids synchronized swimming team (seen here around 1972) performed amazing routines despite the compact size of the Old 77 swimming pool. Installed in the early 1930s, many called it "a bathtub." In the 1980s the pool was covered with a floor and the area became a dance studio.

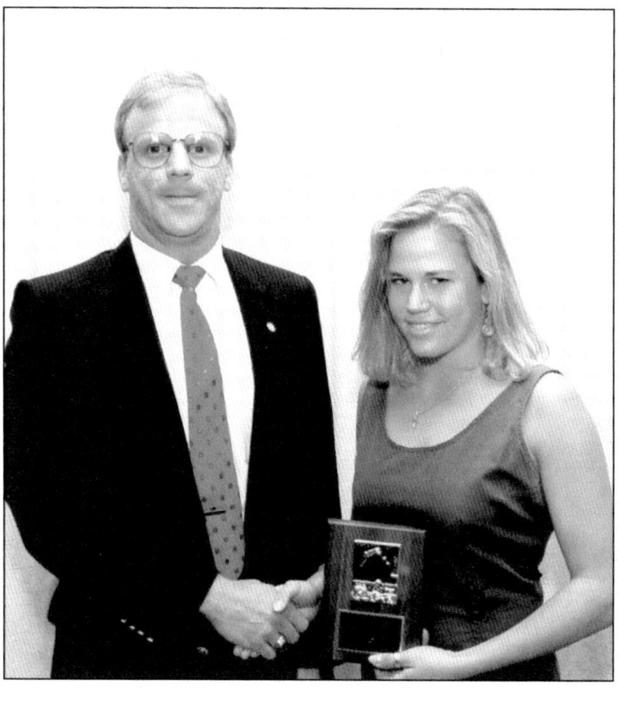

Westminster is a powerhouse in collegiate swimming. The college's success in the sport grew in the late 1970s under the tutelage of coach B. Eugene Nicholson. Record-breaking coach Robert G. Kalmut (left) congratulated Kristen Zukowski, the first Westminster woman to win a national title. She did so in the 100-yard butterfly in 1991 and was the second Titan in the college's history to capture a national swimming championship.

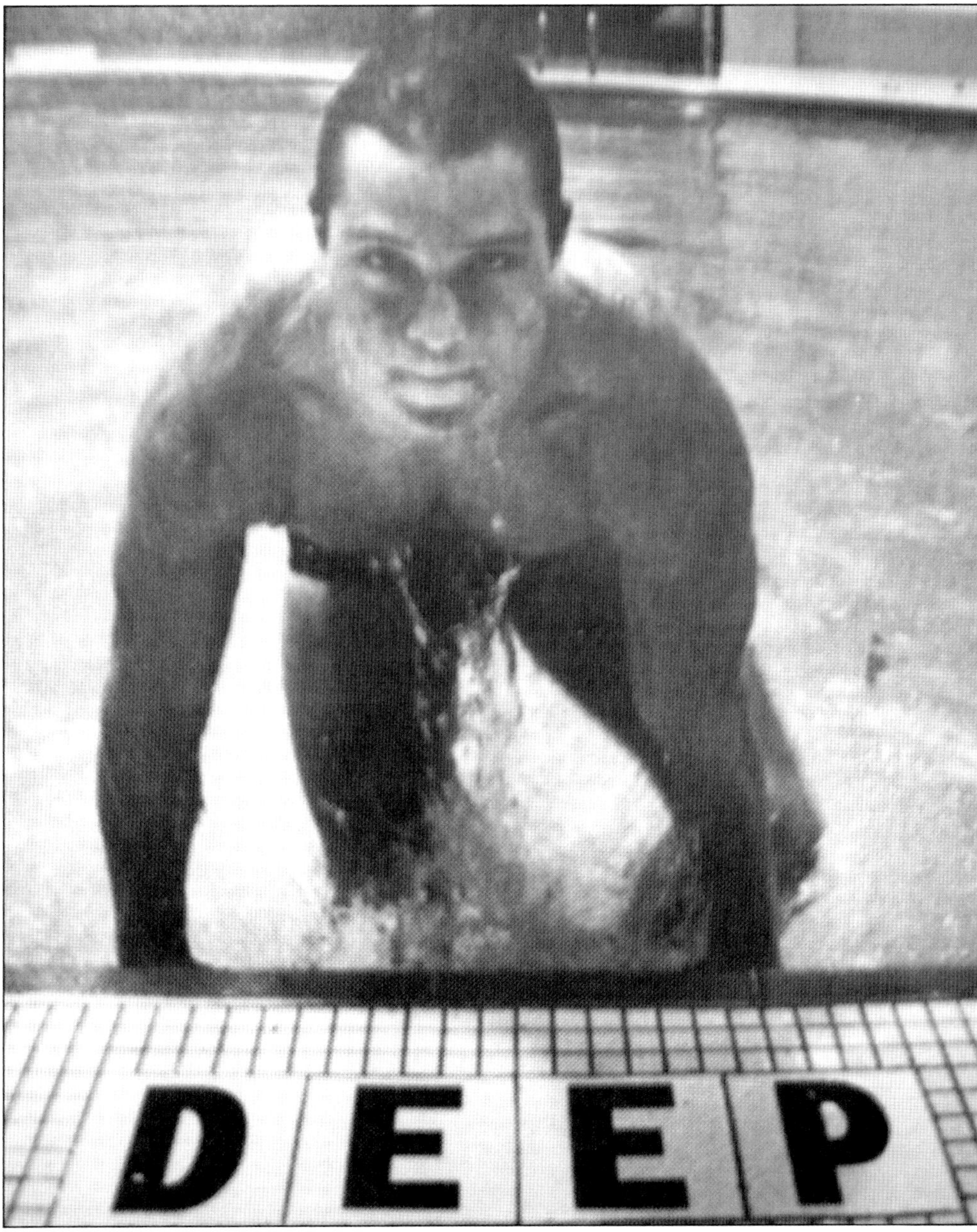

The first Titan swimmer to earn a national title was Myron Luthringer, who, in 1981, won for the 100-meter breaststroke. He also earned NAIA All-America honors in nine events.

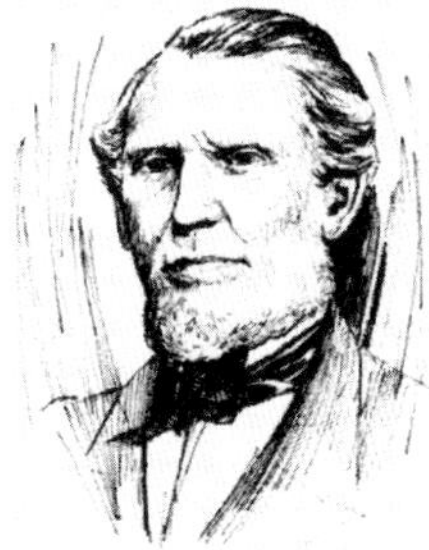

James Patterson, D.D.
1853-1866

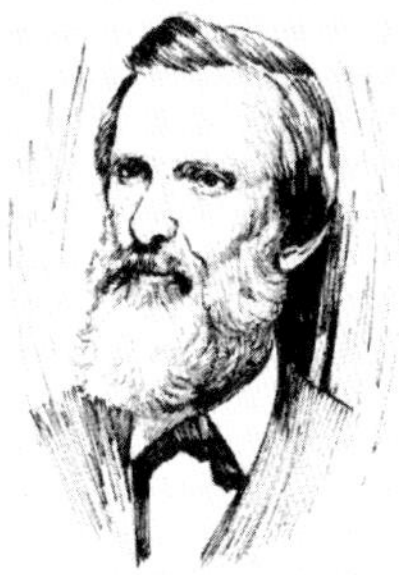

Robert Audley Browne, D.D.
1867-1870

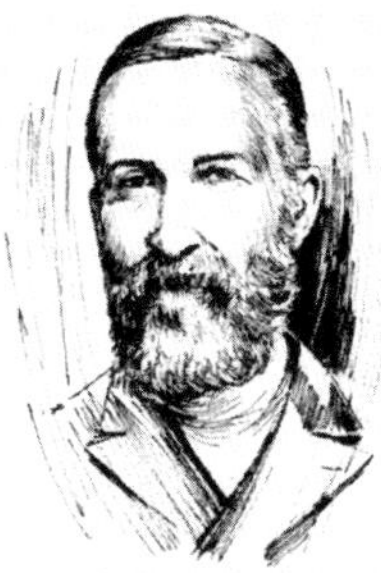

E. Tupper Jeffers, D.D.
1872-1883

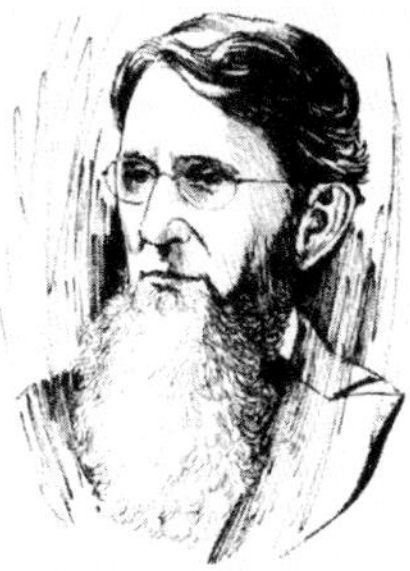

Robert Gracey Ferguson, D.D., LL.D.
1884-1906

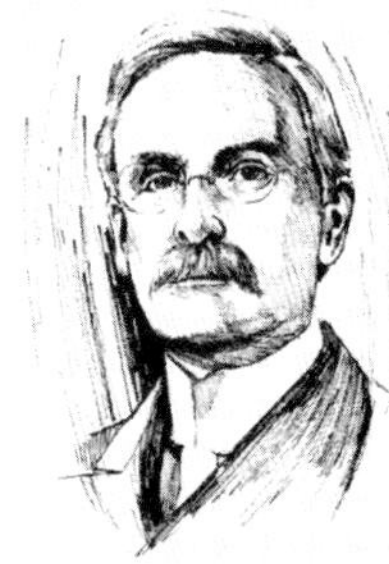

Robert McWatty Russell, D.D., LL.D.
1906-1915

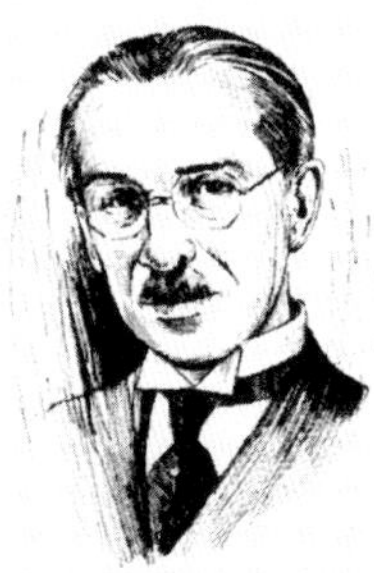

W. Charles Wallace, D.D.
1916-1931

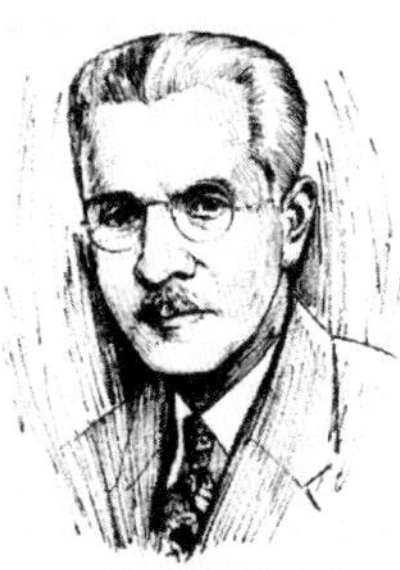

Robert F. Galbreath, D.D., LL.D.
1932-1946

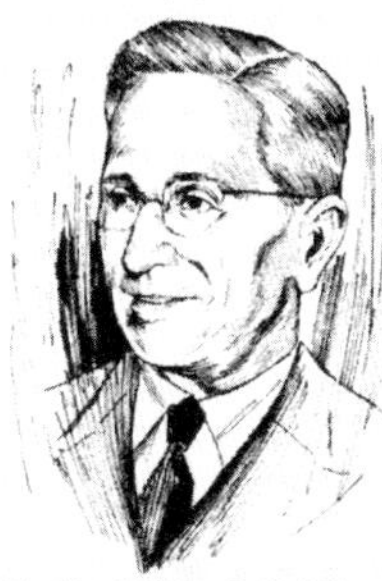

H. Lloyd Cleland, Ped.D.
1946-1947

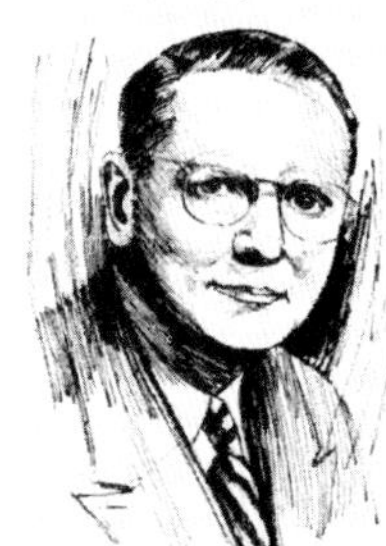

Will W. Orr, D.D., Litt.D., LL.D.
1949-1967

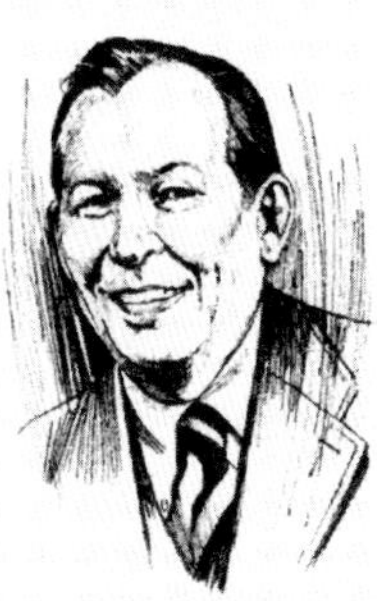

Earland I. Carlson, Ph.D.
1967-1981

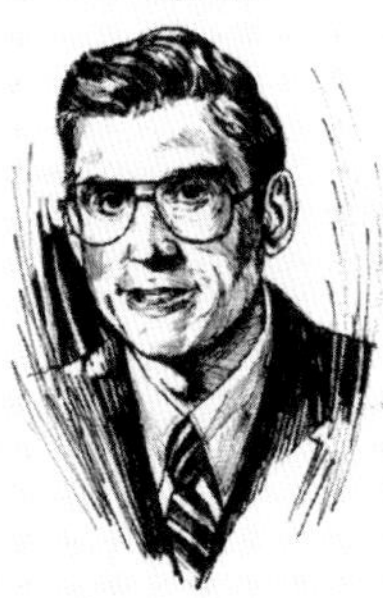

Allen P. Splete, Ph.D.
1982-1985

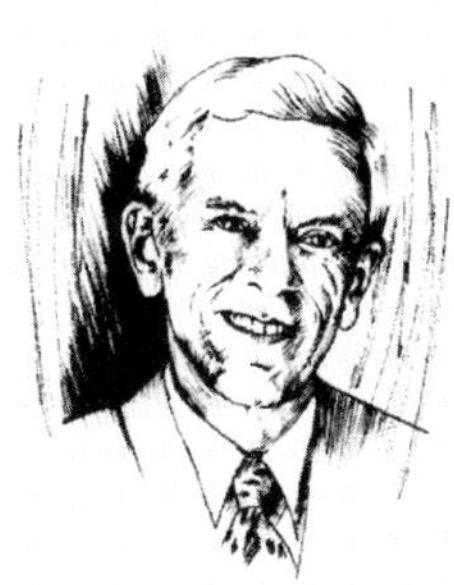

Oscar E. Remick, Ph.D.
1987-1997

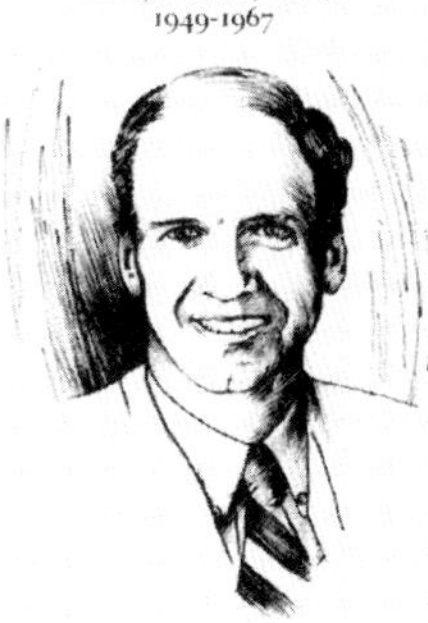

R. Thomas Williamson, J.D.
1997-

Thirteen men, many of them members of the Presbyterian clergy, have led Westminster College since its founding in 1852.

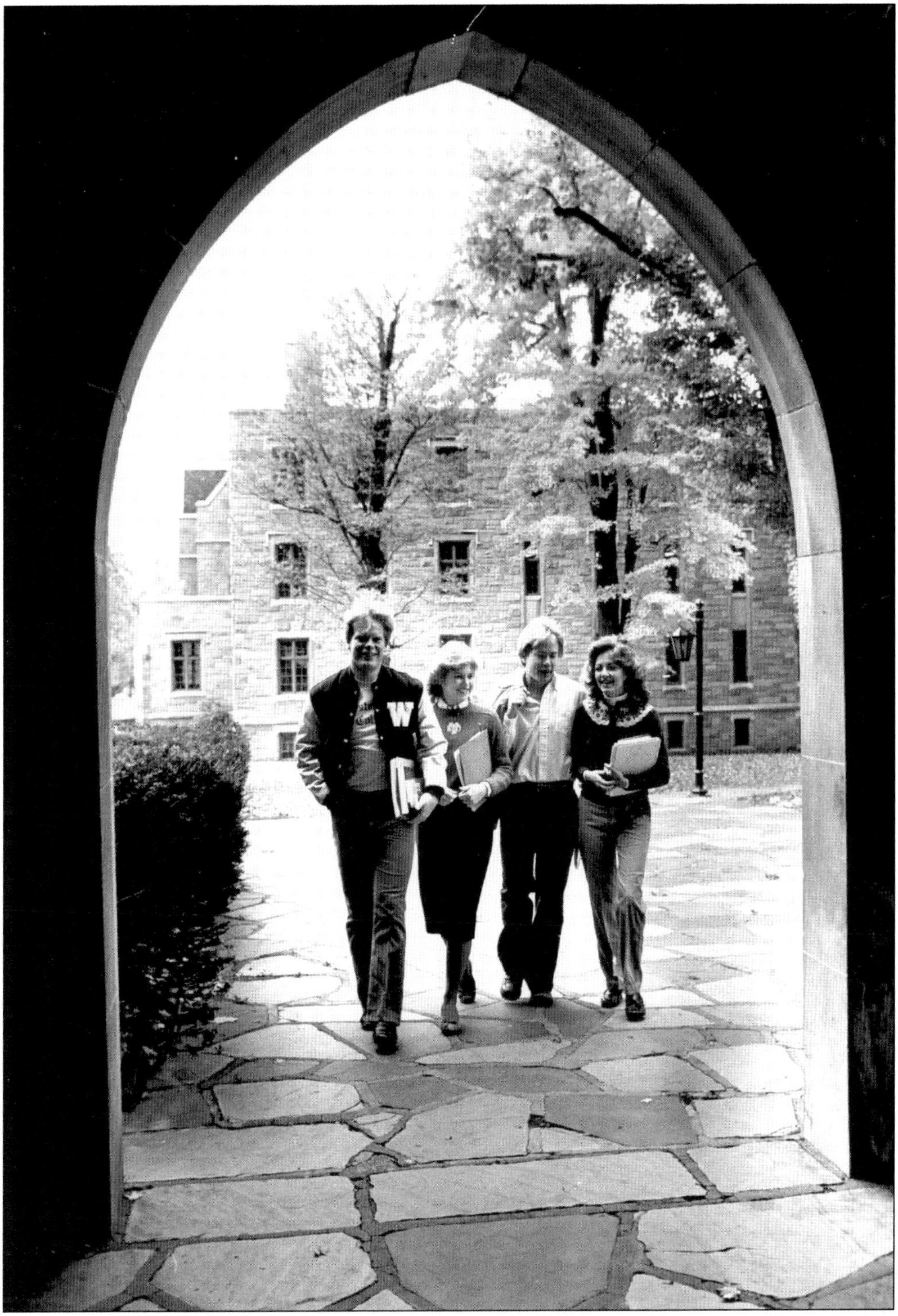

The heartbeat of Westminster has always been its people, those who value education and who are eager to come to learn, and, most of all, those who cherish Westminster's traditions and prepare the college to serve future generations.

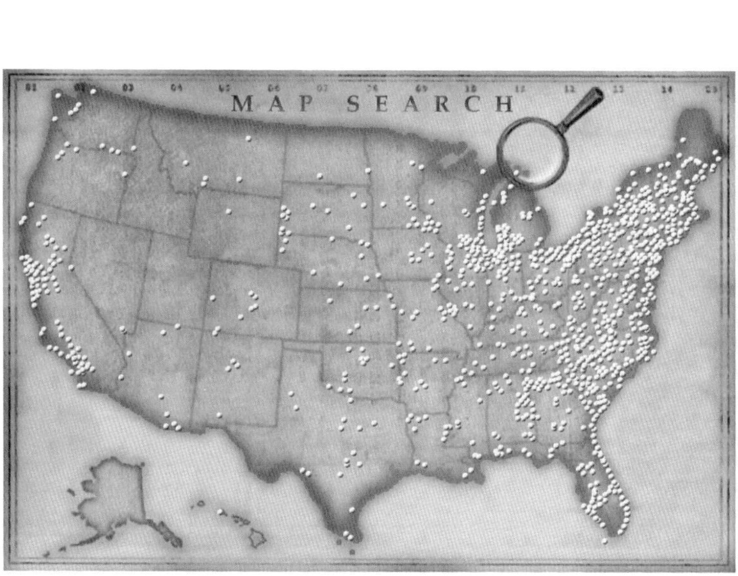
MAP SEARCH